Belmarsh Bang-Up

A Newbies Guide to Prison

Paddy Kane

Table of Contents

Contents

Introduction

HMP Belmarsh is not only Britain's most secure prison, it must also rank among the Top 10 in the World. It's security measures include not only the 'rolling drums', with built in movement sensors, that run along the top of 15M high perimeter walls, interlaced with razor wire, but an equally wide corridor of ground adjoining the wall is also embedded with similar movement detectors. The outside flood lighting is on a par with Wembley Stadium, and there is not a square metre inside, or outside, the prison blocks, that isn't covered by 24/7 camera surveillance. The outside exercise yards are encircled by 5M high mesh fencing, topped off with more razor wire, with heavy cables overhead to prevent helicopters landing. Belmarsh also has some unique features of its own, e.g. due to inmates being permitted to wear their own clothing, all guard dogs are trained to attack anyone not in uniform; and, all meals are eaten in cells, with no more than 6 at a time allowed to go to the servery. This round trip has a 1 to 1 Officer/ Inmate ratio for the length of the permanently mothballed Dining Hall, plus a dog handler hovering at each end. What really sets this 21st. Century Alcatraz (minus the sea-view) apart from similar institutions worldwide, is it's usage as a 'clearing house' for all Courts in S.E. London, plus the

Old Bailey. Remand prisoners, presumably innocent until proved guilty, are locked in small cells with convicted murderers; violent criminals; drug barons; etc, for up to 22 hours a day, for weeks/months on end. Of the 100's that are 'banged up' yearly, many for the first time, some eventually are found Not Guilty, or receive non-custodial sentences. Others arrive with short sentences, like myself, who will be compelled to serve their time in Belmarsh, because it's not worth doing the necessary paperwork to transfer them somewhere more appropriate. One inmate was serving 2 weeks of a 4 week sentence for not having a T.V. Licence. He had to pass the long hours with another 'doing' a total of 14 years for Aggravated GBH, and Armed Robbery. The T.V. Licence dodger was transferred to what passes as a Hospital Wing after 4 days, due to various injuries including 2 broken ribs and 1 nose, having pushed his cell mate's patience too far with constant references to how many days he had left before he could pop down the pub for a welcome pint. Incidents such as this, along with both failed and successful suicides, are regular features of such a bizarre environment. Some will claim that the experience could be a deterrent against reoffending, and for some cases they may be right. Equally it is arguable whether the cost is too high, in both human and financial terms. In the event of such a debate, I would point out that as the cost of keeping an inmate in Belmarsh is over £59K per year, then whilst you are reading this there are upwards of 300 inmates in that penal mausoleum, who could be more appropriately locked up elsewhere for half the price.

One thing that became apparent is that many of the inmates at Belmarsh are there because of a wrong turn or decision made in life, something that anybody could do and pay a price that they never thought they would pay or be in a position they never thought they would be in.

There are many people that glibly take the "Daily Mail" view on what life should be like for prisoners without ever considering that they themselves may all too easily find themselves on the wrong side of the prison gates. For those that do take that view you need to read this book to understand that any day could bring you a situation which by the way you deal with it will determine that you join the same ranks that you so often hold in disdain and contempt.

For those with a slightly more humane outlook on life this book is a useful tool just to forewarn you what prison life is really like should the unfortunate situation arise.

It is estimated that approximately 1 in 8 adults will serve a custodial prison sentence at some time and it is to these that this book is meant for. With odds like those it really could be you that this book needs to be read by.

Chapter 1

The Judge Is Not Impressed.

It was just turned 9 am when my younger son, Joe, dropped me off outside the Inner London Crown Court. I remember thinking how that monolith matched the December weather, grey and full of foreboding. Today, I had been informed the previous afternoon, was the day the judge had decided to dish out the sentences for myself and my six co-defendants. Eighteen months had elapsed since our arrest by officers of H M Customs and Excise, for selling duty free tobacco, cigarettes and alcohol, thereby depriving the government of some income, and now the judge was to exact retribution on behalf of those who had appointed him.

Passing round the gate barrier and heading across the forecourt, the mixture of feeling that had cost me the best part of the previous night's sleep were still churning around inside me. After eighteen months, five magistrates' court appearances and four Crown Court sittings, there was relief in the thought that the whole affair was coming to a head. The relief was tempered though, by a large portion of apprehension as to what the judge was going to inflict on me, especially as the consensus opinion of all involved was that he revelled in the reputation he had built for himself as a judicial "hard-man".

Up the stone steps and through the revolving doors, I joined with other arrivals to file through the metal detector manned by a security guard who already look totally bored, and the day had only just started.   This cleared; I looked around the foyer but could see no familiar face, and pondered as to whether I should pop down to the basement cafeteria to purchase a cup of tea.   The thought was quickly dismissed as, due to previous experience of what was passed as tea, I saw no sense in adding to whatever punishment laid in store for me, so I took myself across to one of the benches that were steadily filling up.   I was about to sit down when my eye caught sight of the board in the corner that carried the various court listings for that day and, on impulse, I went across to read it.   For a moment I had the completely irrational hope that we might have been cancelled, or that we were faced with a different judge who didn't aspire to emulate "Hanging" Judge Jeffries.

The wild hope was soon dashed.   There we were, Court Three, at 10.30 am, and there he was to preside. I went back to the bench, wishing I hadn't looked at the board in the first place.

The foyer was getting quite full now, with most of the people huddled in small groups, conversing in hushed voices.   It was the various expressions that struck me more than anything, ranging from worried and unsure, through casual and resigned, to defiant and indignant.   Some were obviously there in a supportive role, including elderly parents, and two young women with toddlers and buggies.   It was the supporters who seemed to be doing most of the talking, but maybe they thought that was what was expected of them.   In amongst these little islands flowed a constant stream of court officials in gowns; solicitors or their clerks; and barristers, complete in gowns and wigs.   Some of the legal representatives would stop at one or other of the little groups, with the regular effect of the hushed conversations rapidly becoming more heated.   Sitting there alone, I rolled a cigarette, lit it, and retreated into my own thoughts as to what was likely to happen to me.

Throughout my life I have always tended to be an optimist; my glass is always half full, never half empty, so I focused my mind on what I felt were the points in my favour.   Yes, I had been caught with a substantial quantity of cigarettes and tobacco in my van that had started the day on the shelves of a Calais hypermarket and, yes, having tailed me to my lock-up garage, the Customs men had found some more that, if they were for my own consumption, would turn my lungs into coal mines.   On being arrested, though, I had offered no violent reaction and gave them my name and address, as requested.   I even directed them from the rear seat of their car to my home, as it was obvious that they would otherwise get lost.

That night had been spent in a grotty cell in Southwark Police Station, to be collected the following morning and taken to the Customs' cell suite overlooking the Thames, for interrogation. In the company of the duty solicitor, I answered their questions and made a full statement and, at 11 pm, was taken back to Southwark Police Station and bailed to appear at Tower Bridge Magistrates' Court the next day. All along, I had been calm and co-operative, which I thought must count in my favour. During the eighteen months that had elapsed since that fateful day, both mine, and my wife's health, had suffered. Twice I had been rushed into hospital due to exploding blood pressure and angina, due to stress. Surely the judge would take that into account?

Then there was my previous good character. I had turned fifty, with a clean sheet. I was still a serving borough councillor after twenty years, having been re-elected the previous May with a resounding majority, after all the press publicity following my capture. Approximately fifteen hundred voters in my Ward did not regard me as a criminal and wished me to continue to represent them.

A number of notable people had furnished good character references, including the Leader of the Council, who was of another Party, and the local Chief Superintendent, the latter having received special dispensation from Scotland Yard. Even the probation officer who was drawing up my pre-sentence report was recommending probation. I was feeling quite buoyant and could visualise myself back home in a few hours, unpacking the bag of personal items that sat next to me.

Suddenly I was brought back to reality by the arrival of two of my co-defendants, one of whom was gloomier than usual. Since day one, he had been forecasting dire consequences for what we had done and, whereas to him he was just being realistic, to the rest of us he was a pain in the backside. Any hopeful expressions that were made were soon drowned by the cold water he was quick to pour over them. This morning, he was well and truly on form. "I wonder what prison they'll be sending us to", he started, "I hope it ain't Brixton 'cos I've heard they are running alive with cockroaches". "We could all be looking at hefty fines", I replied, "seeing as it's only money we done them out of. Why spend more money locking us up. There was no violence involved". "No", he immediately responded, "it's more than just money, it's government money, and they don't like that. On top of that, there's thousands doing what we did, so they are going to make examples of us".

My buoyant mood had taken a nose-dive because, deep down, I knew he had a very strong point. All our solicitors and barristers had made the same observations with regard to making examples of us, in order to deter the multitude that were making daily trips across the Channel to return with cargoes of booze, baccy and cigarettes, to sell to a waiting clientele. After all, the barriers had come down in Europe to assist big business, not entrepreneurial peasants like us.

Before anymore could be said, we were joined by the others, plus our assortment of legal representatives, whereupon we all received individual last minute situation appraisals, prior to trooping through the series of swing doors to Court Three.

The court, as on previous occasions, reminded me of a large chapel of rest, with all those present wearing expressions that would do even the most grieving mourner proud. With windows at ceiling level and the whole room fitted out with light wood panelling, the only items missing were the vases of flowers and the coffin. As we entered, we were confronted by a middle-aged woman, complete in black gown, who was making a big show of studying a clipboard. Her function within the courtroom machinery was to ensure that we, the defendants, stepped up into the dock in a pre-arranged sequence. Looking back, one of the unanswered questions in the back of my is - why was the sequence the same as on the previous occasions, at a time when most of us were still pleading not guilty, especially, as it transpired, the eventual sentences followed the same sequence of line-up, in degrees of severity. Maybe there is some secret formula known only to court-room attendants, handed down at some secluded initiation ceremony to the new entrants, by the older hands. Possibly a sweepstake takes place amongst the staff with, on this occasion, ourselves as the runners, and the payout being made on the poor sod with the stiffest sentence. Anyway, to me, it is still one of the little mysteries of life.

With seven of us, plus a warder at each end, there was not an inch to spare in the dock and I resented the fact that the warders made sure that they had plenty of leg room. After all, we were the customers and if it were not for unfortunates like us, they would, most likely, be out of work. They would probably be supplementing their meagre dole by selling duty free baccy and booze, obtained on day trips to France. Suddenly my thoughts were interrupted by the woman with the clipboard demonstrating her other function and calling on all present to rise.

The judge entered from a door behind the bench, seated himself in his high-backed chair and immediately began scrutinising some papers on his desk top. A full half-minute elapsed before he looked up and acknowledged there were others in the courtroom, scanning all and sundry with little beady eyes and wearing an expression that was a mixture of boredom and contempt. A cursory nod to Ms Clipboard had her telling everyone they could sit down, except us. We had to remain standing until he had confirmed who we were and accorded to the sequence he had before him. Then we could sit down and listen, while everyone else talked about us. First on his feet was the Prosecution Counsel, who gave a global account of what we had been up to and the estimated amount the Treasury had been denied. He must have been a member of some amateur drama company because his voice, and the way he stood, was obviously modelled on some Shakespearean actor reciting Mark Antony's speech over the corpse of Julius Caesar. Having given the overall picture, he then went on to list our individual roles in the operation, in a voice that had noticeably transformed from stridency into a monotonous monotone. As he droned on, I found my attention wandering around the courtroom and over its occupants. In particular, I focused on the sea of wigs that lay between me and the judge. We had fielded seven barristers who, added to those of the prosecution, the judge and sundry court employees, presented not a few varieties of this antique headwear. Two or three were patently quite new; most had obviously been around for a few years, and a couple looked positively tatty. It may have been the lighting, but from where I sat, the judge's wig looked as if he had given it a pink rinse. I then began to ponder the cost of what was so much theatre. In our own case, we had had four Crown Court appearances, plus four of our originally arrested number having gone through a two-week trial, with two being acquitted. With court running costs, staff wages, our legal aid funding, paperwork that must have accounted for a couple of trees in the Brazilian rain forest, and the judge's substantial salary, the government was definitely throwing a lot of good money after bad. Whilst there is no question that many cases must go to a Crown Court, those such as ours could be dealt with just as effectively in a magistrates' court. I believe that more than ever now, as the eventual punishments ranged from twenty-seven months at the top end, down to a £3,000 fine. One of the ironies of our extremely costly court system is that, even with all the staffing overseeing the ritualistic rules of procedure and making sure the various traditions are maintained, most defendants cannot confirm when they are due in court until as little as 24 hours beforehand.

Now it was the turn of our barristers to litigate on our behalf. Basically, they were seeking to influence the judge not to be too hard on their clients. One by one they stood up and spoke, and I found myself almost becoming impatient for my brief to have his turn, but as I was number six in the line-up, had to content myself listening to the others. The judge displayed a much different attitude towards our barristers than he had to the prosecution brief. To him he had been very polite, apologising on the few occasions he had interrupted him to clarify a point, and thanking him each time for his enlightenment. With ours, he interrupted frequently and very brusquely, with no apologies or thank-yous offered. He obviously viewed their presentations as part of the court ritual he had to suffer and made no effort to hide his feelings. It was during this process that I drew the conclusion he was not at all interested in what was being said to him. His mind was already made up as to what punishments he was going to inflict, in all probability, due to the nature and topicality of the offences, based on instructions from above. I now saw my brief get to his feet to recount the many things I thought must carry a fair bit of weight, even with the "Hanging Judge".

He commenced with what seemed to be the obligatory shuffling of various reports and notes, then spoke in a voice that seemed just right for the occasion, not too deep and full of reasonableness. His client was of previous good character; married with three adult children and a grand-daughter. He earned his living as a market trader but, like many others, had felt the impact of recession, which led him into the temptation to sell duty-free tobacco and cigarettes, as a means to augment his income.

For over twenty years, his client had served his local community as a councillor, and the esteem in which he was held was greatly underlined by the various personal references submitted on his behalf. These included, amongst others, very glowing statements from local dignitaries; a senior police officer and a peer of the realm. Upon arrest he had co-operated with customs officers, even though their heavy-handed approach at his home had caused his wife to collapse and to be rushed into hospital. The following day, his client had made a full statement admitting his illegal retailing activity, and expressed full remorse. During the following year and a half that his client was on remand, the stress suffered had resulted in two separate emergency hospital admissions, once with high blood pressure and the other following an angina attack therefore, when all these factors were totalled up, he would wholeheartedly concur with the probation officer's pre-sentence report recommending probation for his client who, in essence, was a good guy who had slipped off the straight and narrow. Listening to all this and getting carried away a little with the spirit of the presentation, I was almost expecting the judge to query why I was in the dock at all, to order my release and offer me an apology, plus my train fare home.

Then my brief, doubtless on a well-deserved high due to his eloquence, delivered the rounding-off coup de grace. He reminded his worship that the glory of the first Elizabethan Age had been brought about by men of enterprise taking to the seas in ships and that, maybe, the second Elizabethan Age could be rescued from its present doldrums by men of initiative such as his client, and his compatriots.

Even the judge, who up to then looked as if he was doing a crossword puzzle, raised his bewigged head at that one, to comment that crossing the Channel on a ferry was hardly in the same category as sailing the Spanish Main. Declining to respond to that opinion, my brief sat himself down, to enable the final submission to be made on behalf of the Asian shop-keeper seated next to me, who had already commenced praying to himself quietly, in the dialect native to wherever he originated from. His barrister presented a very glowing profile, followed by some sound reasons to justify his client's waywardness, but I had the distinct impression that he, along with everyone else in the courtroom, knew he was going through the motions.

The judge looked completely disinterested, checking his watch twice during the presentation, and I came to the conclusion that the still praying shop-keeper was imploring his God to penetrate where the defence barristers most patently could not. Then it was over, and during the half minute or so that it took the judge to realise it had gone quiet, everyone seemed to be looking at everyone else, with the unasked question

14

etched clearly on their faces as to what he was going to do.

Surveying the court with his beady eyes, obviously enjoying being the focal point of attention, with us in the dock being graced with the most fleeting of glances, he made his first pronouncement. The court would adjourn for lunch, with the prisoners remanded to the cells, all to return at 2 pm., and before we could be called upon to rise, he had disappeared through his personal door.

The two warders shepherded us out of the dock, through a panelled door and down a winding flight of stairs, to the basement cell area. At the foot of the stairs were more warders, who commenced to handcuff us in pairs before unlocking the iron gate at the start of the short corridor leading to the cell block. A second iron gate had to be unlocked at the end of the corridor, the other side of which were the actual cells and once through that, the handcuffs were removed. To this day, I am still unclear as to why we had to be handcuffed in order to travel between two locked iron gates, in a basement corridor, whilst being outnumbered by the warders two to one. Maybe it was a sort of introductory ritual, to prepare us for things to come. On the other hand, maybe warders just like handcuffing people.

We were all locked in a fair sized room, having been told that the cell menu for the day was sausage, chips and beans, with a mug of tea to wash it down. I remember thinking that can't be too bad, but how wrong I was.   Even under those conditions my appetite was unaffected, until a screw unlocked the door to pass the plates around.   The chips were limp and lukewarm; the sausage was a strange piece of beige substance, also lukewarm; and the beans had quite clearly been re-heated numerous times and tasted somewhat rancid.   Along with the others, I left it all uneaten and just sipped the stewed tea; that, at least, was fairly hot.   Three of us were content to sit quietly, clutching our mugs of lookalike tea, and having a smoke, whereas the other four were busy speculating as to what lay in store, with Mr Gloomy playing a leading role.

"We're all going down", he opined, "he's already made his mind up.   Coming down here is just to make us sweat!"   "Not necessarily" responded one of the others, "two or three of us could get hit with a hefty fine, plus a bit of probation!"   "No way!" was the swift retort.   "Some of us are definitely going away!" chimed in another, "but I don't see why you think we all are!"   Mr Gloomy bit on that immediately, with one of his pearls of analysis that, like it or not, one had to admit contained a large degree of sense.   "It's pretty bloody obvious why he's going to lock us up.   He's been told to make examples of us and he will do as he's told!"   "But judges make their own decisions, don't they, within the guidelines already laid down?" interrupted the Asian shopkeeper, with a note of hopefulness in his voice.   "Don't be silly, just think about it.   Look at the whole bleeding set-up.   We've nicked money off the Crown; we're in a Crown Court to be sorted out by a Crown-appointed judge. Not exactly a neutral situation, is it? The judge works for them who gave him the job, and pay his wages. It's almost like me being up on the bench doing you for burgling my house, that's how impartial it all is!"

And so the debate went on and, although I was not participating, my natural optimism was definitely taking a hammering. The only apparent areas of consensus were that the judge looked a sour bastard; the barristers had done pretty well and that they were all having a far better lunch than us. In a resigned sort of way, I was almost glad when the screws unlocked the door, in preparedness for our return to the dock.

Handcuffed in pairs, with the seventh defendant attached to a screw, we passed back through the two sets of locked gates which were, of course, unlocked for our benefit, where the bracelets were then removed. We filed up the steps, into the court, where Ms Clipboard ensured we re-entered the dock in the appropriate order. Barely had we sat ourselves down, when we were called on to stand up for the return of the judge, and told to remain standing. Without even glancing in our direction, he commenced reading from an obviously prepared text, the theme of which was how our activities contributed towards the country's decline by depriving the poor old Treasury of some income; plus the additional financial burden we had created by having to be chased, apprehended and dealt with by his court. Immorality; illegality; or our lack of patriotism by boosting the turnover of French supermarkets, were completely absent from his ramblings.   It was all about money, which had me thinking that, surely, he will want money from us rather than adding many more thousands to the bill, by locking us up.   How wrong I was.

I had temporarily overlooked the historical fact that money is no object to the British state, when it comes to punishing those who come into conflict with it, even if it is just over a few grand in customs' duty. He had now reached the closing stage of his sermon where he offered his congratulations to all those who had played a part in the case, except us, and expressed special thanks to the court players for enabling this latest bit of theatre to run smoothly.   Then he looked at us, or rather, he looked down his nose at us and began to recite from another sheet of paper.   You could cut his upper-class accent with a blunt knife, which went to emphasise that, contrary to Magna Carta and the centuries old myth that flowed from it, 99% of people facing a British court were not judged by their peers.   The world they live in, their social background, their place on the bottom rungs of the ladder of society and the place in the sun that produces, and sustains, judges, are poles apart.   The nightmare scenario for judges and the rest of their class must be situations such as France in 1789, and Russia in 1917, where the gentry were in the dock, being tried by peasants on the bench.   No wonder those occurrences are described as mob rule, because the rules were not dictated by their mob.

My thoughts were brought back to more immediate

things by my name being called and, against the background of the Asian shopkeeper next to me once again seeking spiritual assistance, I listened to a very quick reference to all the points in my favour, irrespective of which, the judge declared, I was sentenced to six months' imprisonment.   My immediate reaction was that he was having a joke; winding me up; that he was going to say he was only considering giving me six months, but due to all the good references and previous good character, he was going to fine me, and put me on probation instead. But no.   That was it.   I was going to have porridge for Xmas.   For a few months, society was to be protected from me, and my family was to forego my company.

Over 20 years as a borough councillor, founding member of the Sutton Police Consultative Group, regular overwhelming support at the ballot box, all my other schools' and community involvements, were to be abruptly flushed down the proverbial toilet because, with one other, I had helped to deprive the Exchequer of a few grand, 15 to be precise.   The same Exchequer now would spend more thousands to keep me, all in a vain attempt to set an example and to enhance the judge's "tough guy" image.   Next to me, the Asian shopkeeper must have got through to his God, for he was fined £3000, with time to pay.

The call for all to rise was made, to witness the judge's departure and the remaining six of us were escorted back to the basement cells.

Downstairs, we were kept together in the room we had occupied earlier, while our solicitors arranged to see us, before we eventually departed for prison life.

The sentences ranged from 27 months for the main man in the operation, down to my 6 months. In between, one had 2 years; one 15 months; and two had 12 months each. Mr Gloomy, who had received 15 months, was on form, telling us how right he had been all along. No one was in the mood for his opinions, so he was told to belt up. The main topics were possible appeals against sentence, and what destination we were most likely to go to. On the second question, either Brixton or Wandsworth seemed the most likely. We asked one of the screws but he appeared to regard the question as tantamount to threatening national security. I didn't realise at that stage, but I had already taken the first tentative step into a world of paranoia, as well as making the mistake of expecting a straight answer from any, but a very small handful, of screws.

One by one, we were taken to a small room to talk with our solicitors. Mine expressed genuine amazement at the severity of my sentence and, in agreement with the barrister who accompanied him, declared his intention to lodge an appeal immediately. My priority concern was getting word to my wife and how she would take the news. She had not been in the best of health recently and, of course, the whole affair had served to depress her somewhat during the 18 months since my arrest. Now, with me facing a prison sentence, she could be plunged into an all-time low, more so with Xmas around the corner and us being apart for the first time in 31 years of married life. My solicitor undertook, following my request, to telephone my daughter to go round and break the news. At least my wife wouldn't be on her own when she learnt the result, which was the main thing. My legal team then took their leave and I was taken by a screw to their office for my first strip search and to have the contents of my bag examined.

The whole situation being a first time experience for me, probably dulled my senses a bit, but looking back I can see that the search procedure I was now going through was, in essence, another step into the bizarre world known as the prison system. One screw, seated at a desk, laboriously wrote down the contents of my hand luggage, whilst another scrutinised each item, getting positively excited when he unearthed my pot of shaving soap. Apparently that, along with my safety razor and a bar of soap, were forbidden items, as they could contain drugs, maybe even a hacksaw, cunningly secreted inside the block of soap. They were put into a separate plastic bag and sealed, along with the bag I had brought with me. The rest of the contents, dutifully recorded, were dumped into a larger plastic sack.

By now I was reduced to my underpants, awaiting the expected body search but, instead, the screw at the desk offered me a boiled sweet. Not being into boiled sweets, I declined, making a light-hearted comment that my Mum always told me not to take sweets from strangers who want me to take my clothes off. That went down like a lead balloon and, half throwing the plastic sack at me, told me to get dressed and sign the form. Clothed again, I was taken back to rejoin the others.

Our destination was still the subject of speculation, with Brixton being thought as the most likely, with its reputation for cockroaches making us even more miserable. The screws, when asked again, still regarded the information a state secret and the subject was terminated when someone declared the obvious that, wherever it was, there was nothing we could do about it. Then a ray of sunshine penetrated the gloom. The main man had picked up a Prisoners Information Pack from the office, which he had spent a good ten minutes perusing. He was now waving the information card entitled 'RELEASE' and, quoting from it, informed us that, provided we kept our noses clean, we would only have to serve half our sentences inside. The card was passed round so everyone could see it in writing for themselves. My mind was already buzzing with the effects of this knowledge. Instead of being away for 26 weeks as I originally thought, it was now going to be 13 weeks, provided I didn't have days added on for misbehaviour. As far as I was concerned, wherever we ended up, my nostrils were going to be the cleanest in the place.

Keys rattling indicated we were on the move. We stepped out of the room, where the screws waited to 'cuff us, then dragging our prison issue plastic sack with our free hand, we were led along the corridor and out into the yard, where our transport awaited us.

The transport resembled a massive strong-box on wheels, which of course is what it is. It was referred to by both screws and prisoners as a sweat box, which is what it also is. Prisoners are locked separately into the equivalent of a vertical, metal, coffin, with a sealed glass slit for a window. Once inside, you have the choice of standing or sitting on a tiny bench, with your knees pressed against the wall panel in front of you. Tough shit if you are claustrophobic. As a gesture towards equality, the prison service moves prisoners all round the country in these sweat-boxes, irrespective of whether they are serving three, or four, weeks for not paying their council tax, or all their natural life for being homicidal maniacs.

Prisoners remain incarcerated inside even when on the ferry to the Isle of Wight, on their way to Parkhurst; Albany, or Camp Hill. If the boat went down, they would have no chance, but at least Davy Jones would not have to provide them with a locker. They would already be in one.

In the event of an accident, or the vehicle turning over, the presumption is that the screw seated in the narrow centre aisle would let the prisoners out. No one wants to consider the possibility that, in a collision situation, the screw might be out of action or decide that, due to the vehicle filling up with smoke, his own safety is paramount. Like most tragedies waiting to happen, when it does, some unknown bureaucrat will express regret and announce a review

23

of procedures.

The transport screws signed us into their custody, took us on board, whereupon the handcuffs were removed and shut us, one by one, into our compartments. With the six of us secured, we had the obligatory slamming of the outer door then, to the accompaniment of grinding gear changes and teeth rattling vibrations, we commenced our journey to Destination X.

The irony, as we learnt later, was that everyone - including our solicitors - was informed of our destination after they had left us in the cell area and assumed we would be notified accordingly. It was a foretaste of the "mind-games" that all too many screws indulge in, to enhance their otherwise sad lives.

It was the loneliest journey of my life. Outside, darkness had fallen, with a fine drizzle adding to the dreariness. The whole situation, to me, seemed unreal, like a dream that I would soon awaken from. Locked inside my metal cupboard, with only the engine noise penetrating, I was totally isolated, yet through the window slit, could see people hurrying home to their families, a sight that only served to add to my already depressed frame of mind. How many times in the past had I seen these sweat-boxes rumbling through London streets and not given their captive occupants a second thought? In future, I will make a point of giving the face at the window a friendly wave, in the hope that it may perk some poor sod up a bit.

We had journeyed for about half an hour, when our transport turned into a large car-parking area, and came to a shuddering halt. My view was limited to the empty, extremely well lit car park, flanked by a wall that looked like the side of a canyon. Then we slowly moved forward, through a very large entrance, coming to a halt again inside a courtyard, this time with the engine silenced. The stillness was soon shattered though. Keychains rattled; doors crashed; boots clumped; and screws shouted as we were taken from our boxes, and escorted into the reception room, to be met by more screws shouting. I suppose they are told to shout all the time as part of the job. Prison life is all down to control by intimidation and, just like the Army; a big mouth is a mark of authority. One must sympathise with the families of screws, having to live with the shouting and door slamming, and the neighbours must get the right hump. The thought occurred to me as to whether they receive a Strepsil allowance.

We stood in a group, clutching our plastic sacks, in front of a desk, behind which two screws studiously ignored our existence. It turned out that until they had signed for us, as far as they were concerned, we weren't there. Looking around, we saw the framed proclamation declaring that it was the Prison Service's ambition to treat inmates with dignity; to enable them to spend their sentences constructively; and eventually release them to become worthy citizens.

It also informed us that we were now residents of HMP Belmarsh, the "state of the art" monstrosity at Thamesmead.

As we absorbed this information, a new noise joined with the rest. It came from a nearby cell, where the occupant was trying to demolish the door. A rush of bodies and five screws surrounded the doorway, whilst one unlocked it after having shouted through the little window for the prisoner to stand back. A verbal battle then ensued between a black man insisting he needed to use the toilet opposite and a screw demanding to know whether he was going to behave himself. I found the altercation quite absorbing and was pondering the possible link between behaving oneself and going to the toilet, when I was savagely interrupted by one of the desk screws shouting at me for my name. My particulars were duly logged and I was told that I had now become No.EP3490, for the duration of my prison life, and not to forget it. That done, another screw, who was at least 3 metres away, hollered for me to accompany him into the room where I was photographed and strip searched.

The strip search is yet another aspect of the control psychology, in this instance to humiliate. No sooner had I undressed, than I was told to get dressed again. Maybe it was out of deference to my age, or a realisation that since my previous strip search, I had been confined either in a cell, or a sweat-box. Either way, it was a pointless exercise but, in the world of

Belmarsh, pointlessness becomes a norm.

Passing through another door, I rejoined my companions, plus some new faces, in a small dining hall, where I was told to get something to eat at the servery. Some dubious sausages, obviously related to the ones at the court, lukewarm carrots and potatoes, followed by rice pudding, was the total fare on offer, so I took a portion of each and sat down with the others. Two mouthfuls of potato and carrots, flushed down with tea, was all I could manage from the dinner, but I was sorely tempted to go for second helpings of the rice pudding, that intention being scotched due to the servery shutter having been pulled down. I rolled a fag instead, surveyed my surroundings and the five strange faces, one of whom, a white bloke in his mid-twenties, kept jumping up and down telling all and sundry how he wanted to get back to Parkhurst. With his wild expression and somewhat agitated behaviour, I found myself keeping a watchful eye on him.

Then an office door opened and a woman in a white coat called a name. It appeared that the modest dining hall also served as a doctor's waiting room. One by one, at five minute intervals, we were all summoned, with me being the last. The doctor must have been a relative of the judge as, without even looking at me, he recorded that I was drug free; not an alcoholic; was not carrying the HIV or Aids virus; had no other transmittable disease and that I would require the tablets that had also been taken from me in the court cells, to control my blood pressure. That was the medical examination completed, without one button being undone. In Belmarsh, the screws undress you more than the doctors.

I rejoined the others, who were in the process of being assembled by a screw with a clipboard, then with a screw in front and two in the rear, we all filed out to see what the accommodation was like.

Along empty corridors, through numerous locked gates, up stairs and down stairs, we were eventually shepherded into a large TV room that didn't have a chair, let alone a television set. With the door duly locked, two of the screws disappeared, whilst the third paced up and down outside. We, in the meantime, stood around smoking, suffering a combination of Mr Gloomy declaring that at least it wasn't Brixton, and the agitated one claiming that we were in one of the biggest shit holes going. I was still hallucinating that it was all still a dream that I would shortly awaken from. The clipboard screw returned, the door was unlocked, and an argument commenced. We were all to occupy double cells, some together and others going in with an existing occupant. Mullin, one of the strangers, was not having that. He had been sentenced but still faced further serious charges and, due to the use of informers, the other bloke may have been told that it would be worth his while to glean some damaging little snippets, to pass along to the authorities. He was aware that, even if you are guarded in your conversation with a stranger, after a few days of being locked up for 22 hours together, the tendency is to become less guarded. Things may even be mumbled when asleep. The screws promptly resolved that issue. Mullin was put on report for refusing an order, handcuffed, and marched off to do solitary in the isolation block. With that little matter sorted, the screws commenced to take us in one's and two's to the reception wing cells until, to my horror, there was only me and the exile from Parkhurst left. Feeling rather depressed and only wanting to be left alone in a quite corner, the prospect of being cooped up with that hyped-up individual, constantly twittering on about how much better Parkhurst was, assumed nightmare proportions. Then we were called and I trudged along behind him and the screw, dragging my plastic sack. Through another two barred gates, along the landing, down the metal stairs, to eventually be halted outside a cell on the ground floor. With a flourish of keys, the door was unlocked and in we went, to have the door immediately slammed shut behind us. The cell was tatty more than dirty, and my companion straightaway commenced to unroll what passed as a sheet and blanket at Belmarsh, to make his bed up. It was pretty obvious that he had done it too many times before. I began to do the same, then saw the large round stain on the cotton mattress cover, clearly the produce of someone's bed-wetting, and decided that I would either sleep sitting up, or on the floor. Danny, for that was his name, spotted the cause of my concern and, embellished by much profanity about screws in general for expecting people to sleep in such conditions, pressed the buzzer button to summon one of them. Nearly 10 minutes went by with no response, so he began kicking the

29

door, which generated an almost immediate result. The shutter clicked back, and a pair of eyes peered through the observation window. "He can't sleep on this, guv!" shouted Danny, pointing at the soiled mattress, "we'll have to change it!" "Turn it over!" came the response. Danny grabbed it, and flipped it over, exposing a large, smelly, hole in the centre. "It's bleedin' rotten, guv, you'll have to sling it out!" Keys rattled, and the door crashed back against the wall, revealing one irritated screw. "That'll be alright, with the sheet over it!" he claimed, then we can sort another one out in the morning!" I wasn't going to argue about the matter, in case it made things worse. I didn't want to be arguing with screws on my first night, but Danny wasn't going to be fobbed off. "No way can he sleep on that, guv, it's bleeding alive. He'll end up with typhoid, and what with the stink and things running around in it, his asthma will go through the roof!" Not being asthmatic, that possibility had not crossed my mind, but it definitely had an effect on the screw. The consequences of me requiring medical attention during the night clearly entered his thoughts, and screws will always act to cover themselves. "All right, then!" he conceded, "stick it outside and we'll pull another one out where it's not being used!" Danny immediately yanked the mattress off my bed, stood it outside the door, and followed the screw to a neighbouring cell, returning a couple of minutes later with a replacement. Without so much as a goodnight, the screw slammed the door shut and hurried off; no doubt hoping that the mug of tea he had left was still warm. My companion was well pleased with what he viewed as a victory over the system in general, and screws in particular. Turning to me, with a satisfied smirk on his face, he said, "That's lesson number one for you. Always keep on their case; otherwise the lazy bastards will do nothing for you!" Both of us knew that without his efforts, I would have suffered the rotted mattress, so I emphasised my thanks to him, but Danny had already turned his back on me, to make up his bed. I just sat on mine watching him, still mentally adjusting to my present circumstances, and half-heartedly began rolling a fag. It took him less than five minutes to lay his few belongings on the cupboard shelves; hang his items of clothing up; arraign his toilet equipment around the sink taps; carefully place his little box of letters, cards, and photographs inside his cupboard; check the state of the lavatory; roll a cigarette, light it, and lay on top of his blanket, idly watching the smoke curl upwards. He had obviously gone through the same routine many times before. His cigarette lighting equipment had caught my attention. It consisted of solely the wheel and flint part of a lighter, and what appeared to be very thick string but, in reality, was a piece of mop head. The spark from the flint actually caused this to smoulder, thus saving on buying matches. I couldn't help visualising though, thousands of scalped floor mops in prisons up and down the country. It was the first of many innovations I was to witness during the coming months.

I had no inclination to unpack my plastic sack, which still sat on the floor at the foot of my bed, confining myself to rolling up my overcoat, to use as an extra pillow. Danny had transformed in the meantime, and was now much calmer. He had weighed me up quietly, and now commenced to strike up a conversation, prefaced with what was to become the regular opening query from other inmates during my stay, asking as to whether I was alright. It was probably due to the fact that, age-wise, I was old enough to be most inmates' father. Surprisingly, apart from clarifying a few details, such as my name, and home area, Danny talked mostly about himself.

He was 26 years old, and during the previous ten years, had become something of a veteran of the penal system, referring to various prisons in the same way as men on the outside would discuss the varying merits of pubs, and holiday destinations. His fiancée was currently in Holloway; why he didn't say, but they were hoping the prison authorities would permit them to see each other sometime, as they were both claiming to be common law husband and wife. In the event of them being unsuccessful, he was considering requesting permission for the two of them to marry. Listening to him talking away, whilst still mentally adjusting to my new environment, I found myself slipping onto a plane of unreality, like Alice stepping through the Looking Glass. I was actually visualising a prison wedding!! The chaplain symbolically handcuffing them together; the bride and groom posing for the wedding photos', with the two of them holding number plates across their chests; then driving off on their honeymoon in a sweat box, to the Isle of Wight, to spend the night in the Parkhurst bridal suite.

I was brought back to reality by someone in the cell next door thumping on the wall, and calling for a light. Danny shouted for them to hang on a few minutes, and he would send one across to their window. Taking hold of the edge of his blanket, which was manufactured like a big string vest, he pulled out a whole length of weave, and tied one end round a roll-on deodorant, leaving a few inches to spare. This was then tied round a short length of mop head, which was in turn ignited. Dangling the smouldering article out of the window, weighted down by the deodorant, and his face pressed against the bars, he called on our neighbour to be ready to catch it. Swinging it pendulum fashion, he progressively played out the length of blanket weave, until the hand protruding through the bars next door was able to catch it. Cigarette lit, it was then released for Danny to haul back in. To any casual observer outside, the smouldering mop head string, swinging to and fro in the darkness, must have looked like a firefly unable to make its mind up where to land, and making itself dizzy in the process.

Danny clearly recognised my less than buoyant mood, and tried in his way to cheer me up. Comparing the three months I would actually have to serve, provided I didn't lose any remission, with the fact that he wouldn't be released until the year 2001, he calculated I would use no more than three tubes of toothpaste. In the morning, he explained, I would be taken on a very short conducted tour of our part of the prison, along with the other new inmates, where I would have the opportunity to 'phone home and arrange for up to three visitors to see me. That piece of information did actually perk me up a bit. He then went on to say that we would probably be separated the next day, as being a transfer inmate, he would be allocated straight away to one of the permanent wings. I found myself actually regretting that, as I was not only taking a bit of a liking to him, but in the unknown world I now occupied, I felt he would be a valuable companion. On the subject of allocations to cells, he stressed the need for me to push to share with one of my co-defendants, provided we got on with each other. The thought of being locked up for hours on end with Mr Gloomy, ruled one of them out straight away. One reason to emphasise with the screws, was that you were both appealing, and therefore, needed to be able to discuss the various points as the appeal progressed. Apart from that, he said, you're better off sharing with someone you know, rather than take a chance with a stranger, who may turn out, at best, to be forever scrounging, or a junkie; and at worst, someone with whom you will rapidly develop an urge to throttle. He went on to give me other snippets of advice, but due to tiredness creeping up on me, some of it failed to register. Danny took the cue, slipped underneath his string blanket, bade me goodnight, and went asleep almost immediately. Standing up to survey my bed and its dubious cleanliness, I removed my boots, turned off the light, and lay, fully clothed on top of the bed. In the gloom of the cell, illuminated by an outside floodlight, the events of the day raced through my mind, mixed up with concern as to how my family, particularly my wife, were coping with the situation.   The pointlessness of locking me up, when it would have made more sense to heavily fine me, could only be explained as pure revenge by the state, and as an illusionary attempt to deter others.   The cost of the lengthy court farce, and now the expense of keeping me in prison, far outweighed the sum I had denied the Treasury.

Having been a political activist for over thirty years, I couldn't help comparing the few thousands of excise duty I was sentenced for, to the billions that the Tory government had fleeced the country for, by selling off nearly all the public assets at substantially knocked down prices.   I heartily cursed the judge for the misery he had unnecessarily inflicted on myself and my family, and wished him the most painful illness imaginable.   Maybe if they were made to serve a prison sentence, and all that it entailed for their families, they would only send others there as a last, rather than a first, resort.   With all those thoughts churning round in my head, I eventually drifted off to sleep, on my first night in the bizarre world of Belmarsh.

* * * * * * * * * *

Chapter 2

Belmarsh Baptism

I was awakened by the sound of the toilet being flushed. The pan was about half a metre from my head, with a thin partition wall between us. Looking at my watch, it was 7.45 a.m., and apart from the gurgling urinal, there was not a sound to be heard. Danny emerged from the cubicle, expressing the hope that he hadn't disturbed me and advising me that, in the event of having the bed on the same side as the toilet, I should have my head at the opposite end. More so, he added, if I was sharing with a bloke who may have extremely ripe bowel contents. Thanking him for his advice, I made use of the facility myself, then returned to sit on my bed. In addition to the two beds, the cell, like all the others, was also furnished with two small tables, two wooden chairs, plus a large cupboard complete with shelf above each bed. The chairs were used for a variety of purposes, such as piling clothes on, and only used for seating when the beds could accommodate no more guests.

A small hand-basin completed the fittings, above which a small, polished, stainless steel plate was glued on the wall, as a shaving mirror.

Commencing to make a roll-up, Danny informed me

that we would be opened up for breakfast very soon and, sure enough, dead on 8.00 a.m., an outer metal gate crashed back, and to the accompaniment of the obligatory shouting, key chain jangling, and clumping boots, the screws opened up all the cell doors.

Having put my boots on, I followed Danny outside, to join the other inmates milling around in what was the association area. In amongst the 40 to 50 blokes, I spotted my co-defendants, and made my way towards them to have a chat, but before I reached them, a screw came bustling around telling everyone to line up at the outer metal gate. Two screws manned the gate, and were counting off six at a time, to go to a servery at the opposite end of the building, to get their breakfasts. Screws stood at intervals on the route, with one positioned at each end of the servery, issuing plastic mugs and cutlery. As each six returned clutching their metal trays, with the food laying in recesses, another six would be sent on their way. The reason for ensuring that the screws always outnumbered the inmates at the servery was, I learned, because it was always regarded as a potential trouble spot, with inmates either accusing the inmates serving of holding back on some of the preferred items, or complaining about the quality of the food. In both instances, it must be said, with full justification.

I noticed that Danny stayed at the back of the queue, so I joined him, which wasn't difficult as everyone else seemed eager to push to the front. He explained that as prisoners returned to their cells, and had obtained hot water from the dispenser that stood on each wing, they were locked up by the screws. By being last, it lengthened the overall time out of the cell.

On top of that, he added, being the last usually meant a bit extra, as anything left was only tipped down the waste disposal. Eventually it was our turn, so we strolled down towards the servery, no point in rushing, taking a stone cold tray from the "heated" cabinet as we got there. The choice confronting us was either a hard boiled egg, or two lumps of luke-warm tinned tomatoes. Danny spotted two cracked eggs, that didn't count, and then said we would both have tomatoes, as they would have been our first choice. The screw confirmed they were both cracked, and begrudgingly let us have them. Porridge, unsurprisingly, was also on offer, so I had some of that as well. The selection was completed by some lightly tinged bread that was regarded as toast, and as many slices of bread as we wished. An inmate scooped lumps of margarine from a container, to stick on the corner of each alternative piece of bread. I'm sure he thought he was a bricklayer, building a garden wall.

The screw waiting for us at the end of the counter plonked a plastic mug, complete with tea bag, sweetener, and whitener sachets, on each tray; and then stood a plastic cutlery set up in it as well. Returning to the wing, with my egg rolling around with the tomatoes, and a lump of bread plummeting to the floor, the only attraction was the prospect of a drink of tea.   There was no danger of the mug escaping like the bread, due to the screw having thoughtfully stuck it half on my porridge.

Back in our cell, and having filled our mugs with hot water, a screw promptly banged our door shut. Sitting on our respective beds, the trays on a table between us, Danny immediately passed me his hard boiled egg.   I was soon to realise during the new few days that, although they were served up daily, a lot of inmates had no liking for them, therefore, once they learnt how I relished them, I was to end up with never less than a dozen on my shelf.   What they weren't to appreciate was the inevitable tail wind, that always seemed to emanate whilst I was in their company.

The porridge, I thought, was quite tasty, and the eggs, tomatoes and toast, soon followed it.   My cell-mate, I noticed, ate half of the tomatoes, a piece of toast, then standing up, threw the remainder, plus about four slices of bread out of the window.   Then, having rolled a fag, which in prison language is referred to as a burn, he lay back on his bed, blowing smoke rings in the air.   A couple of minutes passed by, whilst I rolled a burn, then, breaking the silence, he opined that it was my first time in prison.   I replied in the affirmative, following which he proceeded to give me what turned out to be good advice.   Examples were - don't start counting the days until you are past the half-way mark, because it will only depress you; be firm with the scroungers, otherwise they will clean you out; avoid the tearaway element, otherwise you risk losing remission if you are caught up in their antics; and generally keep your head down, but don't let the screws take too many liberties. Three things to particularly avoid were (1) Going into a cell uninvited; (2) Talking about other prisoners in front of screws; and (3) Helping myself to other inmates' belongings. A cell thief was generally despised, and very often had to be transferred for their own safety. He went on to comment that, at my age, and serving a short sentence, I wouldn't have too much to worry about from either prisoners or screws. On the last point, I must say, there is much more respect shown towards older people in prison, by both sides, than they obtain on the outside. Frequently, I was pleasantly surprised by little acts of consideration by individuals one would normally cross the road to avoid.

My education was interrupted by the doors being unlocked, so the trays could be put on the floor outside, to be collected by an inmate cleaner. Then a screw, with a clipboard, called the names of the new prisoners to assemble outside, whilst the transferees, like Danny, were to be relocked in the cells. I linked up with my co-defendants, to compare notes on the situation so far. Apart from myself, Mr Gloomy was the only one who had seemed able to eat any breakfast, but it hadn't improved his attitude. He reckoned the place was full of junkies, and psychos, who would slit your throat for a fag, and no way was he going to use the shower recess without someone he knew and trusted being there as well. In his opinion it was better to be locked up, so at least he'd be safe. One of the others warned him not to bank on it, as whoever he was banged up with would probably throttle him, just to preserve their own sanity. As he pondered that scenario, the screw with the clipboard informed us, there were about fifteen of us altogether, that he would be taking us on a short tour, taking in the library; a visit to the probationers; obtaining some toothpaste and disposable razors, plus a towel; from the stores.

The highlight was to be an interview with the Principal Officer, the screw in charge of the house-block, which consisted of three wings, holding a total of 171 prisoners, where we would be able to make one telephone call home, to arrange, if we wished, a visit to take place as early as the next day. Even Mr Gloomy was cheered by that bit of information. We then followed him off the wing, which in Belmarsh, we were told, was referred to as a spur, each receiving what was to be the routine rub down search, as we passed through the gate. On this occasion the rub down was carried out by a female screw, who bluntly told one bloke who wanted to go back in and come out again, that there would be no point as she couldn't feel any concealed item the first time.

The library was a medium sized room, half stocked with cast-offs from the London Borough of Greenwich, staffed by a civilian librarian who had difficulties writing up the name cards for those wishing to take books out. Having locked us in there, the screw disappeared, presumably for a smoke and a cup of tea. Returning after about half an hour, we were then taken to the probationers, who, seeing us individually, asked if we had any problems we would like them to help with.   In our naivety, we nearly all unloaded our various concerns on them, only to learn later that, either through a genuine inability, or laziness, that the Belmarsh probation service was, in the main, a waste of time and space. The P.O. also received us one at a time in his office and recited what was obviously a standard speech, that boiled down to keeping one's nose clean, and do what one was told.   I took the opportunity of asking him about my prospects of being transferred to an open prison, such as Ford, to which he advised me to put in a written request, but not to hold my breath waiting.   I also raised the matter of my blood pressure tablets being taken from me, and not having had one that morning.   That actually seemed to concern him, as he straightaway rang the medical wing to have a tablet sent over.   Screws of all grades will cover themselves.   Then the 'phone call.

Security dictated that a screw had to dial the number and stay within earshot of the subsequent conversation; why, I could never fathom out.   Maybe they thought I might be arranging for my wife to organise a helicopter to swoop down and pluck me out through a barred window; or that I may divulge sensitive information such as what I had   for breakfast.   Hearing my wife's voice cheered me up, especially as she seemed to be handling the situation O.K.   One of the few positive features of Belmarsh was that inmates could wear their own clothing, so I listed the items I would require, plus my chess set.   One could also have an unlimited private

42

account that, in addition to whatever prison wages were earned, could be spent in the prison shop, known as the Canteen, so I requested her to pay in £100 when she came to visit me. As a new arrival, I could have a visit as soon as I wished, and it was great to know that my wife, daughter and youngest son, would be visiting the next day. Subsequent visits would revolve round my bi-weekly entitlement, valid for any day; and an additional privilege one, valid only on week-days. The maximum number of visitors each time was three adults. Like most inmates, I was totally unaware of the ordeal visitors to Belmarsh were subjected to until after my release, but more of that later. The screw then terminated the 'phone conversation and I rejoined the others gathered in the TV room. As least, that is what the sign on the door said, but as such a usage would entail supervising inmates off their spurs, and additional work for screws, it was only used for herding prisoners in, rather than having them cluttering up the corridor. Apart from that, there was no television set in there anyway, just an empty room with a lock on the door. The screw with the clipboard was in the process of reciting the various occupation options available to us. Everyone in Belmarsh had to work, or attend education classes. Refusal would result in loss of privileges and/or remission. Work consisted of the Farm and Gardens, although there was no Farm, just vegetable patches and flower beds full of rose bushes, or working in what was known as the Plug Shop, packing items ranging from plastic cutlery to light bulbs. Earnings in the Plug Shop were based on the piece work system and could, rarely, amount to

£20 per week; whereas working outside, but inside the prison walls, on Farms and Gardens, paid £16 per week.

Our group, it transpired, was not unique amongst the prison population, for its lack of enthusiasm to go pottering around outside in the middle of winter. Education classes were morning or afternoon only affairs, with subjects restricted to basic English and numeracy; computers; cookery and Psychology, all subjects dependent on retired, or part-time, staff from the South London Poly turning up. Those on education would receive £4.50 per week. When one prisoner queried about the Decorating and the Motor Mechanics workshops, the screw replied that the first was temporarily closed because they had expended their budget for paints and wallpaper, and that the Governor had shut down the latter. We learnt later that he had become aware that the screws were having their own cars serviced and valeted there, for the price of a pouch of tobacco, although the official reason was, once again, cost. What was available for those with a practical bent, was the recently introduced floor polishing course, where one could learn about the different materials, and solutions, for a whole variety of surfaces, especially those that existed in Belmarsh. It was a course that suited everyone, as the Governor could impress important visitors with some of the shiniest floors in the Penal System, if not the whole country; and in addition to the princely sum of £8.00 per week, prisoners got to move around the prison to see old mates and pick up any gossip. Some even thought the certificate they could obtain might enable them to obtain employment, when released, with a cleaning company. What the reaction of the business community might be to having a cleaner with a certificate stamped with HMP Belmarsh on the loose, after hours, in their offices, was a matter of much conjecture. It struck me as ironic that on the outside, millions couldn't work, whether they wished to, or not, yet inside you were punished if you didn't. Maybe it had something to do with the rates of pay. I calculated that with minimum requirements, such as a smoke, and a 'phone card to use as, and when, I could get on the spur 'phone, that were more than covered by my personal account; plus a belief that I would benefit more from mental stimulation than physical activity, I put my name down for Education.

The final work option, the screw concluded, was cleaning inside, and outside, the house-block, including the collecting of the dirty trays, to be returned for washing to the servery.

Those functions, and the job of actually serving up the food, were subject to the whims of the screws on the house-block we would shortly be allocated to. There was never a shortage of those seeking to be made cleaners because, apart from the wages ranging between £6.00 and £16.00 per week, depending on the actual duties to be performed, it also meant time out of the cell when others were banged up, therefore easier access to the one and only telephone.

The screw duly noted a preference against each name,

some of which were actually expressed, then, like the Pied Piper, led us out of the room and down the stairs to the houseblock stores. There we were confronted by another screw, who made a big thing of checking the names on the clipboard, before unloading all his problems onto his colleague.

Apparently, the screws took turns at being what they designated, the Cleaning Officer. That made them responsible for stores coming in, and going out, plus organising the cleaning inside the houseblock, and outside. The cleaning on each of the three spurs was left to the senior screw on each spur. We stood there listening while he groaned on about the admin. people messing up the rota; how stores items never arrived; and the obvious belief of those "up above" that he had at least six pairs of hands. The "clipboard" screw looked totally bored, no doubt having heard it all before, and suggested that he should be getting us back to our spur. Belmarsh screws share a common aversion to prisoners being out of their cells, and the suggestion stimulated the Cleaning Officer into curtailing his moaning, going inside his store-room to return with a box of goodies. As our names were called, he ceremoniously issued each of us with a small tube of S.R. toothpaste; a roll-on deodorant; a bar of soap; a shaving stick and a disposable razor. That done, we were shepherded back to our spur, just in time to line up for our mid-day meal, our stores issues rammed into our pockets. Being a hot meal, the metal tray was stone cold and I returned with what was claimed to be stew, with a scoop of potato mix rolling around in it, like a golf ball. The door being locked, I had to ask a screw to let me into the cell and immediately noticed that Danny's possessions were gone. Querying the situation, the screw informed me that Danny had been moved onto one of the permanent spurs, and not to get too comfortable, as I would shortly be doing the same, then the door crashed shut. Having nothing better to do, I consumed some of the now lukewarm stew, then rolled a fag to smoke as I gazed out of the barred window. I could see where most of the piles of bread given out at the servery ended up. The ground outside was littered, to the obvious delight of the hordes of pigeons that had descended. Belmarsh, I thought, must have the fattest pigeon population in London, if not the country, with some of them only taking off again with real difficulty.

Belmarsh prison consists of four houseblocks, containing three spurs each, plus the Special Secure Unit, a prison within a prison, of which more later. Apart from the hospital block, also of which more later, that is the sum total of "accommodation". Each spur holds 57 prisoners in a mixture of double and single cells, 171 altogether in each houseblock. During the course of the afternoon I could hear prisoners being moved, against a background of doors crashing and names and numbers being called out. Eventually, Patel, one of my co-defendants, and myself, were escorted to spur 2, Houseblock 2, with assurances that all efforts would be made to put us together, as requested. On arrival, he was locked up with Tony, a young black drug dealer from Lewisham, whilst I was to share with Mo, a West Indian from

Brixton, who was finishing off serving the mandatory 11 years of a 16-year sentence for armed robbery. Much of his time had been spent elsewhere, mainly Parkhurst, but he had been brought back to Belmarsh so he could be released the following month in the London area. Mo was down the gym when I arrived and as I entered the cell, the sight of his "ghetto blaster" taking up the whole of the window sill generated spine chilling thoughts of being locked up for hours on end, having to suffer non-stop rap and reggae. Thankfully, as it turned out, it was not the case, as Mo mainly preferred listening to plays and panel programmes.

Lacking any enthusiasm to start unpacking, I left my big plastic sack on the floor, lay on the unused bed and began reading the four day old newspaper that had been left on the table. I must have dozed, because the door banging back against the wall brought me back to reality. In came Mo, dressed in prison issue blue singlet and shorts, giving me a look that made me feel like Goldilocks when the bears returned home. Before the screw could shut the door, Mo asked to be able to fill his mug from the dispenser outside, so as to make tea. Without waiting for a reply, he was out of the door, returning to query whether I wanted some hot water for the same purpose. I did, and with the screw reminding us we were not in a hotel, dug my plastic mug from my sack and followed him across to the machine. Not a word passed between us until we were back in the cell and a tea-bag floating in each mug. Then we introduced ourselves and he proceeded to demolish

48

the first of many of my preconceptions regarding black people. "Was I on drugs?" he asked, and I automatically thought he wanted to trade some. When I replied in the negative, he said that was O.K. then. My predecessor had been and Mo, who was hostile to anything stronger than marijuana, (weed), or cannabis, which he regarded as medicinal, had got the screws to move him. As it turned out, I had fallen on my feet being banged up with Mo, because not only did he have the experience to help me to cope with my new environment, but he also commanded a lot of respect among the other inmates and, as his cell mate, I also benefited from that.

We both lay back on our beds, our backs propped up against the wall, puffing our burns. Mo made what appeared to be small talk but, in effect, was learning the background of his new cell-mate and, once aware that it was my first time "away", proceeded to give me some tips. Some of what he said, particularly relating to scroungers, had already been said by Danny, but two pieces of advice proved especially valuable, as I was to appreciate in the coming weeks. Firstly, I was not to let myself get wound up by the "mind games" that many of the screws indulged in. This was where they would undertake to follow up an inmate's request, be it for information about transfers; getting to the canteen (prison shop); or for some toilet paper, and then do nothing about it. Prisoners who were dependent on the paltry wages would find they were not required for work and, in Belmarsh, no work meant not only no wages, but also resulted in being banged up for 22 hours per day.

Prisoners who started educational or training courses would find themselves overlooked when the names were called for classes, with the later excuses given being of either a typing error or they must have been asleep.

The results of these "mind games" often resulted in frustrated prisoners kicking hell out of their cell doors, or getting into arguments with screws, leading to governor's punishments ranging from loss of privileges; solitary confinement; or loss of remission. What those screws that indulged in this routine sadism achieved could only be some perverse satisfaction for a condition that should be identified, and treated. The second major point was to try and stay on Spur 2., as compared with the others it was relatively free of junkies, cell thieves and other undesirable elements, that were a pain in the neck to those inmates who just wanted to get through their time. He shared the P.O.'s opinion that I was most unlikely to be transferred due to the shortness of my sentence and said nothing when I expressed my intention to pursue the matter. The main reason we had the best spur was Mr B., who was the screw that ran the show. Twenty-eight years old and ambitious for promotion, he was conscious of how it looked on his record to be seen to have everything under control. To that end, he would have those who caused him problems transferred, either to other spurs, or another prison. He would also facilitate the transfer of prisoners to his spur to further his objective, a practice made easy as nearly all his counterparts were indifferent as to whom they were in charge of. The end product was a spur consisting, in the main, of mature prisoners like Mo, getting through long sentences, and me, who was to be stuck there because I wasn't doing long enough, a situation adding to the sense of unreality that was to permeate my enforced stay.

We chatted generally as I unpacked my plastic sack and arranged my bits and pieces in the wall cupboard, suspended over my bed. I mentioned my regret that I hadn't been given more time to speak with my wife, both to reassure her I was O.K., and to bring my chess set the next day, but even if I possessed the necessary 'phone card - which I didn't - my prospects of getting on the telephone during the next two hours of association time were zero. All the prisoners were let out of their cells between 6.00 pm and 8.00 to obtain their evening meal and mix with others, within the confines of the spur. It was during that limited time that access to the one telephone, on the first landing, was available to the overwhelming majority. The exceptions were cleaners, who could make calls during the additional time they were let out of their cells, as their main privilege. The mathematics of the situation was up to 40 men wishing to make a 10-minute call, in 120 minutes. It was a source of great amusement to many screws, to watch the inevitable scramble and the resultant arguments. As part of their mind games, they would open the same cells last, so their occupants were always confronted by a queue, and routinely forget to turn the telephone on from the houseblock office, known as the Bubble.

When inmates protested, the screws would claim to be busy supervising those getting their meal, who would be equally upset if they were delayed whilst one of the six screws walked 30 metres to the Bubble for the purpose of flicking a switch.   In order to deny the screws their pleasure, some of the prisoners had taken on the job of organising a telephone list, whereby a rota was developed and those unsuccessful one evening started off first the next.   The only real abuse was inmates putting their names on the list, for the sole purpose of trading their place when it came up for a burn from another who had no chance that evening.   Whilst the practice generated protest, it was reluctantly tolerated as a small price to pay to avoid the alternative free for all.

Most of the screws, with exceptions such as Mr B., resented those who organised lists, whether for the telephone or the pool table, perceiving it as a threat to their total control.   Mo told me not to worry as he would get my name on the list as soon as the door was opened, and borrow a 'phone card on my behalf. Not long after we were opened up and before the screw had got his key back out of the lock, Mo was out the door and up the stairs, like a greyhound, while I ambled over to join the throng lining up for the hotplate (servery).   This was the one meal where the prisoners were not immediately locked up, being the start of association, so there was no hanging about getting their meal.   I returned to the cell with what was alleged to be egg flan, drowned in gravy, crowned with a scoop of potato.   In another tray recess was a ladle full of mixed carrot and turnip, likewise submerged, and in a third was a flat slab of jelly held down by a rock cake.

Mo was in the process of mixing a tin of sweetcorn and one of tuna in a plastic bowl that had originated in the hospital wing. Being a health and fitness enthusiast, he would only eat very selectively from the hotplate, maintaining that the food was low grade to start with and reduced to crap in the preparation process. Belmarsh, he claimed, was the only prison where the Governor avoided the symbolic sampling ceremony. Mo's concern with his diet and exercise was not a fetish, but very important to long-serving prisoners, where the environment was extremely conducive to letting oneself deteriorate. Another source of friction at the servery was the question of diet. The screw who was designated as the Cleaning Officer would stand at the servery, supposedly to ensure that each inmate received his fair portion. He would also note down any requests by prisoners to be classified as vegetarians or vegans, so that they could be adequately catered for. Most inmates requested to be put down as pork free, not because of any mass conversion to Judaism or wishing to be followers of the Prophet, but as a means of obtaining boiled fish or beef. When they next went for their dinner, a different screw overseeing the servery would claim to have nothing written on his clipboard about any requests, therefore the choice would lay between a couple of anaemic meatballs swimming in fat, or go without, and a couple of trays of boiled fish would go down the waste disposal chute as surplus to requirements. Hardly a session went by without arguments on this issue, much to the obvious delight of the watching screws, who got their kicks out of winding up inmates.   For my own part, I would eat almost anything, and after a short while arrived at a situation where all I had to do was to indicate what I wanted and got it, for reasons that will be revealed later.

Sitting myself down on the edge of my bed, I noticed the phonecard laying on my half of the table.   Mo had borrowed it to lend to me, to be reimbursed as soon as I was able to visit the canteen.   He also informed me that as soon as I had finished eating, I was to go to the telephone on the first landing and see David, who had taken on the function of overseeing the waiting list.   Needless to say, the contents of my tray came second best in the contest between it and getting on the 'phone, and barely one minute later, I was up on the first landing.   One inmate was in the process of making a call with his spare hand pressed over the other ear, with another dozen or so standing around waiting their turn.   A Rastan, dressed in a blue nylon track suit, with dreadlocks down to his waist, stood nearby, clutching a sheet of paper, listening to a bloke protesting about his placement on the list.   Seeing me standing there, he terminated the complainant by telling him he had no case, and came over to me.   Confirming that I was Mo's cell-mate, he gave me the pleasant news that I just happened to be the next on the list to make a call but, in future, I would have to take my turn with everyone else and, so as to not make myself unnecessarily unpopular with my new neighbours, who knew I was being slotted in at their expense, to keep my call short and sweet.   This I did, and the surprise expressed in my wife's voice, when she didn't expect to be speaking with me until the next day, really cheered me up.   It would have been easy to just natter away, enjoying the tangible link with the world outside, knowing that she was most probably in the house on her own, but the line-up behind me provided a very powerful incentive not to.   We clarified what items of clothing she would be bringing, plus my chess set, and buoyed yet further with the reminder that my youngest son, and daughter, would also be coming on the morrow, I reluctantly ended the conversation.   I didn't actually hang up as, seeing that I had finished, the next man in the queue took the handset off me, pressed the cradle down and was tapping his number in, before I had even stepped away.   I thanked David and returned to my cell, to eat the jelly and munch the rock cake.

Mo had gone off somewhere, so I ate alone, but not in silence as, being on the ground floor, I was only a few feet away from the T.V set; the pool table and half the population of the spur, all seeming to be talking, arguing, or shouting, simultaneously.   My meal finished, I rolled a burn, popped one of Mo's teabags into my plastic mug, left the cell and walked across to the hot water dispenser to make a cuppa.   On top of the machine lay a paper bag with some sachets of whitener inside, so I emptied two into my drink.   It was a chalk-like substance that lay on top of the water like a layer of dust.   Seating myself on a battered chair that must have started its working life in an airport departure lounge, with my mug of tea placed on the floor underneath, I lit my fag and surveyed the surroundings, particularly my co-inhabitants.

The two focal points were the T.V. set, that was to mainly churn out soaps; sport; and the always popular travel documentaries; and the pool table. This piece of equipment, quarter size, was to be a constant source of dissension, with the waiting list always being challenged, often with justification. On one occasion, an aggrieved Glaswegian named Greaves resolved the dispute he was having, by grabbing the white ball, running into his cell, slamming the door, and throwing it out of the window. For days after, a red ball with a biroed cross had to substitute, until a replacement was pilfered by a cleaner who had access to a neighbouring spur. The game in progress on this occasion seemed normal enough, until I realised the pool cue was a broom handle due, looking back, to probably another light-fingered cleaner replacing one that went astray on another spur. Inside the barred gate that let you off the wing, three warders, one a woman, sat chatting round a large desk, allowing themselves to be disturbed every so often by an inmate querying some issue or other. Periodically, a call from the control Bubble would come through to the telephone fixed to the bars behind them and they would yell out for a prisoner to go to the pharmacy to obtain something to help them sleep. The only time they would actually move off their chairs before lock-up time was to respond to the alarm going off, or to let individuals in, or out, of the spur. I noticed very soon that some inmates, who turned out to be cleaners, could come and go quite freely, to either visit friends on the other two spurs, or use a second telephone located outside the Bubble.   Close by to where the screws sat, a prisoner was attempting to iron a pair of jeans, that kept sliding off the board. There seemed to be a fairly even balance of black and white inmates, with only two or three that would seem to be older than myself.   Later on, when I had got to know most of my fellow prisoners, the breakdown, give or take a couple, worked out as a third Afro; a third whites from around South-East, and East, London; Belmarsh being the prison serving the various courts in those areas; 10 or 12 Irishmen; and the remainder a motley collection, including myself, Patel, a couple of Jocks and two from Portugal.

My thoughts were interrupted by a black man asking me for a burn, but remembering what Danny had impressed on me, told him that I had only a bit of dust left until I could get to the canteen when next it opened, which was after the week-end. As he moved away, Patel came across to bemoan the fact that he started the day with twenty Benson and Hedges cigarettes, and having smoked three himself, only had two left.   His cell-mate had consumed most of the remainder, with others zeroing in as soon as the cells were unlocked.   Patel, possibly feeling vulnerable between the blacks and whites, had tried to buy friendship from those who only viewed him as a soft touch.   I told him to either start learning to say no, or pack up smoking.

Like myself, Patel was looking forward to a visit the

next day when, in addition to items of clothing, his father would be depositing funds into his private account and bringing him his Nintendo computer game. A major matter to be dealt with during the visit was to ensure his father understood which newspapers went to what addresses when their team of paper-boys did their morning rounds. Apparently Mr Patel senior was not very proficient in the English language, so his son dealt with that part of the business, and kept the list in his head. He had spent all that afternoon writing it down with the intention of passing it to his father the next day, and in recognition of his father's limitations, the list was written both in English and Guajarati. The only problem was that his Guajarati was as good as his father's English, so he hoped there would be sufficient time to go through it at least twice. I couldn't help thinking what a jolly visit they would be having; a sobbing mother worried about her little boy; a father coping with a self-inflicted sense of shame; a wife there to hold hands, provided she wasn't required in the shop, and Patel trying to explain who has the Daily Mirror and the TV Times, in very basic English interspersed with broken Guajarati. In the meantime, I had drunk my tea and decided to take an exploratory walk upstairs to the other two landings, rather than listen to a minor dispute at the pool table; Patel wondering who would be buying at the Cash-and-Carry in his absence, all set against the hysterical voices of a B-rated American soap, emanating from the TV. Rinsing my mug at the water dispenser, I returned it to my cell and, whilst there, rolled another fag, then headed off up the iron stairs.

David was still supervising the 'phone queue on the first landing as I continued on up to the second.   It was quieter up there, due to most of the occupants being downstairs, but walking to the locked gate at the end, I couldn't help smelling the distinct aroma of puff drifting out of a couple of cells.   Officially it was an offence to possess it and occasionally the screws would search (spin) a few cells, but unofficially, it was tolerated due to its calming influence on those smoking it.   What was of real concern was crack, which produced the opposite effect.   I retraced my steps to the head of the stairs, to look out of the one and only window on the landing. It afforded the choice of either looking across at some tower blocks in Plumstead, with traffic moving tantalisingly freely about half a mile away; or looking down at a sombre building that stood eerily bathed in floodlights, approximately 100 metres from the one I was in.   This, I learnt from Mo later, was the Special Secure Unit (S.S.U.), a prison within a prison, that housed up to 28 top security prisoners.   It was referred to as the Double A unit, where 25 and 30 year plus sentences were the norm.   Opening the windows, I could see that a light rain was falling, but the fresh wind blowing through the bars was a welcome relief from the staleness inside.   My fag finished, I had just flicked the remains out into the night when a screw began yelling "Get your water, lads"!   That cry routinely signalled the end of association, when mugs would be filled for the last cuppa of the day, and plastic bottles wrapped in newspapers would become makeshift thermos flasks, for those who wished to have a top-up.   I looked at my watch.   It was exactly 8.00 pm.

Retrieving my mug from the cell, I joined the throng at the water dispenser.   It was another queue where everyone wanted to be last.   The usual banter of the prisoners, sorting out who was lending who a magazine, or trying to obtain the makings of a fag, was broken up by a screw trying to keep them moving.   There were no shortages of volunteers to take the pool balls back to the Bubble, in order to delay their locking-up for an extra 10 minutes. Clutching my mug of hot water, I returned to my cell to find Mo discussing some family snaps with a couple of inmates.   It would appear that he was one of those popular figures in prison, the pencil portrait artist, with a never-ending supply of clients, that also included some screws.   Payment from prisoners would usually be in the form of tobacco, or phonecards, and screws would either pay the same way or deposit cash into his private account.   They would also be the source of his materials.

I dropped another of Mo's teabags into the hot water and lay back on my bed to listen to the discussions, which were eventually terminated after a few minutes by a screw chasing them up to get their mugs filled, or go without.

Finally, the door was locked and whilst I drank, Mo busied himself sorting out the pile of portraits, all in varying stages of progress, that were kept under his bed.   A number of them would never be finished, due to the clients having been transferred unexpectedly to other prisons, and as Mo himself was due for release in 4 weeks, screws were the better customers to have, as they were in a position to pay into his account.

On release, such monies would be paid out to him and, in the meantime, he could confirm at the canteen that the appropriate deposits had been made. We spoke little, until Mo picked up a newspaper from a pile on the end of his bed and, turning to me, asked whether I liked doing crossword puzzles. They were a pursuit I very rarely indulged in but, to be sociable, said I did, and regretted it ever since. In addition to being a very competent artist, Mo was also a great crossword enthusiast, more so as he viewed them as a counter to the potentially mind-deadening effects of prison life. Whenever the opportunity presented itself, he would hunt for any publication that may include one and regularly other prisoners would drop them into him. Midnight was long past when I fell asleep, fully clothed, across my bed, as we struggled for the answer to the clue "in abundance". There was no 'lights out' time at Belmarsh and each cell could be switched on or off by its occupants, but there were more than a few nights I would have regarded the lack of such a facility as a blessing. No doubt the thinking behind the availability of 24-hour lighting was not of generosity or to be nice to the chaps, but rather the calculation that having been awake most of the night, a prisoner would be less of a nuisance if he slept half the day. I will never forget Mo nudging me awake to tell me the answer must be "prolific", and me muttering something back to him from the twilight zone. Through bleary eyes, I focused on my watch. It was just turned 3 a.m.

* * * * * * * * * * *

Chapter 3

Welcome Visitors

The noisy routine of opening up brought me back into the real world much sooner than I would have wished. I was glad to be already dressed as the only inducement to get off the bed was the thought of making myself a mug of tea. The screw had left a paper bag on the chair inside our door, that contained a quantity of teabags; sachets of sugar; and some of whiteners, that took the place of milk. Before joining the line-up for breakfast, I made myself a drink that would be cooled enough to drink as soon as I returned, that way I could make a second one before they re-locked the cell door.

Breakfast was some porridge, the choice of a little curled up rasher, or a hard boiled egg. I obtained both by spotting a slightly cracked egg. The usual mountain of bread was available but I settled for two slices of toast, one of which was actually slightly browned. Mo, unsurprisingly, was foregoing breakfast, preferring to sleep on, so I had to quickly gulp down my tea before the screw, hovering with his key chain, pounced and cut off my access to the dispenser. Sitting on the edge of the bed munching, I was sorely tempted to wake Mo, to see if he wanted to do another crossword, but desisted in case he said yes.

The week-end routine had the cells unlocked between 9.30 a.m and 11.30 a.m., when lunch was served. They were unlocked again from 2.30 p.m. until 4.30 p.m. when the evening meal was dished out. With the exception of most of the cleaners who operated on a rota, everyone spent the rest of the time locked up, only to be disturbed between 7.30 p.m. and 8.00 pm., when a screw went round with a cleaner, to fill up mugs from a big jug. Breakfast finished and with my companion still totally submerged under his blanket, I passed the time shaving with my recently acquired disposable razor, in the process inflicting numerous cuts on myself. It was later explained to me that before using one for the first time, it was advisable to smooth the blade edge by rubbing it a few times on a piece of cardboard. Anyway, I got through that ordeal without too much blood loss, although the water in the hand basin was a very deep pink.

Shortly before opening up time, Mo was up, washed and dressed, straining at the leash to get to the gymnasium and urging me to go along as well. Keep fit was never a strong point with me, less so with a quantity of prison porridge in the process of bedding itself inside me, so I firmly declined. Gym was very popular with a great many inmates, but its availability and who went, was subject to the whims of screws. In an enclosed prison environment such as Belmarsh it is better not to want too much; that way one avoids many of the frustrations and the wind-ups, which inevitably result from the mind games that get played.

There were not a few times when my name was called for gym, even though I was not interested, yet enthusiasts, banging on their locked doors, were studiously ignored. When our door was opened, Mo was out through the entrance and straight across to the screw sitting at the desk, to find out what the prospects were. I dropped my tray on the floor outside and ambled over to the dispenser to fill up my mug again.

Much of prison life is repetitious and every time we were opened up presented the same scenario. The scramble to get on the 'phone list, or the pool table list, usually at the same time. The TV being switched on, with mainly the younger inmates scraping their chairs into the best viewing position, happy to watch anything provided it was a moving picture. After a while you could recognise the same blokes going round trying to scrounge a smoke; going for a shower or utilising the ironing board. The same faces were equally noticeable by their absence, preferring to play cards; backgammon or chess, in each other's cells. It was also more discreet that way to pass a joint round amongst themselves. It became fairly easy to recognise the cells where a bit of dealing took place, by the frequent visitations they generated, plus the look-out who spent almost the whole association period draped over the landing railing outside.

In a closed regime such as Belmarsh, the trading has to take place during the very limited periods that prisoners can visit each other; therefore, the cells where it took place soon became noticeable and spun unexpectedly, with the occupants suddenly being transferred to another spur, or prison. Business though, doesn't get disrupted for long and usually within a day or two, another couple of cells become little hives of activity, complete with the human fixture outside.

The desk by the gate would always have its complement of two or three screws sitting round it, who would listen to the usual bout of complaints, or requests, from generally the same inmates, who would in turn receive the same responses of either being reminded that they put themselves in prison, or to fill in one of the non-existent request forms. Even the screws undertaking to make enquiries, or obtain an appropriate form, neither of which they intended to carry out., became repetitious. It was on this occasion, as I was filling my mug, that Mr B. made me aware of his existence. Leaning back on his chair, he called me over to, as he put it, have a word. I thought, here we go, I'm going to have all the do's and don'ts spelt out to me, only to be proved wrong when he actually asked whether I was settled in OK. Replying in the affirmative, he then went on to ask me what I was doing there in the first place and, on briefly telling him, expressed his opinion that I must have had the misfortune of coming up in front of a health freak judge, who was anti-smoking and drinking. Nearly 2 metres tall, from his close cut blonde hair to his highly polished size 10 boots, my initial impression of Mr B. was of someone who was sharp enough, very self confident and most definitely full of his authority. I also decided that whilst I was resident on his spur, it would be in my better interests to play to his ego and not to underrate him, bearing in mind at all times that he was in a position to make my stay either tolerable or not. He cut me short as I was about to give my opinion of the judge, suggesting I get a teabag in my mug before the water went cold, at the same time turning his back on me, and resuming his conversation with the other screws.

I walked back to my cell, thinking what an ignorant git he was, but realised later that, in effect, he was doing me a favour, as most prisoners get very suspicious of one of their number, especially a new one, if they are seen to be too chatty with screws. Patel, who had been hovering nearby, followed me into the cell to tell me he now had no cigarettes at all. I offered him a roll-up, which he gladly took, and nearly choked himself. He told me that his cell-mate, who had helped to clean him out, was going to introduce him to another inmate who would trade him 2 cigarettes for 3, to be repaid as soon as he got to the canteen. I asked why his cell-mate didn't utilise this service, to learn that he couldn't as he had no private money and his meagre wages were committed for the next few weeks to repay numerous debts. The thought crossed my mind that he must have viewed the arrival of Patel in the same way as a fox seeing the chicken shed door wide open. Whilst it is true that very long prison sentences can change people, those serving short, or medium, terms usually remain mirror images of themselves on the outside. The active ones are always clamouring for the gym; the lazy ones will sit out the whole association period glued to the TV, irrespective of what is on; the clean and tidy ones are constantly showering and keep their cells pristine; others remain smelly, with cells that would look neater after a bomb went off in them; and the penniless scroungers continue to prowl around with empty pockets, looking for a handout.

Within a short space of time they exhaust any goodwill and rely either on new faces appearing, or being transferred where they can start afresh. Loans, repayable generally in either 'phone cards or tobacco, have to be redeemed within the week, due to the frequency of short notice transfers. Many are the debtors who have prayed for either themselves, or their creditor, to be given 24 hours' notice of a move elsewhere.

Patel expressed his intention to obtain some cigarettes from the 3 for 2 man, to tide him over until he could get to the canteen on the Monday, and asked me to keep hold of them, so his cell-mate couldn't scrounge them. When I pointed out the minor problem of him wanting a smoke and his cigarettes being locked in another cell, he said he would retain 2 or 3, and claim they were all he had, and replenish each time we were unlocked. I agreed, but told him I still thought it would be easier just to say no. He then proceeded to go on about how he wanted to make sure his old man understood the intricacies of the newsrounds, and what his brother should concentrate on getting for Xmas at the Cash-and-Carry, when I was mercifully released from learning how to run a shop by remote control, by Mr B yelling my name. Poking my head out the door, he told me I was required at the Pharmacy and to leave the spur via the gate on the first landing. Up the stairs I went, past the 'phone line-up, along the landing to the screw manning the barred gate. Confirming my name and number, he gave me a rub down search, then let me through, indicating a door past the Bubble with a serving hatch, outside of which a handful of inmates were clustered. A surly, very large, woman was handing out various potions at a tortoise-like pace. I never did clarify whether such individuals were screws that had learnt a bit of first aid or actual nurses with a big bunch of keys. The only thing that this woman would have had in common with Florence Nightingale is that all the men they administered to wanted to go home.

Standing there, waiting for my turn, a white inmate with a tea-tray paused to speak. He introduced himself as Tom and that he knew I was banged-up with Mo, also being on the same spur himself. His job was making teas and toast for the screws in their mess room, which was located a few yards from where we stood. I asked him how one became a cleaner, to learn that although many asked, it was dependent on the 6 or 7 screws that effectively ran the House-block. In my case, Mr B. would be the one with the main say. Apparently Tom obtained his job solely on the basis that the screws felt reasonably sure he wouldn't spit in their teas when they weren't looking. A bit of banter with a couple of others, he then went about his business, claiming he couldn't stand around rabbiting all morning.

After a while my turn came and I was told to enter to have my blood pressure measured. The way she put the strap round my arm indicated that she was heavy into bondage, and while she pumped away, I'm sure my lower arm and hand were going dead. My request to know the reading was completely ignored, but as a week's supply of tablets was shoved in my hand, she growled that I would obtain more when they ran out.

One way of making my enforced stay not a total waste of time, I'd decided, would be if I could lose some of my abundance of surplus weight. I had heard that this was usually achieved, to a great extent, by the unappetising food that was dished up. In order to see whether or not I was realising that objective, I thought it would be useful to know my weight at the beginning, so I asked if I could be weighed. The answer was an immediate no, as it didn't state on my record card that I was to be weighed. My attempt to explain my request was cut short by being told to leave as she had others to attend to, although there was no-one else waiting behind me. I returned to the spur clutching my pills, distinctly unimpressed with the Pharmacy. With regard to my aim of losing weight, I actually put it on, which probably makes me somewhat unique among the prison population.

Mo was not to be seen, presumably having got down the gym, and Patel was sitting in front of the TV., in conversation with Gopal, the only other Asian on the spur.   I decided to take another wander round the landings as the slightly better option to sitting inside a cell with the door open.   Following Mo's advice, I rolled one burn to smoke straightaway, with a second prepared in my pocket, as to roll them outside would immediately attract the scroungers.   I then headed off up the stairs to the first landing, which is where I met Kevin, more generally known as Semtex, and through him became introduced to the Irish community.   He had heard David the night before refer to me as Paddy when confirming I was Mo's cell-mate, and his curiosity had got the better of him. Seeing me coming along the landing, he broke off the conversation he was having with two others to ask me whether I had any connections with the "Ould Country".   I recited the counties my parents had come from and it turned out that my father's home town was only 20 miles or so from Kevin's, who hailed from the historic town of Athlone.   He was doubly impressed to learn that I had visited his town earlier in the year, only regretting that as I didn't know them, I hadn't popped in to see his Mum and Dad.   Beckoning to 3 or 4 others who were loitering nearby, he introduced me, at the same time highlighting the point that two of them, John and Martin, were natives of my Mother's County of Kildare.

Irish hospitality being what it is, even in a place such as Belmarsh, they insisted I joined them in one of their cells where, as one put it, morning coffee was about to be served.   The coffee was instant and there were only enough biscuits for one each, but the company was great. Seated three on each bed, and a seventh on a chair, we smoked and chatted about Ireland, London, families, life in general; all interspersed with humorous anecdotes based on our varying experiences. It was noticeable that no-one asked what I had been locked-up for, but when I volunteered the information, the main response was that I should have sent it straight on to Ireland where, due to higher tax levels, a better price would have been obtained for the cigarettes and tobacco. In their company, it was easy to forget that you were confined in a maximum security prison; their cheerfulness and good humour actually pushing the cold oppressiveness of the place into the background.

Semtex, who appeared the more dominant one of the group, impressed on me that if I needed anything, such as baccy or puff, to just ask, as they functioned on the basis of sharing what they had with each other, but equally emphasised that it was a two-way thing. He also repeated Mo's assertion that Spur 2 was the best one to be on whilst in Belmarsh and although they tended to keep to themselves as a group, they co-operated with the other prisoners to keep it that way. Only one fellow inmate was specifically referred to with disdain and that was a Jock, known as Swooper, because of his adeptness at swooping on any cigarette butts laying on the floor. Reference was made to him never washing; his apparent record of beating his wife; and how he was a Rangers supporter. I never was too sure as to what aspect of the man's pedigree actually provoked their contempt. We were on the second round of coffee, Martin having gone for a jug of hot water to refill the mugs, when I was dismayed to hear a screw shouting that association was over, and for those wanting dinner to get it, or go without. It is so true that time flies when you are enjoying yourself, and the hour or so that I had spent in their company had flown by.   Making a move off the bed, Dermot - one of the quieter ones - offered me a book to read which, as he put it, would have my mind flying as free as a bird, even though my body was caged.   Etiquette, plus a recommendation such as that, compelled me to accept his offer.   It was a book of Irish Poems and Legends which, although turning out to be pleasant reading, still left me distinctly feeling locked up. I emptied my mug of coffee, bade farewell for the time being and returned downstairs to join the line up for the hotplate.   My second roll-up, well and truly bent, was still in my pocket.

The middle lock-up period of the weekend routine was 11.30 am until 2.30 pm, and it was always an eerie, unreal, experience. A deathly hush fell on the place and if you weren't banged-up with someone, you could easily believe that you were the only living thing there.   Those with transistor radios either listened through ear-phones, or saved the batteries for the long evening that was to come.   Now and again the silence was broken by an inmate holding a shouted conversation through his barred window to another, but they soon petered out.   It always reminded me of a day nursery, with all the little kids laying in a line on the floor for the obligatory after lunch nap.   Having finished our meals, mine

73

consisting of a very dubious spam fritter with chips and beans, and Mo polishing off another tin of sweetcorn, mixed up with tuna, I lay back on my bed smoking whilst he concentrated on a portrait. My mind was full of the forthcoming visit, only regretting that as it was my youngest son's birthday, I would be wishing him 'Many Happy Returns' in such a place.

Speaking over the telephone with someone in the outside world definitely helped to break down the sense of isolation one readily feels in such an environment, so an actual face to face chat with loved ones, I thought, must be the next best thing to going home. I found myself scrutinising my watch, mentally debating as to whether the coming visit would seem to be sooner if I calculated the time to go in minutes, rather than hours. In the expectation that it would take place about 3 pm., and it was now 12.30 p.m., I decided that 150 minutes seemed less than 2½ hours. Next was to run a list through my mind of all the things to be said in the 30 minutes we would have, and the items rapidly built up. Ensuring my wife was OK., and explaining how the solicitor was going to lodge an appeal against the severity of the sentence; how to explain my absence, especially over the Xmas period, to my 8 year old grand-daughter; reassuring them that I was alright and could cope; taking care of my van; disposing to friends some of my Xmas stock that I would now not be selling, and for my wife to make use of the money; people to notify, in England and Ireland; explaining the facilities for future visits and to ensure I had some money deposited in my private account, were just for starters. I was just deciding that it might be a good idea to jot down a "shopping list", when Mo interrupted my thoughts, with the suggestion that I'd better answer him.   For a moment I wondered what he was on about, and why I should answer him when, as far as I was aware, he hadn't said anything, when I heard my name being called from another cell window.   It was Semtex, who was located two floors above.   Getting off the bed and with my face up against the bars, I shouted back an acknowledgement, whereupon he announced he had something to cheer me up and to stay by the window.   A few moments later, at full blast, the whole spur was treated to a stirring rendition of the rebel song "Kelly, the Boy from Killane".   Whether in appreciation, or protest, the effect was to have a number of our neighbours kicking their doors, long before the final chorus.   At its conclusion, I shouted back to Semtex, only to have my thanks drowned out by his yelling to all and sundry that "Our Day Will Come".   The spur then relapsed into its previous grave-like silence.

One effect of Semtex's treat was to disrupt Mo's artistic concentration, so putting aside the portrait he had been working on, he rolled a burn, laid back and engaged in conversation.   Surprisingly, he seemed to want to talk more about himself than I would have expected, bearing in mind that a little more than 24 hours previously, neither of us knew of the other's existence.   He spoke at length about his birthplace in Barbados, the people and of the poverty that existed amongst so much natural beauty.   I learnt of his family in Brixton, and the strains that his long incarceration had caused.   He slipped easily into his teacher role, to explain to me the intricacies of reggae music and what Rastafarianism was all about. We discussed some politics, where he displayed a full understanding of Britain's colonial history, with particular reference to the slave trade and the psychological basis it laid for modern day racism. It was quite an absorbing passing of the time and it was with a slight tinge of regret that I heard the noise of cells being unlocked, but equally recognised that there would be plenty of time ahead to resume the discussions.

Immediately our door was opened, I was off to top up my mug for tea, in the process colliding with an inmate hovering outside, who was waiting to see Mo about his portrait. Before I even reached the machine, Mr B. was shouting at me to forget it, as I was wanted for a visit. Within minutes the mug was back in the cell and I was up to the gate on the first floor landing, waiting with 3 or 4 others for the ritualistic rub down search. That done, it was along to the Bubble, to join more inmates from Spurs 1 and 3, and then wait whilst the prison management, with the full support of many screws, played more "games" with both visitors and prisoners. Belmarsh, as prisons go, is new. The equipment for monitoring and controlling is state of the art. There are surveillance cameras in abundance; screws with walkie-talkies all around; computers in nearly every office. The buildings and the three or four miles of corridors linking them are airtight, so even a mouse has never got in uninvited. You cannot walk anywhere in any direction, inside the buildings, without coming up against a steel barred gate within 50 metres of the last one.   The buildings are a mixture of brick and steel, with every window heavily barred so that even an anorexic midget couldn't squeeze through.   At each of the barred gates a screw would be loitering, with a clear view to the screws at the gates before and after. Outside the security measures make Fort Knox look "open plan". Cameras and floodlights on both poles and walls, constant dog patrols, sensors buried in the ground and perimeter walls, that are crowned with coils of razor wire encircling the whole prison.

Visitors are not welcome and are treated in the same contemptuous manner as the inmates.   They are all automatically suspected of smuggling in drugs and, deep down, the forcible recognition of the fact that so many inmates actually have people who care about them, rubs in to the screws what sad personal lives they must have.   By definition, a prison is going to have visitors and, whilst the cramped conditions of older establishments, such as Brixton, can be to some extent excused because of age, whoever designed Belmarsh must have been under instructions to deliberately make it visitor unfriendly.   People of all ages, including babies, are kept waiting in the open, outside the outer gate, in all weathers, for periods up to an hour.   Then they are permitted into a small reception area and subjected to a dragged out identification procedure, and a scrutiny of their visiting order.   Having achieved the main objective of getting everyone thoroughly pissed off and all the children crying, a screw will then call for everyone to file through a narrow doorway leading out to an internal courtyard, that affords absolutely no cover in the event of rain. To jolly the occasion up even more, the screws wait until visitors are going out of the door before telling them that buggies, pushchairs, crutches, walking sticks, zimmer frames, and anything else that may be deemed a threat to prison security, or potentially of assistance to a prisoner planning to abscond, will not be permitted into the visiting hall. The average waiting time in the courtyard is 30 minutes, with no seating or toilet facilities, and all the doors locked to prevent you going forwards or back the way you came. Effectively, up to 50 people are confined in a big open cell. After a while, an electronic door is opened on the opposite side of the yard and a screw will instruct no more than 6 at a time to enter. The number six must be programmed into screws during their induction courses as it corresponds with the number permitted to leave the spur at a time, to get their meals. One can only speculate as to the confusion that would be caused if the Home Office issued a directive altering the number. Once through the door, the whole ritual of identification and V.O. checking is repeated, plus a search of items being brought in for prisoners, prior to them being removed to a storage area. All visitors are then checked with a metal detector and subjected to a rub down body search. In the case of babies, nappies are checked to make certain no unauthorised goodies are secreted inside, and turbans are treated the same way.

Finally, visitors' attention is drawn to the dire

consequences, including arrest and prosecution, that will descend on both themselves, and the prisoner, if they are caught passing anything, especially drugs, during the visit; and that if they don't mind spending half the visit in a queue, refreshments are available at the small servery in the visiting hall. This is all topped up with a request for their co-operation in making the occasion a pleasant one for all concerned. Then a second electronic door lets them into the hall where some screws sitting behind a raised desk immediately demand the V.O.'s before directing them to what table to seat themselves at. By this time, one may assume that the prisoner would have been brought to the visiting area, that a telephone call to his spur had set the train in motion, but no, not in Belmarsh. What happens in Belmarsh is that a couple of screws are detailed to be "runners" between the visiting area and the four house-blocks. Their function is to fetch prisoners from the wings and escort them back afterwards. Once the visitors are seated in the hall, the screws at the raised desk notify one of the "runners" of the prisoner's name, number and location who, in turn, will take a stroll to the relevant wing, as and when they get round to it. Generally, they will wait until there are 6 or 8 inmates to collect from the same house-block, as part of their energy saving programme. On arrival, they will give the details in at the Bubble who will ring through to the three wings for the screws there to bellow out the names. Each inmate receives the ritual search as they leave the wing, assembling at the Bubble, where they will inevitably stand around for 10-15 minutes waiting for the inmate who had his personal stereo on when his name was yelled. There is always one!! When all have arrived, another rub down search is gone through in order to leave the house-block, then off we tramp for 10 minutes along sealed corridors, through half a dozen gates, to eventually arrive at the visiting area. By this time, the visitors have sat in the hall for anything up to an hour, with babies crying, young children fretting, as they watch, wide-eyed, sour-faced screws prowling around, rattling their key chains. Screws, by definition, are not required to have a friendly, bed-side manner, particularly in high-security prisons, but the ones who staff the visiting area must be hand-picked for their sourness; pettiness and for having a general grudge against humanity.

Queries by visitors as to how much longer will they have to wait, are met with helpful responses such as "long as it takes", or "you can always leave if you're in a hurry". They know that most visits are emotional occasions where, very often, the visitors are under stress coping with various problems, so the nastier screws help matters along by interrupting to tell them to get the kid off the table; or telling them that "times up" just as a visitor, having queued for 20 minutes at the snack-bar, returns with a hot cup of tea. Such screws really get a buzz when the inmate complains that they haven't had the minimum 30 minutes, so they can blow their whistle for the hit squad, waiting in a nearby room, to steam in and drag the protesting inmate away, leaving the visitors screaming and crying. Belmarsh, like all prisons, has its full quota of sad people and sick minds, all too many of them hiding behind uniforms in the visiting area. On arrival, the inmates are locked into a short corridor to file, one at a time, into the pre-visit room, where one screw will take and record anything in your pocket; a second will search you and a third will watch the other two. Then, with the appropriate colour bib on to make you look silly, orange for remand prisoners, blue for convicted, entry into the visiting hall is finally achieved. Name and number to the screw at the raised deck elicits a grunt as to where your visitors are located, and you feel you have made home base.

Altogether there must have been in excess of a hundred adults sitting in the hall, plus 30 to 40 young children, yet it wasn't noisy as one would expect. It was more of a loud hum, interspersed by the high pitched sound of an excited child's voice when they finally spot Daddy coming through the door. Waving arms indicated where my visitors sat and, moments later, we were together, reassuring each other that, collectively, we were O.K.

Over teas and snack biscuits I learned how my wife was constantly answering the telephone to well-wishers expressing their indignation at my sentence, especially on top of Xmas, and how the normally ten minutes' walk to the local shops now took an hour, for the same reason. It was pleasing to hear it as, alongside family support, such occurrences would serve to bolster my wife's morale for the weeks ahead. We clarified the different things that would require attention, either immediately, or in the near future, and I was informed that as far as my grand-daughter was concerned, I was over in Ireland helping a cousin with the influx of newly-born lambs. Personal clothing had been handed in but my chess set had been refused, due to the pieces being regarded as too big. Whilst it is a large set, the only rationale I could think of was, either the screws thought each piece was packed with drugs or, more likely, it was another example of the Belmarsh "mind games".

They had compensated their refusal, though, with a contribution towards prisoner rehabilitation by allowing me to receive two books, one a chronicle of "Famous Poison Murders" and the other "Serial Killers of the 20th Century". There had been a delay over depositing the money in my private account, due to my wife not being able to recite my prison number. The screw was only prevented from refusing it by my daughter drawing his attention to it being written on the visiting order in front of him. His half-hearted effort to assert that all visitors should still be able to quote the prisoner's number was rapidly quashed by the rising tide of protest from the impatient queue behind.

With all the relevant matters apparently dealt with, we moved on to lesser subjects, but were soon interrupted by a screw telling us "time was up". It was not an easy parting, although I felt we had all benefited from the visit and, as we moved away in opposite directions, constantly waving, I realised as an inmate not only how fortunate I was having a good family but, also, the fact that my children were adults. Scenes of families parting with young wives barely able to cope, and toddlers screaming and crying, is something you can never fully get used to. Some of the young inmate fathers are scum, being more concerned that there was no money to be paid into their accounts, or that the "silly cow" forgot to bring their other track suit, or trainers, in, whilst claiming that it was down to the "Soash", (Social Security") and the Council to look after their kids; but others were visibly upset and even depressed after visits, and the emotional trauma of parting. Slowly making my way back to the high desk to be booked out, I was intercepted by the screw who had continually hovered nearby for the duration of my visit. "Eat it, bin it, or your nicked" was his advice to me. He was, of course, referring to the uneaten bar of chocolate I had slipped into my pocket as I stood up from the table, having failed to read the big sign prohibiting the removal of food items, or indeed, any item except yourself, from the hall, with attempts to do so inviting severe penalties. My suggestion of donating it to a family nearby earned me the knowledge that even the thought of so doing would land me in big trouble. I began to point out that the item was "clean" having been purchased from their snack-bar, as no food is allowed through anyway, when the screw cut me short to tell me he wasn't debating the issue, just telling me to get rid of it so to a great extent due to his persuasive manner, such as getting his whistle out, the offending lump of chocolate ended up in my stomach almost in one piece. I realised afterwards that, within the paranoid world of Belmarsh, the screw had really done me a favour, as I would have definitely been nicked in the search room that you enter immediately on leaving the hall, but then, he would have had his knuckles rapped for not having spotted me slipping it in my pocket earlier.   What his motive was remains a mystery, but one thing is crystal clear, the record of prisoners getting out is matched by the total failure of chocolate bars to get in.

The screw at the high desk ticked me off and I left the hall to join the small queue being called one at a time into the search room.   This consisted of a rub down search, accompanied by a scrutiny inside the mouth, mainly looking for drugs, and the return of any item removed prior to the visit, such as burn, watches, or matches.   Approximately one in ten prisoners would receive a full strip search that was supposed to be random, but more likely applied where the screws had real suspicions, or just wanted to humiliate a particular inmate.   In such instances, the door was locked so other inmates couldn't enter and join in the inevitable row that took place.   After the search room, inmates were locked into the corridor that led to a waiting room, where once a screw unlocked the door, personal goods were collected and everyone stood around until a runner appeared to shepherd us back to the different house-blocks.   This was another area for "mind games" where screws would claim that items handed in two hours previously weren't there. They would suggest that the visitor who had assured the inmate shortly before that they had deposited goods must have made a mistake, or that the goods may have accidentally been given out to another inmate.   Either way, the other two screws sitting down smoking and chatting haven't got time to double-check at the moment, but will have another look as soon as they can.   In the event of the items being located and due to this particular room having to be cleared each night, ready for the next day's influx, they will be deposited in the permanent store, to which the inmate can address a request form to obtain his belongings, provided a screw can be found with the time to escort him there and back.   This particularly nasty stunt has deprived inmates of a change of clothing, plus other items, for as much as a month, when they were available for issue on the day they arrived.   I learnt of this practice later and, thankfully, was not a victim of it myself. I also learnt that, due to transfers being implemented at short notice, it was not uncommon for prisoners to still be trying to obtain their belongings after weeks in another prison where prison clothing must be worn, and much of what was deposited at Belmarsh was of no use to them except on release.   The goods ended up in limbo in the prison system until they arrived where the inmate was currently incarcerated and he could arrange to have them returned to a visitor. They couldn't be returned whilst still at Belmarsh because a visitor wouldn't be let in without a visiting order, that was only available if they had someone to visit there.

Whilst sitting in the waiting room, clutching my sack full of mostly clothing, Patel appeared with a face that looked as if he had just had his sentence doubled. The cause of his extreme distress, it transpired, was that the detailed list he had written out regarding the paper rounds had been taken from him in the search room. In addition to the list, he had also jotted down notes relating to the shop in general, with particular reference to items required from the Cash-and-Carry, and things to be avoided. Although the major part of his visit had been spent in explaining it verbally to his Father, he felt that much of it had not fully registered, with the inevitable result of a disastrous Xmas that may result in no shop to return to on his release in six months. My efforts to console him achieved nothing and by the time we eventually got back to the spur, just in time for the last meal of the day, I really thought he was on the verge of a mental breakdown. Dumping my sack on the bed and leaving Mo chomping a lump of water melon, I responded to Mr B.'s call for last orders for dinner, in the process putting my head into Patel's cell next door to see whether he intended dining, or not. He was curled up on his bed, with his Nintendo bleeping like a demented morse code machine, so I left him to it and joined the final handful of stragglers strolling down to the hotplate.

The feast tonight was a choice of mince, or toad-in-the-hole, mixed carrot and turnip, and mash, followed by jelly or water melon, rounded off with the obligatory rock cake. I settled for the mince and prayed my stomach would do the same, but as I was literally the last to be fed in the whole house-block, the screw spared me having to make any further decisions, letting me have both a slab of jelly and two slices of water melon. Taking full advantage of his obvious good mood, I helped myself to a second rock cake which, to be fair, I found to be quite tasty.

Back in the cell and my mug filled with hot water, I gave Mo one of the melon slices and tucked into the rest with a surprisingly good appetite, bearing in mind the amount of chocolate I had consumed not so long before, saving one of the rock cakes for later.   It had been a good day, I thought, as I sat on my bed munching.   I now had the comfort of knowing that all important things outside were catered for and that my wife was O.K. under the circumstances; I had made my acquaintance with Mr.B., and was regarded as an associated member of the Irish contingent, which was of value in a place where you can't have too many friends.   In the bag on the bed next to me was a selection of clothing which, being my own, provided yet another real link with the outside world, thus serving to help break down the lingering sense of unreality, plus a couple more books to supplement the two battered Westerns from the library, and the collection of Irish Poems and Legends so kindly donated by Dermot.   On the subject of inmates being permitted to wear their own clothing, a big thank you is in order to whoever sanctioned it.   Cynics, myself not included, claim that it's a cunning ploy to cut running costs, but the reality is the long days do pass somewhat easier when you are wearing comfortable clothing that fits.

In a world where an individual's identity can get submerged, especially with longer serving prisoners, personal T-shirts and jumpers do provide a tangible link with a former life without barred windows and locked doors.   Inevitably, the more affluent inmates are seen posing around in their designer track suits and Reebok trainers, whereas the vast majority are dressed more mundane, but the prison laundry service is a great leveller. Whether it's the water, the powder used, or the machinery itself, remains a complete mystery, but whatever colour a garment goes in as, it comes out battleship grey. I, myself, have put whites in the personal wash-bag on their own and on other occasions, mixed with coloureds, and on every occasion each item has come back in varying shades of grey. The recollection is still vivid of one affluent prisoner, Stringfellow, who dispatched a very nice turquoise Amani jogging suit to the wash-house, that not only came back somewhat misshapened, but in a colour that could only be described as very old seaweed. For days after, his moods swung like a pendulum between highly homicidal and extremely suicidal, and just the thoughts of what he wanted to do to all concerned, from the laundry man up to the governor, would have gained him a life sentence.

Yes, it had been a good day and I felt quite content as I rolled a burn and lay back on my bed. In a few minutes, I would unpack the bag into my cupboard, have a read or listen to my companion's radio, then when the screw brought the water round, I would have the second rock cake with my tea and finish the evening off reading until I fell asleep. Glancing at my watch, I saw that it was still only 5.30 pm. Any other Saturday I would not even be home yet from the market, yet here I was settling down for the night. It reminded me of a short stay I'd had some months previously in hospital and it was that thought that helped me mentally get through the weeks ahead. The time involved equated with the length of stay that would follow a major operation, or serious injury; the regime was similar and the lack of visits would be offset by both the livelier company and a distinctly better menu; with the bonus being having all my physical bits and pieces intact.

With the bag emptied and another burn lit, I decided to browse through some Irish poems, not because of any cultural urge but so as to be able to demonstrate to Dermot that I had at least looked at them. I would stick with it until the hot water came round, then would switch over to "Serial Killers of the 20th Century" until my eyelids collapsed. My fervent hope was that Mo wouldn't want to involve me in his crossword fetish but, like Napoleon at Waterloo, I was soon to learn you can't win them all.

* * * * * * * * * * * *

Chapter 4

A Sunday Stroll In The Yard

My first Sunday started the same as any other day. It was an effort to drag myself out of bed, not only due to "burning the midnight oil" over yet another bloody crossword, but mainly because one of the outside flood lights shone straight into our cell, with my pillow seeming to be in the centre of its bright amber glow. Many inmates, including Mo, regularly curtained the window with a spare blanket, wedging roll-on deodorants between the bars to keep it in place, solving both the bright light problem and that of draughts. But now, as part of the security paranoia, such a practice was banned and those persisting with it would be subject to dire consequences. The "reasoning" was that when the screws looked through the little window in the door during the night, to make sure we had not all flown out into the night sky, like the kids in Peter Pan, a darkened cell made it harder to ascertain we were still there. Once opened up, as part of my routine, I filled my mug for tea that would be cool enough to drink on my return from the hotplate, to enable me to make another before the door got slammed shut, and even on those occasions when the screw was quicker off the mark than usual, I would empty the mug on my way to the dispenser.

Joining the throng at the gate, I eventually got despatched to the hot-plate with five other similarly bleary-eyed residents. On the way, in addition to the usual array of screws, we were confronted by a real monk, complete in brown robes, with toes sticking out of his sandals, solemnly blessing everyone as they passed. The last thing I wanted that morning, or indeed any other morning, was something out of the Middle Ages bestowing meaningless platitudes on me when I'm getting my breakfast so, quickening my pace, I conceded a polite half nod of the head in his direction, for the sake of the watching screws. Shortly after, I learnt that he was Father Donald, the subject of not a little speculation, who actually lived in one of the cells in the isolation block, presumably with his own personal key. Nobody, when asked, seemed to know what exactly his functions were, or if he had any at all. Some opined he was more than just a spiritual friend of one of the Governors, whilst others reckoned, due to his obviously pensionable age, that he was an ex-screw that had completely flipped upon reaching retirement, and in the interest of the Prison Service, it had been deemed desirable to keep him tucked away from the public eye. He was definitely a strange individual, who was probably made much more welcome on the nonces wing.

During morning association my name was called for gym, due mainly because I hadn't requested to go, whereas many that had, weren't called. Mo had also been called and, partly due to his urging and a bit of curiosity on my part, I hastily completed the request form Mr B. had obtained, to see a Governor regarding a transfer, then trooped off with a dozen others to pump iron.

On arrival, first timers, such as myself, were issued with the official blue singlet and shorts, plus a pair of canvas shoes with rubber bottoms, then left to get on with it. The two instructors, having locked us in, spent the whole hour or so we were there with their feet up in their little office. To someone who had not seen the inside of a gymnasium since leaving school 37 years previously, the place looked like a highly polished torture chamber. Many there were obviously regulars and had the shape to prove it, with a fair amount of posing taking place, but alongside that, they all helped each other, which I'm told is the gym ethos wherever you are. For my own part I felt a complete prat. Standing there in shorts and singlet; dark grey, three-quarter length woollen socks disappearing into canvas gym shoes, substantially overweight and wearing glasses, I most definitely did not look - or feel - like Gladiator material. The overwhelming majority of athletes I was locked in with were the same ages as my daughter and sons, and it was from that gathering I received the nickname "Fletch", after the Ronnie Barker character in the TV series 'Porridge', that I was to carry until my release. I did manage a modest session on an exercise bike without sustaining any real injury, and helped to lift a bar-bell off one bloke who was turning a very funny colour, before deciding I'd had enough exertion for one morning. The time was not wasted, though, as I enjoyed a nice leisurely shower all by myself, before the sweat and grunt brigade came jostling for space. That was my first and last visit to the gym, but it was worth it. The shoes were most comfortable for internal wear and the cotton kit served as bloody good cloths when things got spilt on the floor. We arrived back on the spur in time for the mid-day meal, and then it was "bang-up" until 2.30 pm. Doubtlessly due to a combination of a semi-sleepless night and the exertions of the morning, I enjoyed a very satisfying after lunch nap, while Mo scraped away with his pencils, vainly trying to recreate the photo of a screw's wife, without her moustache.

For the afternoon "time-out", I thought I would have a chat with Patel, and then mooch around to see who else's acquaintance I might make. One thing I wanted to sort out, was a bag from the laundry man for my dirty washing. I had rinsed out socks and underwear in the small hand-basin in the cell, draping them in the time-honoured way over the hot pipes to dry, but now we were talking about shirts and trousers, following my acquisition of a full wardrobe the day before. I located him in the line-up for the pool table and it was with great reluctance, coupled with repeated assurances that he would not sacrifice his place in the queue, that he went to his nearby cell, returning with a large string bag that zipped up at the top. Borrowing a ball-point from a screw sitting at the desk, I superimposed my name over the faded one of the previous user, returning to my cell to throw it on the bed.

Poking my head into Patel's cell, I saw he wasn't at home and, in response to my query, his cell-mate, engrossed in Patel's Nintendo, mumbled that he was visiting Gopal, the Asian on the top landing. Having nothing better to do, I thought I would go and see what they were up to, but as I reached the top of the first flight of stairs, the screw whose biro I had borrowed, bellowed out that exercise in the yard was on offer to those who wanted it. It had been four days now since I had been out in the fresh air and I did miss it, so quickly checking at the landing window that it wasn't actually raining, I decided to partake of his kind offer. Back to the cell, to re-emerge a few minutes later in boots, jumper and overcoat, I went outside to join the handful of other poor sods trudging round in a big circle, with hands firmly wedged inside their pockets.

The heavy grey sky overhead, threatening rain any minute, made the exercise yard look even drearier than it would normally, but at least the air tasted sweeter than inside the house-block. It was rectangular, approximately the area of half a football pitch, with the tarmac surface littered with assorted rubbish, emanating from the cells on two sides. The other two sides consisted of heavy steel mesh fencing, 10 metres high, with two coils of razor wire running the whole length along the top and, to make sure there were no scenes from a James Bond movie attempted, the total yard area was covered with anti-helicopter cables. It was certainly not the same as a stroll in the local park. Exercise provided one of the few opportunities to fraternise with inmates from the other two spurs and, in some instances, to renew old acquaintanceships. Three or four were actually running, either to keep warm, or as part of the self-imposed keep fit regime, earning not a few smutty comments from the stragglers, whilst all the time, two screws, looking like big old crows in their regulation black raincoats, stood huddled by the doorway, watching us go round in circles. One thing that struck me particularly was the absence of the gym brigade whom I thought would have been out en masse. Maybe it's harder to pose outside when the temperature is hovering just above freezing point, the old macho image becomes almost impossible to generate when the nose is running and one's willy has all but disappeared. Being an old market trader and deriving the benefit of having a thick coat, I stayed out for the whole hour allocated, until one of the screws shouted that time was up. Returning to the doorway, I noticed that the other screw had gone to check that the small gates at each end of the wire were still locked, and couldn't help speculating as to the panic that would undoubtedly erupt in the event of one not being intact.

Returning to the cell, I discarded my outside wear and decided to treat myself to a mug of coffee, using one of the two sachets bestowed on each inmate at weekends. There was no sign of Mo, and Patel was in the process of demonstrating his pool skills, pocketing the balls quite regularly with the broom handle, so I thought I would go upstairs to say hello to a couple of residents who were in my age bracket. Their side of the spur consisted of single cells and I had already clocked the ones they occupied so, coffee in hand and burn in the mouth, I headed off up the iron stairs to socialise, locating them together playing an intense game of backgammon.   A knock on the door was rewarded with an invitation to enter, and I spent the next 10 minutes sat on the bed, watching a game that was - and still is - a complete mystery to me.   Eventually, the play was over and Harry, whose cell we were in, offered round apples from the bowl full on the window ledge, and the three of us chomped away like rabbits.   They were both long serving prisoners I learnt later, with John almost half way through a 9-year sentence for a series of arson attacks, motivated by no other reason than getting a buzz out of watching blazing buildings; and Harry was four years into a life sentence for murder.   A few weeks later, when we had got to know each other a lot better, he told me he was in for killing his wife with a hatchet, but that he hadn't meant to kill her.   When I responded by suggesting he should have been tried for manslaughter, he enlarged on the subject. Apparently, he had returned home unexpected one day, to find his wife in bed with her boyfriend, prompting Harry to run out to the tool shed, returning with the weaponry.   In the process of taking a swing at the lover, his wife jumped in the way, catching the blade full force with her head, allowing the intended recipient a precious couple of minutes to leg it out of the house and down the road, minus his trousers. What he really meant was, he intended to kill the boyfriend first, and then the wife.   It would appear that if, at the point of finding them, he had bludgeoned them both with the table lamp he would have been dealt with more leniently, but he had made it a whole lot worse for himself, due to going out to the shed and returning with the hatchet, before laying into them.   Something about showing intent, the prosecution said.

Having devoured the apples, John offered his baccy tin to make a roll-up, demonstrating another irony of life inside.   The vast majority of scroungers were blokes serving relatively short sentences, leading me to conclude that maybe the longer serving inmates paced themselves better with their earnings, coupled with a reduction in luxuries. With the passage of time they leave out buying sweets and biscuits, and as the number of people to contact outside reduces, so does their need to buy phone-cards, stamps and stationery. I probably made more telephone calls and sent more letters during my three months' incarceration, than most long-serving inmates indulge in during a whole year.   We chatted away whilst smoking, with both of them already aware of how long I was in for, and why, going to great lengths to reassure me that the time would soon fly by; and upon me stating my intentions to seek a transfer to a lower category prison nearer home, earned myself another slice of "old lags" wisdom.   According to my companions, I would be better off doing a short sentence in Belmarsh, for a number of reasons that they almost competed with each other to outline.   Firstly, I would probably have to wear uniform and sleep in a dormitory, where personal items would become more vulnerable to thieves.   Then there were all the petty rules and temptations in an open prison, breaches of which normally led to losses of remission.

To lose a couple of weeks when one is serving 10 years does not have the same impact as 13 weeks becoming 15 or 16, all things being relative.   In Belmarsh I could spend any amount of private money, whereas in the open and semi-open prisons I would be restricted to about £2.50 per week, having to earn any more by working a 40-hour week, for the princely wage of approximately £20.   Visits tended to only take place at weekends, unlike my current domicile, where they took place 7 days a week, subject to one's quota.   Then there was the question of bullying and intimidation.   In a maximum security nick, with most of the time "banged up" and loads of screws wandering around, the scope for such practices were severely limited, unless it was the screws dishing it out.   It was a different ball game in the C and D category establishments, where a combination of much more time out, a far lower staffing level and too many secluded areas, gave the wolves almost unlimited opportunities to harass the sheep.   In a situation, for example, where you have upset one of the "hard men", you would be looking over your shoulder all day and reluctant to close your eyes at night.   Other reasons were included, such as the proliferation of drugs, plus the impossibility of leaving any choice edibles in one's locker, and the inevitable late return from a day out with a pass that would be punished by loss of remission; that all added up to making me see the issue in a far different light.

Whilst I had no doubt whatsoever of the validity of what I was being told, I still intended to press for a transfer nearer home for the purpose of making things easier for my visitors, especially my wife.   Harry himself had prevailed on the Governor to block any transfer regarding himself, for their mutual benefit. He was like a dog with two tails pottering around in the prison greenhouses, being an avid gardener, and thoroughly enjoyed planting flower beds or pruning bushes and fruit trees.   His daughter, who was his sole visitor, lived locally, and he enjoyed a single cell on a trouble-free wing where, largely due to his age (he was 57) nobody gave him any hassle.   Due to his diabetes, he was given extra food, thus the full up fruit bowl, and his earnings were sufficient for his modest personal requirements.   The Governor benefited by having someone reliable working on his gardens, whereas most inmates would be inclined to do as little as possible and sabotage anything they laid their hands on.   He much preferred to impress notable visitors during Spring and Summer, with vegetable plots and flower beds that would do justice to a Gardener's World TV programme, than have them surveying the results of an "accidental" watering with a solution of weed killer.   To many of the younger inmates that were delegated to work on the gardens, Harry was a bit of a fatherly figure, and they would do far more for him than they would ever do for either screws or the civilian staff.

Before long, 4.30 pm to be exact, we could hear a screw bellowing for everyone to get their meal or go without, and with my new found friends I dragged out the procedure the best I could, because once the meal had been obtained, we would be "banged up" until 8.00 the next morning.

The evening meal on Sundays never varied.   One slice of corned beef and another of waxy cheese, were straightaway buried under a ladle full of beetroot, plus another of coleslaw.   This was bolstered with a jacket potato, any amount of bread, a slab of jelly with a rock cake stuck on top.   Being a cold meal, including the potato, asbestos gloves were required to lift a metal tray from the stack.   Throughout the week it was always hit or miss whether the tray cabinet worked or not, but you could always guarantee the heating elements functioning full blast on Sunday afternoons.

Later, laying back on my bed, digesting both my meal and half of Mo's, I pondered the situation of mixing short term prisoners with those doing a lot of years. Every cell had the occupants name, number and length of sentence written on a card, and displayed outside on the door, a number of which I had read during association periods.   Some were serving as little as four weeks, of which they would do half, for such matters as motoring offences and non-payment of fines.   At the other end of the scale there were those in for 12 and 15 years and even longer, for serious crimes including armed robbery, heavy drug dealing and murder.   13 weeks seemed eternity to me but try as I did, I just couldn't begin to imagine the mind-deadening hopelessness of looking forward to a possible release date sometime into the next century.

The breakdown of relationships that inevitably occur and the pace of change generally would leave very little to return to, and for those serving such long periods when genuinely innocent, each day must be hell. Those loved ones on the outside that maintain the vital support, whilst serving their own sentence; who cope with the sheer despair and gnawing loneliness; who face the daily struggle to raise families and keep a home together whilst maintaining a brave face on heart-breaking visits, deserve the highest praise. Unfortunately, all too many also carry a torch for men who don't deserve their commitment. Within the prison, the mixing of short and long sentence prisoners, provides an element of torture for those facing many years when, during the 6 to 12 months between transfers, they see so many barely arrived before they are off home. In the regular circumstances where such inmates share the same cell, it is not uncommon for the long server to snap under the pressure of the other constantly twittering on about how many weeks, or days, he has to go, culminating in the "short stay" inmate winding up in the hospital wing and, on occasions, in the mortuary. But more of that later.

I was fortunate insofar that Mo had less than four weeks to go when I moved in with him so, if anything, I could envy him, conveniently omitting, of course, the years he had already done.

I wrote my first letter on official prison notepaper that evening, remembering to leave the pre-paid envelope open as per instructions, so some very sad screw could study it to make sure I wasn't undermining security or hatching a plot to overthrow the government. The censors read all letters, both in and out, which reminded me of the time that Fletch, in the aforementioned TV series 'Porridge' actually got the local constabulary to dig his back garden by hinting in a letter as to how he'd buried stolen property there. Screws also listened into telephone calls, presumably in the hope of picking up some useful snippets, and quickly pulled the plug when the ethnics resorted to their Mother tongues. Did they really expect inmates to go into details about their criminal activities, I sometimes wondered, in a letter or telephone conversation, when they had the opportunity to discuss such things on visits? Maybe the screws in the visiting hall are trained to lip-read. Whatever the supposed reasons, the practice of reading personal letters was, and still is, regarded with extreme contempt by prisoners. My letter completed and my "top up" mug of tea helping to flush Mo's rock cake down my throat, I managed to get halfway through the third crossword before escaping into a good night's sleep.

* * * * * * * * * * * *

Chapter 5

Back To School And A Spot Of Shopping

Next morning, after breakfast, I was summoned to join about 6 others for education classes. Patel was one of the number, which afforded the opportunity to have a chat, that effectively boiled down to his earnest hope to get to the canteen to, amongst other things, buy some cigarettes and batteries for his radio and Nintendo. Due to the enthusiastic assistance of his cellmate, the brand new ones inserted two days previously were now completely drained. I was also wanting to do some shopping, especially as I had learned that on my arrival, the governor had generously advanced me £2.50 from my future earnings, that I intended to splash out on such goodies as a carton of milk, sweeteners, orange squash and a packet of peppermints. In the event of my private account functioning, I would top up my baccy and purchase some matches. For some strange reason, my lighter had been confiscated and to be caught in possession of one was a serious offence, yet it was OK to have any amount of matches. Enquiries to a couple of hovering screws regarding our prospects of going shopping that day, drew the standard replies to any query of "Don't know" and "You'll have to ask so and so", who was never around to ask anything. Then we were off and three rub down searches, six locked gates and 500 metres of corridor later, arrived at the Education Block. I had put my name down for English, Numbers (Sums) and Psychology, so was allocated to the Cookery class, whereas Patel got drafted into the Social Awareness class, to listen to a retired vicar expounding the Real Meaning of Xmas, which I thought, being a Hindu, he should find particularly stimulating. After all, he did sell Xmas cards in his shop so it seemed only right and proper that he should understand why. It turned out a good result being locked in the Cookery room, where under the guidance of a fussy old dear, six of us had to prepare a Chinese dish, followed by lychees and cream, on completion of which we all sat down and promptly devoured.

I managed to blot my copybook though, by needing to go to the toilet during the preparation stages, with the old biddy getting somewhat irate when I expressed an inability to comply with her suggestion to "hold on". Due to the comprehensive selection of knives in the room, plus other assorted implements, she had to call up a screw to check me over to ensure I wasn't trying to smuggle a meat cleaver out in my underwear. That was my one and only visit to the cookery class, no doubt due to my record card listing a weak bladder, which clashed with their system of once locked in, you don't come out until the end.

Towards the end of the morning, once the washing up was done, we were all given a rub down search and released from the kitchen, to join 40 or 50 other inmates milling around in the communal area, waiting to be escorted back to our various spurs. During this time, I took the opportunity to be nosy and wandered from classroom to classroom to see what they were like, having to settle for a peek through the narrow glass panels in the doors, due to each one being promptly locked once vacated. From what I could see, each one seemed fairly well equipped, but during the following couple of weeks, until my eventual resignation, one could not escape the conclusion that the facilities were wasted in Belmarsh. The case for educational opportunities in the prison system is to be totally supported, what is lacking is the monitoring machinery essential if it is to avoid being a mockery. When one considers the formidable array of opposition to such provision even existing, both within and on the outside, then what has been achieved by the more enlightened almost borders on the miraculous. The bulk of the media regularly ridicules it, purporting to reflect popular opinion; reactionary Home Secretaries routinely threaten it to promote their "tough guy" image at party conferences, seeking the applause of the ignorant; civil servants view the provision as a soft option for budget cuts; within the prisons themselves the administration view it as an expensive nuisance at best and a sheer waste of time at worst, with no effort made to ensure the calibre of tutors, or to encourage inmates, many illiterate, to participate. This attitude is highlighted by the fact that an inmate can earn up to 3 times more picking up litter than learning to read and write. This negative, even hostile, attitude, permeates all prisons in varying degrees and the minority of governors, and staff, that actively promote the provision, face a continual uphill struggle. In the context of Belmarsh, the whole concept is further perverted by the screws, who view anything that entails prisoners being let out of their cells as not only a threat to security, but also as more work for themselves. Thus we have a situation where they play their mind games, either by omitting to release inmates for classes, altering their expressed preferences, or sending them for classes that weren't even taking place, such regular practices presumably condoned by the management, as they never appeared to do anything about it. During a 10-week day period, I was called 6 times for education, including the cookery class. Twice I ended up in computer studies and one occasion each for Sociology, Numeracy and Psychiatry, the latter two probably by mistake, as I had actually entered my name for them.

The Sociology class was, to say the least, a very strange experience where, complete with lurid pictures, we spent the first half discussing the human brain, which was very tasteful immediately after breakfast; and for the second half the tutor, an elderly lady clothed by Oxfam, bored us all with the misfortunes of her life, whilst continually rubbing herself. The only redeeming feature of that lesson was that she did pass round her bag of boiled sweets, where we all took a couple for later. One other factor undermining education pursuits at Belmarsh, was the frequency of short notice transfers. Those inmates that sought to achieve the various qualifications on offer, having persevered with the meagre wages and the mind games, faced the further hurdle of a sudden transfer to another prison.   In such circumstances, the Prison Service undertook to ensure the inmate could continue their studies at their new "home", but the reality was all too often that the subject was not available when they got there, and due to the shambolic administration at Belmarsh, relevant details were not forwarded on, even if the new prison did run similar courses.

There must be tens of thousands of inmates, past and present, that had their efforts at advancement cut off in mid-stream through no fault of their own.   Until such times as there is a firm commitment from the top down to promote education in prisons, and those who currently sabotage the facility are removed from any active influence, it will continue to be a combination of both whipping boy and Cinderella, devalued in the minds of those that would benefit most from it, with society receiving back into its midst men, and women, whose prospects of obtaining work in a very competitive labour market, reduced from very modest to zero.   The length of my sentence, plus the game playing, influenced by the acquisition of some interesting books to pass the time, had me requesting to be transferred to any other work two weeks following my arrival.   After all, I had only 76 days to go and classes were closing for two weeks for Xmas anyway.

That afternoon, with Mo gone back to work in the Plug Shop, I settled down to read about mass murderers, that might even culminate in a snooze, but with barely a page read, the door was unlocked and I was told I could go along to the canteen.

The canteen was like a little corner shop, located near the servery, and Patel and I joined the small queue slowly edging its way in to the counter where a civilian woman sought to outscrew the screws in both speech and attitude. The stock was displayed on shelves behind her, way out of reach to the inmates, with the inevitable screw propped up at the end of the counter to make sure no one gave her a hard time. His other major function seemed to be to ensure you did not take more than one large brown paper bag to stack your purchases in, American style. We were in no hurry to get served and even let two others go in front of us, who, for reasons of their own, wanted to get back to their spurs; after all, it was all "time out". Eventually, it was our turn to be served and on giving our numbers, the nice lady was able to quote from a printout what our financial status was. It felt quite painful paying the full retail price for tobacco, but I gritted my teeth, whereas for Patel the whole operation became positively tortuous, as every item he bought he couldn't but help compare to what he paid for the same goods at the Cash and Carry only a week before. I bought enough to see me through for the coming two weeks, just in case there were difficulties in returning, remembering an extra 'phone card to repay my debt. Feeling a bit flushed, I even treated Mo to a packet of cream crackers with a small box of cream cheese, as I had noticed he was quite partial to them. My goodies filled one bag nicely, which was just as well as I had to carry one of Patel's three back to our spur. Even the screw muttered something about needing some supermarket trolleys. My companion had gone a bit over the top and judging by some of the looks received on the way back, he was due to become a focal point for more than a few scroungers. He realised this also, because as soon as we got to our cells he asked me to take two of his bags for him to sort out later. Whilst the screw hurried Patel up, who was trying to sort out what items to take in his own cell, I nipped over to the dispenser to top up my mug. It was certainly handy being on the ground floor.

Behind a locked door again and savouring one of my newly acquired peppermints, I returned to reading about the art of mass murder, until Mo's return shortly before the evening meal and association.

I had just polished off my helping of shepherds pie and mixed veg., (I had decided to stay off the chips and potatoes to preserve my waistline), and was about to start on the semolina, when Patel appeared at the door, wanting to sort out his bags. The scroungers were already buzzing round him, like flies around a camel's arse, with his cell-mate helping to drive them away, not out of any sense of solidarity, but purely on the basis that the more they took the less there would be for him to ponce. I told him they were under my bed and that it was OK to sort them out on top, provided he didn't make me spill my semolina. When my cell-mate saw the quantity of goods in the bags, including chocolate biscuits, cigarettes and cans of soft drinks, he told Patel he must be mad buying so much and that he would be making things very hard for himself for doing so. In a lower category prison, with much more time out for inmates, he would not even be able to stand guard over it, as they would just trample him into the floorboards to get at his locker. We decided he could sort out the goods and leave some under my bed as, due to Mo's standing on the spur, they would enjoy a substantial, but not total, degree of safety in our cell. It was also impressed on Patel, in his own interest, not to have so much in his possession in future, but he never really took the advice, much to his cost. Quite a few scroungers were to benefit from his shop's takings during the ensuing weeks.

With my meal finished and my co-defendant's bags back under my bed, I decided to take a shower. Patel and Mo were both waiting to get on the pool table, provided the screw trying to fix a tear with a stapler was successful, and I was beginning to feel stale due to the lack of fresh air. One of the other few good points about Belmarsh is the constant supply of hot water, an achievement that would put many hotels, not just in Spain, to shame. What they also lack is the screws desk, positioned in such a way as to afford a full view into the shower units, but I thought if the woman screw sitting there with her two male colleagues wasn't bothered, then why should I?

Chapter 6

Punch Up In The Visitors Hall

The remainder of that first week passed fairly uneventfully, with me consolidating friendships already made, whilst adding more to the number. I learned from the outset to ignore the various offences of my neighbours, some of which, such as drug dealing, I would be generally hostile to, and to view them solely as individuals trying to get by in the same artificial environment as myself. Some were good blokes, whose company I thoroughly enjoyed; others I just kept on sociable terms with and there were a few I made a point of avoiding as best I could. On the Friday, I had a privilege visit to look forward to, when my wife, elder son and my daughter's partner, would be turning up in the afternoon, so straight after breakfast that day I took extra care to have a shave without cutting myself to ribbons. That function had been achieved with minimal blood loss and I was half way through brushing my teeth when Mr B. shouted through the observation panel that I would not be going to Education that morning, as my request to see the Deputy Governor had been granted.

My original request was to pursue the question of a transfer to a lower category prison nearer home, preferably Downsview in Surrey, but in the meantime

111

a second issue had arisen, namely my categorisation. In the security ratings, A was the highest and D the lowest security category.   I had been made a C cat., for reasons that were only explained as the result of sloppiness, when I received an apology after my release.   My 5 co-defendants, all with longer sentences, and 3 with previous convictions, had all been made D cats.   I felt I had a justified grievance, especially as it was an obstacle to obtaining a transfer.

Within the hour, I had passed through two gates, each one meriting a rub-down, on the 50 metre journey from the spur to his office, located next door to the Pharmacy.   Once inside, I was confronted by an elderly Welshman, seated behind a large desk, who managed to conduct the 10 minute interview without once looking me in the face.   My request form to see him, with the reason clearly stated, lay in front of him, so he commenced the discussion by asking me why I wanted to see him.   He was momentarily confused when I replied that, in addition to what was in front of him, there was the second matter regarding what must be a mistaken categorisation.   Regaining his composure, plus straining his limited mental faculties to breaking point, he resolved that issue for the time being by telling me to submit another request form specifying the new item to be raised.   When I suggested the two matters were related and asked that we dealt with them both here and now, he snapped back that he was a very busy man and couldn't have inmates requesting an interview to deal with one issue, then turning up with a shopping list.   Before I could respond to that blatant exaggeration, he immediately switched to what was an obviously prepared mini speech, to dismiss the prospects of a transfer. Essentially, it boiled down to me only doing a "five minute" sentence, therefore it would not be worth the time and expense to relocate me. With particular reference to Downsview, they were currently heavy into drug rehabilitation which, according to my records, I was not in need of. I cut in at that point to suggest I could let them wean me off the occasional paracetamol I took if I had a headache, thus helping them to bolster their success statistics, but I could see he was distinctly unimpressed with that idea. As far as me only doing a five minutes sentence, to repeat his words, I declared that it may only be five minutes to him, but as far as my family, and myself, were concerned, it was going to be a bloody long 3 months. That observation served to make him really ratty and he actually raised his voice to point out that my language and general attitude could earn me an extension to the 3 months I had just quoted, whilst simultaneously pressing a desk top button to summon the screw, waiting outside, to take me back to my cell. I learned later he was a religious freak, who was known to sing hymns with Brother Donald on Sundays, calling on God to save mankind, many of them, no doubt, from the likes of himself.

Back on the spur I helped myself to a request form, from the drawer on the screw's desk. They were referred to as applications, seeing as the users were usually applying for something or other, and consisted of sliced up sheets out of a dismembered exercise book.   That done, I sat myself at the desk, reading a newspaper that was also tucked in the drawer, whilst waiting for a screw to appear to let me back in the cell.   Finally, one came clumping round and did the honours, to immediately re-open the door to take back the newspaper.   Once inside, with half a mug of orange squash beside me, I made out the request to see the Governor regarding my categorisation as a medium grade security risk, passing the remainder of time until lunch was served reading more about mass murderers.

When the time came to stroll to the servery, I was treated to a reminder of how fast news travels inside, plus the all-too-often vindictiveness of prison decision making.   Half way to the hot-plate, a senior screw took me to one side to give me a word of advice.   He was aware of the reason I had requested to see the Deputy Governor about, and how voices had become raised during that recent confrontation and was therefore taking it on himself to warn me I was risking making the situation worse for myself. Like most bureaucrats, the D.G. took great exception to his decisions being challenged by what he regarded as riff-raff and, to be nastier than usual, could appear to concede to my transfer request by shunting me off somewhere miles away, in the opposite direction of my home, thus making a difficult journey for visitors virtually impossible.   He reminded me that Home Office guidelines, recommending prisons accessible to inmates' families where possible were for public consumption and pressurising reformers, but rarely acted upon.   I thanked him for his effort, appreciating he need not have bothered, but the prospect of what he said did play on my mind, resolving me to say nothing about it at my visit that afternoon, knowing full well how it would upset my wife and family.

Over lunch I aired my fears to Mo, who expressed complete agreement with what the senior screw had said, easing my mind a little with the added observation that all prisons are reluctant to take another's unfit inmates and I was, after all, receiving medication for high blood pressure, with angina also on my record.   It was something to do with keeping their costs down and it was an accepted fact that it cost more to keep a sick prisoner than a healthy one. I was to ponder that one further, as the recent advice had opened up a whole new dimension and no way did I want to end up exiled to some God-forsaken spot in Norfolk or Suffolk, with my loved ones in Surrey.   To underline the point, Patel's consistent efforts to go to Ford Open Prison resulted in him serving the second half of his sentence in an "Open", only it was stuck on the coast outside Ipswich.

My visit that afternoon was a bit more relaxed than the previous one, although the proceedings ended on a distinctly lively note.   The initial shock of it all had subsided, with all concerned adjusting to the situation, although I knew my wife was putting a brave face on things for my benefit.   My reassurances that things were OK with me, I recognised, were taken with a large piece of salt, but in reality they were.   The only two difficult aspects for me to cope with was concern for those who were worrying about me and the total sense of the all-round waste of locking me up for what I did, rather than an appropriate financial penalty. It was good to see my elder son, plus my daughter's other half, and I knew they would both be fulfilling a vital supportive role in the weeks to come. Due to priority matters having been covered the previous occasion, plus during two telephone calls I had subsequently made, our conversation revolved around more general topics, including the forthcoming Xmas arrangements. It was heart-warming hearing about all the good wishes my wife was receiving, some from people I would have least expected, her only complaint being that she was up and down to the telephone like a yo-yo, and that it was taking her three times longer than usual to do a bit of shopping.

Whilst we chatted, I kept half an eye on the hovering screw, ensuring that the cheeselets and the couple of chocolate bars were polished off in good time. The next visit I was entitled to would be Saturday week, which was Xmas Eve, when my wife, my younger son and his girl-friend would come to cheer me up, and they would try to arrive earlier due to the expected pressure for visits that particular day. My suggestion that, whilst I really appreciated the efforts being made, I would be equally happy for them to spare themselves the hassle and to make the trip another day, was immediately shot down in flames by my wife. The subject was most firmly not for discussion. We chatted on for a few more minutes until the screw told us we'd run out of time. Then it happened.   Chairs flying; children screaming; women shrieking; men shouting and screws blowing whistles, whilst two of their number held a young black inmate face down on the floor, landing some heavy thumps on his back as he squirmed in great distress.   Their efforts to wallop and restrain him at the same time were being greatly impeded by some women visitors crunching handbags down on their heads, with unerring accuracy, whilst two or three men tried to pull them away.   Alarm bells were ringing away and screws were shouting for everyone to stay seated, as the hit squad, complete with dogs, steamed into the fray.   Bedlam reigned; fists and truncheons flew as the dogs tried to bite lumps out of anyone they could get at, with one extremely large lady almost taking a screw's head off with a punch that would have made Mike Tyson envious.   Bodies rolled on the floor and crashed onto tables, with one dog breaking loose to race around the hall terrorising all and sundry, provoking more curses and screams from the non-combatants.   Screws seemed to be coming out of the woodwork and, eventually, through sheer weight of numbers, managed to restore some order, reducing the battle from a physical to a verbal one.

The inmate who had been half trampled by both friend and foe, was hauled up off the floor and cuffed, to be dragged away through a side door, all the time shouting back to his visitors.   He could have saved his breath, though, as a couple of minutes later they, and a selection of others likewise shackled, were led after him.   By now a voice was announcing over the P.A. that all visits were cancelled for the rest of the day and would the public depart at the exit, whilst inmates lined up along the wall at the opposite end of the hall.   We were all waving vigorously to our departing guests, as those screws who hadn't left to replace torn shirts or receive first aid, ran back and forth to hurry us up, like sheepdogs marshalling a flock.   We were returned to our spurs in record time, as so many prisoners out of their cells and grouped together, make the Belmarsh screws very twitchy.

Speculation was rife as to what had caused the bust-up, but a few days later the truth was known.   In the words of the official jargon, it was drug related.   One of the common methods of getting drugs into prison is to tie a modest amount up in a condom, then for the visitor to pass it from mouth to mouth when giving the inmate a big kiss.   He then swallows it, to fish it out of the toilet pan 24 hours later.   The system works quite efficiently, except in this case too much had been packed inside the condom, with the result that as he tried to swallow it, the inmate ended up choking himself.   The two screws belting him on the back were trying to dislodge it, as much to save his life as to recover the package.   Unfortunately, as far as a number of visitors were concerned, already thoroughly pissed off with the ordeal they had been made to suffer just to get in, all they saw were two white screws beating up a black boy and they weren't going to put up with it.   The end product was 2 weeks loss of remission, plus loss of wages for the same period for the inmate, with all visits for the following 3 months to be held in "closed conditions", ie., behind glass with any physical contact made impossible. The girl friend faced criminal charges for handling and supplying illegal substances, whilst the others were charged with varying degrees of assault. It would appear not to be an uncommon feature of Belmarsh, whereby people turn up to see prisoners and end up joining them, a situation greatly exacerbated by the way visitors are treated by staff, and the paranoid ethos of the place. Maybe that is why they conveniently built a nice shiny court house next door and explains the regularly heard opinion that, if you are visiting Stalag Belmarsh, make sure you inform your solicitor first.

Banged up alone in the cell again, Mo not having returned yet from his afternoon stint in the Plug Shop, my thoughts returned to the prospects of being moved yet further from home, with the additional strain on those who would want to visit me. It did not take long to reach the conclusion that, if I couldn't be moved closer to them, then I'd be better off ensuring I didn't get shunted further away than I already was. Mo's comment regarding less than fit prisoners also figured strongly in my thinking and I decided to kill two birds with one stone as the saying goes. That evening I would complain of the symptoms associated with an angina attack and, hopefully, achieve two results. Firstly, I would rule out any great enthusiasm for another prison to take me and, secondly, have myself admitted to the hospital wing that, in the event of it turning out to be more comfortable, I would try to prolong my stay there as long as possible. Well, until my release date anyway. That settled, I lay back on the bed, smoking, soon to have my peace shattered by the return of my cell-mate who, judging by his loud protests, had not had a very good afternoon. It would appear they had run out of work half way through the period and the screws were going to reduce their wages accordingly. Mo's argument was that it was not the fault of the inmates if those who organised the workshop were useless, and if anyone was to suffer a wage cut, it should be them. To make matters worse, Mo had spent the afternoon seated next to Swooper, who smelled like a manure heap. The screw who was on the receiving end of my cell-mate's protestations radiated complete indifference to the issue, yet Mo persisted even after the door was locked, shouting his opinions through the narrow gap between it and the frame, accompanied by a few hefty kicks. Eventually he subsided, accepting the peppermint I offered, whilst I fought back the temptation to ask him if he had had a good day. Laying back, I listened to his account of it all, plus a few lurid ideas on what should happen to the Governor, the Assistant Governors, the screws and the whole place itself. Financially, the loss amounted to roughly £1.00, the real pain, I suspected, was as a person who paid a lot of attention to personal hygiene, having to sit next to Swooper. If the screws had done it deliberately in order to wind him up, they had certainly succeeded.

When the subject was finished with, I explained to my companion what I was planning to do, to which he urged me not to. Hospital wings in prisons like Belmarsh, he explained, were definitely not like your average General outside, and were regarded as distinctly high risk areas. Many of the occupants were mental cases, or drug addicts, with the A.I.D.S virus in abundance, and there was no telling who I would be sharing a ward with; plus the medical staff, including the doctors, were an insult to their profession. I was to learn later how true his assessment was, but for the time being my mind was made up. He undertook to look after my possessions, including Patel's, which made me appreciate again how fortunate I was to have him as my cell-mate, as I would have had a serious re-think if I was sharing with some of the others. We agreed that later in the evening he would press the button until a screw answered, all the while with him impressing on me to be very careful and not to be away too long in case they decided to re-allocate the cell. I was touched by the thought that he didn't want to lose me.

Meal time came and went, and during the association period, confined myself to laying on the bed for the sake of appearances. It was not to be an exercise in solitude though, as undoubtedly assisted by Mo just happening to let it slip a few times that I was not feeling well, I had so many neighbours popping in that, on occasions, it was standing room only. At one stage, a screw put his head round the door to see what was going on. He probably thought we were puff dealing, or in possession of some hard core porn magazines. Patel spent the whole time sitting on the end of my bed, distinctly uneasy at so many getting close to his bags of goodies stashed away underneath. It was really great having so many blokes, some I scarcely knew, showing such concern, though some of their opinions as to my suffering left a lot to be desired. The suggested causes ranged from the food; the heating system; the food again, through to my age; home sickness and worrying too much. Harry brought some apples along as, according to him, most ailments are cured by keeping the bowels fully open; whilst another recommended I should join the Yoga class that he ran up on the top landing. Dermot claimed that my symptoms compared to the ones experienced by a bull his Father owned back in Ireland, and it was a great comfort to learn that the poor beast subsequently died All in all, it was a stimulating experience, with the occasion turning into quite a social event, and with so many smoking in such a confined space, the cell becoming a real health hazard.

The screw yelling for everyone to get their hot water brought it all to an end and my visitors departed, allowing Mo to get back in to open the barred window to the night air; then ambling off to get his water. Having filled his own mug, he then made a show in front of the hovering screw of doing the same for his poorly cell-mate, thus postponing the door slamming routine. During the extra time, I had Martin - who was actually quite devout - impressing me with the knowledge he was going to include me in his bedtime prayers, and Leroy, a big black man from the first landing, telling me to "hang loose". I was half expecting the waiting screw, poised with his key chain, to say something, but no, as soon as Mo was back, the door crashed shut and he was off to the next one. Obviously he was due to go off duty and didn't want to delay his departure.

We drank our teas, taking sips in between dunking cream crackers, with Mo stressing once again his misgivings over me getting involved with the hospital wing, but my mind was made up. I did really appreciate his concerns, to such an extent that I actually proposed we had a go at a crossword puzzle, both to pass the time and to change the subject. Nearly two hours later, with the second one almost complete, Mo was reluctantly pressing the call button, whilst I lay puffing on the bed, having made myself all clammy with a flannel soaked in hot water from the wash basin. It was just as well my condition wasn't a real emergency, as it took a screw over 20 minutes to respond from the Bubble, all of 60 metres away. I couldn't help thinking how the ambulance service gets heavily criticised if they don't arrive 2 or 3 miles away within 10 minutes or so, and they have to contend with heavy traffic and road humps.

Eventually the cover was pushed back and a pair of eyes appeared at the glass panel, accompanied by a muffled "What's up"? to which Mo responded by shouting back that I needed a doctor. The eyes swivelled in my direction, to witness me groaning on the bed, bringing forth the very pertinent query "What's up with 'im then"? My cell-mate's reply was along the lines of "How the bloody hell would he know, but 'e's in a lot of pain"! that seemed to satisfy the screw's diagnostic instincts, because he promptly shut the flap and plodded off for assistance. Ten minutes elapsed, then a key rattled in the lock and the door opened, revealing three screws, one wearing the white jacket of an orderly. In reply to his question "Where is it hurting"? I recounted the symptoms of the angina attack I had suffered some months previously, and was rewarded with a thermometer being stuck in my mouth. The reading was normal and I'm sure that the combination of Mo going on about my blood pressure problem, with me wincing in pain whilst breathing in short gulps, was all that prevented him from leaving it at that. This was one orderly who was going to cover himself. A brief debate took place between him and his colleagues, ending with his announcement that he was taking me to the medical wing. I cheered inwardly, but expressed extreme reluctance to go, on the basis that when released I could be put anywhere, whereas I was settled where I was. Stress, brought on by worry and uncertainty, I declared, was the last thing I needed. The orderly emphasised he was only having me admitted to the medical wing for my own good, primarily for observation purposes, and that he would have a word at the Bubble to ensure my current bed wouldn't be re-let in my absence. Muttering relief at his assurances, I laboriously heaved myself into sitting on the edge of the bed while Mo quickly popped some personal items into a bag, including my baccy tin and matches. The orderly screw made a point of taking my blood pressure tablets and soluble aspirin out of my cupboard, tucking them firmly into his pocket. Sitting there, I thought one of the screws would be rustling up a wheelchair because, after all, as far as they knew, I could be having a heart attack.

124

How naive of me. Even if such a contraption was available, no screw was going to risk a hernia, or worse, manhandling it up and down all the stairs and steps that lay between us and our destination. The orderly said I would have to walk, but as a concession to my condition, we could take it slowly, stopping any time I felt in need of a rest. To make the journey easier still, he informed me that I could hold on to his arm for support, whilst in the other one he would be carrying a chair in case I actually required to sit down. Mo's generous offer to accompany us on the trip and carry the chair was brusquely refused. Off we set, with me hanging onto the orderly with one hand, whilst clutching my bag of possessions in the other, stopping at the gate for it to be inspected and to receive the ritualistic rub-down. While that was being done, the orderly borrowed one of the chairs at the screws table, then we limped on our way, like a couple of geriatric removal men.

Walked at a normal pace, the distance between our spur and the medical wing would be covered in about five minutes, but I excelled myself that evening, stopping frequently and requiring the chair on four occasions. When we finally arrived after an hour, I had one thoroughly pissed off orderly, who undoubtedly resented people falling ill and depriving him of an evening in front of the television. On arrival, he promptly handed me over to another orderly, who took me along a short corridor without offering me any assistance, stopping at a door to unlock it. Shuffling along to where he waited, making full use of the wall for support, I entered the

125

ward, which consisted of five beds, four occupied and the fifth soon to be. Two of my fellow patients were already in bed with the covers pulled over their heads; another was reading and the last one lay on his back with a head-set on. Being prison, my bed wasn't made up, so I just kicked off my gym shoes and laid on it as it was, to be immediately told that not only was I to make it up, but that it was against the rules to get in it fully clothed. The orderly was a screw first and a nurse barely second.

Leaving me to it, he left the ward, locking the door behind him, to reappear in an office located in the corner of the ward, where he could watch us through the sealed windows. For the sake of appearances, I made up my bed and then got undressed, both slowly and in obvious discomfort, all of which didn't even distract him from the paperback he was reading. Maybe if I could have managed to cough up a pint of blood or, better still, collapse on the floor, his interest might have been aroused, as it was probably also against prison rules to sleep anywhere other than in the bed. The sheets were like real hospital ones, crisp and white, which was a very welcome change to the grotty brown things issued on the spurs, and the pillow-case was the same, so when I eventually pulled up the covers, sleep was soon in coming.

****

Chapter 7
The Only Hospital With A Health Warning

Prison must have the effect of heightening instincts relating to self-protection that, in a normal environment, become relatively dormant. Walking in a park or standing at the bus stop, one is likely to generally observe what is around them, without actually scrutinising everyone or weighing them up. Sitting in a comfortable armchair or laying in bed, relaxation comes quite easily, and it is not unknown to nod off when sunbathing in a public place with strangers all around, thinking nothing of it. In prison, though, a mental antenna becomes activated, picking up any signal that may indicate danger. That is what must have brought me back to consciousness, part way through the night. My half open eyes took in the immediate surroundings, illuminated by both the light from the corner office and the glow from the outside security lights that shone between the window bars, as my memory bank reminded me as to where I was. Nothing seemed untoward until, as I was deciding which way to turn over, I heard the soft mumbling coming from a point nearby. By now my eyes had become accustomed to the half light and I could make out the huddled form of the bloke in the next bed, barely two metres away. Thinking that all I wanted was a neighbour who held conversations in his sleep, I decided to turn over in the opposite direction, when the realisation came to me that it was

127

not him at all.   The mumbling was coming from beyond my feet.   Peeking cautiously over the top of my blanket, at first I couldn't detect anything, but lifting my head slightly, I was able to make out the top of someone's head.   Kneeling in the gloom at the foot of my bed was one of my fellow patients, quietly chanting away to himself, his head gently rocking back and forth, like one of those dogs people put in the rear window of their car.   My first reaction was to tell him to sod off, but I didn't, due to the uncertainty of how he might react if interrupted.   Neither could I just pull the covers over my head to blank him out and maybe get back to sleep. Some of the things Mo had said went through my thoughts and I was very seriously concerned that, after the prayer offering, it may be on the cards to sacrifice me to whoever was being chanted to.   None of the other three occupants seemed to be disturbed by what was going on, but that was not surprising, as they were probably recipients of some of the volumes of drugs dispensed every evening to make prisoners sleep.

I peered across at the office window, but received no reassurance from that quarter as it was empty, and decided the best thing to do was to stay awake, ready to defend myself if needs be.   In order to enhance that possibility, I decided some weaponry was required but all that was within reach on my bedside locker was my plastic mug and cutlery, a book, my glasses and a leaflet about prison hospital rules. Very discreetly, I slid my hand out and plucked my fork out of the mug, to clutch tightly under the blanket. Any hostile move on his part would be rewarded with a

128

severe pronging.   Laying there, armed and ready, I tried to comprehend what was being mumbled, but couldn't understand any of it, at one stage even speculating   whether   Belmarsh   might   be experimenting in some form of alternative medicine and that the bloke at the bottom of my bed was actually the doctor.   The minutes dragged by and an orderly reappeared in the office, who, after taking a brief look through the window into the ward, turned on the TV and settled down in an armchair to watch some late show.   He could not have failed to see what was taking place, but obviously regarded it as nothing to be bothered about.   The thought of him with his feet up in front of the telly whilst I, who was supposed to be in his care, lay in bed a few metres away ready to defend myself with some plastic cutlery, made me feel thoroughly pissed off.   I decided to hit the buzzer over my head, to hopefully generate some interest on his part, but before my hand reached it the chanting stopped and the bloke stood up.   My hand stopped in mid-air, whilst the other one tightened its grip on the fork, but to my surprise and relief, not only did he make no move in my direction, he didn't even look my way.   Stooping down to pick up what appeared to be a small door mat, he moved to the foot of the next bed, re-laid his mat on the floor, knelt down, and re-commenced his barely audible chant.   Seeing this, I began to relax and when the inmate in the neighbouring bed lifted his head to see what was going on, then disappeared back under the covers, I decided it was safe for me to do the same. Discreetly replacing the fork back on top of the cupboard, I burrowed down to try and regain that which had been interrupted.

The next morning I enquired from my neighbour as to what it was all about, to have it explained that the night-time chanter, who was now a mound under his blanket, was a self-professed Buddhist, or Shinto-ist, or some such thing, and dedicated half of every night to offering up prayers for the sick. As we were the ones most readily available and the ward door being securely locked, he would recite them at the foot of each bed as a way of personalising them for the attention of his God. Why he was in the hospital wing was not too clear, but apparently the reason he was in prison was his persistent habit, during the winter months, of seeking four-star accommodation, free of charge. From spring through to late autumn, he travelled around the countryside, sleeping rough, but as the cold nights set in, he would break in to any of the finest hotels in London, to be eventually arrested whilst sound asleep in bed, having polished off the complimentary drinks. He would only zero in on the best establishments because, not only did they have the most comfortable beds, plus some modest liquid refreshments available, they were also sensitive regarding adverse publicity and quite often declined to press charges. The latest one, presumably, hadn't been quite so sensitive.

Breakfast was a miniature version of what took place on the houseblocks, same food with the inmates from each five-bed ward being let out at a time, to be served at a small hotplate along the corridor. The one pleasant difference was that we ate from plastic plates and bowls, instead of a big metal tray. Back in the ward, we could eat sitting on the bed or up at the table. I chose the latter and, whilst munching my cornflakes, discreetly observed my co-residents. The nocturnal faith healer was still an inert heap under his blanket, so I concentrated my attention on the other three. Dave, whom I had already spoken to, was about my age and sat on the edge of his bed, absent-mindedly chewing a piece of toast. The second bloke, Adam, had eaten half his food during the short walk back from the hotplate and now stood peering through the door window, obviously waiting for someone to come along the corridor. He kept muttering to himself, whilst all the time clenching and unclenching his hands, his nose flattening on the perspex whenever he heard a door opening or closing. He was a stocky bloke, in his early forties, and I suspected what he was getting agitated about was the medicine trolley. I decided to tread warily with him.

The last one was a little old fellow, well past retirement age, sitting at the opposite end of the table, drinking his tea, whilst watching me like a hawk. I'd temporarily forgotten that others might be doing the same as me. To break the ice, I asked him if he wanted a roll up, to learn that his one remaining lung would give up if he did. He seemed quite happy to have someone to chat to, explaining that he was moved to the hospital wing so the doctor didn't have to walk too far to check up on him. Also, if he was to die in prison, it would look better for it to happen there than in a cell, when it came to an inquest. It struck me that he would probably be better off in a smoke-free single cell than in the ward, where smoking was permitted, but of course the bed wouldn't be so comfortable and there was also the other considerations he'd referred to.   I asked him why he wasn't moved to a healthier environment, such as a prison near the coast, to be told that he'd only recently been transferred from Parkhurst, on the Isle of Wight.   He was serving a life sentence with a judge's recommendation that he serve at least 20 years, of which he'd completed 16, and the move to Belmarsh was one of the periodic transfers applied to long term prisoners.   He knew it would be his last. Looking at him it was hard to imagine this pathetic looking figure doing anything serious enough to receive such a severe sentence, but I was to learn later from one of the cleaners, whom I met back on the spur, that he'd torched his shop for the insurance money.   Unfortunately, the fire had spread to the flats above and by the time he had found a telephone box that hadn't been vandalised, to make an anonymous call to the fire brigade, three people had died in one, and two in the other.   He had tried to commit suicide twice and could only sleep with the help of strong tranquillisers, due to recurring nightmares.   So far I wasn't too impressed with my present company, consisting as it did of a born-again holy man, an arsonist with suicidal tendencies and a junkie that was currently clawing at the door.   Hopefully, Dave - who was still seated on the edge of his bed - only now he was studying his toes, would be closer to normality. My musing was disrupted by the unlocking of the door and the entry of a fat female orderly, who immediately grabbed Adam to prevent him getting to the medicine trolley, parked outside. Whilst she kept him pinned to the wall, fully utilising all of her very substantial body, a male orderly mixed up a concoction in a small beaker, giving it to Adam, along with some pills. He downed the lot in one swallow as if his life depended on them, which to him they probably did, then on being released from the full body hold, almost ran back to his bed, throwing himself on top of the blanket.

The rest of us were given our allocations, the chanter being woken up for his, to immediately burrow back under his covers like a big dormouse. Whilst this was going on, a cleaner collected up the breakfast utensils and left us a mop, broom, plus dustpan, to clean the ward with. Prisons being a test site for various experiments, the day may not be too far off when some penny-pinching accountant suggests this practice to a Hospital Trust. In an era where operations depend on the luck of the draw, patients sleep on trolleys in corridors and women give birth on the floor of store cupboards, is the possibility of patients leaning on a crutch with one hand, whilst pushing a floor buffer with the other, so unthinkable?

With the door relocked, I pondered on how to pass the time. None of my four ward companions seemed inclined to socialise, as the holy man was still buried, Adam lay in a trance-like state on his bed, Dave was plugged into his personal stereo and the last was immersed in a comic, so I rolled a fag and went over to the window to smoke it. The view was out onto a small enclosed yard, that even though a few rose bushes grew there, I subsequently learned was used as an exercise yard. A fine drizzle of rain was falling, which made the middle-aged bloke, dressed only in a shirt, trousers and carpet slippers, pushing a broom around the tarmac, look pathetic. There was nothing else to look at, so I idly watched him as he pushed a piece of paper to the far end, whereupon he took out his penis, to wave at the surrounding windows. This performance lasted a couple of minutes, then having put it away, he proceeded to sweep the same piece of litter towards my end where, on reaching it, he repeated his "winkle-waving" act. He was half way back to the far end again, when someone called him from a first floor window, at the same time waving a cigarette out through the bars. Going across, obviously expecting to be catching the cigarette, the arm withdrew, reappearing almost immediately to hurl a turd down at him, hitting him squarely on top of the head. Peals of high pitched laughter erupted as the flasher ran around the yard screaming obscenities, while the turd, aided by the drizzle, oozed down his forehead. His tantrums were definitely livening up an otherwise boring Saturday morning and I felt a bit disappointed when, in response to his random stoning of windows, two screws rushed out to drag him inside. Finishing my fag, I returned to lay on my bed, just as the door was unlocked to admit the cleaner bringing a jug of hot water for tea making, and to retrieve the broom. In addition to filling my mug, I managed to obtain from him a couple of old newspapers, to while away the time with. The high point of the morning was when an orderly issued canteen order forms to those who had any money to spend, with the items ordered to be dropped in during that afternoon. I made extra heavy ticks next to playing cards; stationery and stamps; a biro and, in the hope of getting to the telephone along the corridor, a 'phone card. Then, in between sipping my tea, I read the news of the previous week. The mid-day meal was served at 11.30 a.m., for which even the chanter surfaced, followed by the distribution of some more tablets and potions, after which the ward lapsed back into a state of lethargy.

Halfway through the afternoon our goodies arrived from the canteen, accompanied by the invitation to be taken upstairs if we wanted a hair cut. In my ignorance, I actually thought a prison the size of Belmarsh would have its own barber, and feeling like having a trim up, declared my wish to go. It would also be an opportunity to get out of the ward for a short while, which would be a bonus. Adam fancied going as well so, having linked up with six or seven others in the corridor, we were shepherded by two screws up to the floor above. The hairdressing salon was one of the plastic chairs found in the cells, placed halfway along the corridor, and the barber a fellow patient, armed with a battery operated shaver. He was already working on one bloke's head, ploughing away as if determined to leave grooves in his scalp. It was immediately apparent to me that the hairdresser, some time in the past, had been employed on a sheep farm. The going charge for this "treat", as in the rest of the prison, was negotiable, but usually resulted in either a £2 'phone card or 12½ grams of tobacco.   Any inmate was eligible to wield the shaver, provided he could demonstrate to the screws that he had a "customer".   I decided I didn't want a trim up after all and when my turn came, informed the hovering orderly accordingly, whereupon I was locked into a ward with those who had gone through the operation.   It was a larger ward than the one I was in, consisting of a small corner office and nine beds, all of which were occupied, with us intruders standing around in between them.   I felt distinctly uncomfortable with the door locked and made a bee-line for the window wall, so no one could get behind me.   The four I was in with looked 100% compared with those occupying these beds.   Two sat on their pillows, with their chins resting on their drawn up knees; two lay stretched out in a trance; another one kept rolling over and the remainder just kept twitching and scratching themselves.   They all looked emaciated and although appearing much older due to their condition, not one of them was over 25 years of age.   The one nearest to me broke off scratching his arms to ask me for a burn, to which I had to say no, as I genuinely hadn't brought any with me.   Looking at his gaunt face and sunken eyes, reminded me of pictures of concentration camp victims, and his bony arms were smeared with blood where his perpetual scratching had broken the skin. This ward, unlike the one I was in, was monitored by a camera and when the call of nature compelled me to use the toilet; I saw that area was likewise covered. The whole room was filled with a hard to define, but distinctly unpleasant, odour and when the time came to take us back, I was one of the first out the door.

A television set had turned up in our absence and Adam immediately joined Dave, and the bloke with one lung, to get excited over some children's cartoons. Next to drugs, nothing keeps the majority of inmates from being a nuisance as much as a TV set. Put one in each cell, with plenty of valium on tap, backed up with a few spliffs, and you could cut the number of screws required by half. Not being in the mood to watch cartoons, I sat myself on the edge of my bed to sort through the canteen bag. Everything I had ordered was there, including the deck of cards I thought would help to pass some time with, and a 'phone card, which posed the question in my mind as to when I might be able to use it. I called across to the three huddled round the TV set, asking what the arrangements were regarding the telephone, and after the third attempt, obtained a response from One-lung that it was straight after dinner being served, provided you had your name down on the screws' list. I refrained from seeking an enlargement on the bit about a screw's list, seeing how engrossed they were with Popeye the Sailor Man currently having a punch-up with Pluto, in order to rescue Olive Oil from being molested. Adam, I'm sure, was on the point of wetting himself, the way he was jumping up and down, in the process of which he managed to shower Dave with the contents of the crisp bag clutched in his waving hand. Dave didn't seem too bothered though, proceeding as he did to pick the pieces of crisp off his pyjama jacket, to pop in his mouth. It was probably just as well Adam wasn't drinking a mug of orange squash.

137

The question of the screws' 'phone list was still unresolved and I recognised it would remain so until I got hold of a screw, with or without a list. In the hospital wing all the screws wear white jackets so they can be called orderlies, and the only one that I could see as being available was currently buried in an armchair in the office, watching the football results on TV. I ambled across to the window and knocked on it, to obtain his attention, but a combination of his concentration to see if he'd won anything on the pools, the volume being turned up and the substantial thickness of the perspex window, made my efforts totally fruitless. And this man was supposed to be observing us. I gradually increased the strength of my knocks, until eventually I was bashing away with the side of my clenched fist, still to no avail, and was contemplating graduating to the use of a chair, when he turned his head in my direction. With my face up close to the window, I shouted to him that I wanted to have a word, but due to both his inability to turn the volume down or to lip-read, I might just as well have been talking to myself. It was obvious that he would rather ignore me, to get back to seeing how his team had got on, but prompted by the inbuilt instinct all screws have to cover themselves, after all, I might have been telling him of my intention to slash my wrists with a plastic knife, he reluctantly came out of the office and round to the ward door. A flourish of keys had the door opened, and with the charm of an agitated wart hog, he demanded to know what it was that was so urgent, to which I replied with the query as to how I could get on the telephone. One would

138

have thought I was asking to take his new car, if he had one, on a cross-country rally. After getting a few observations off his chest, such as "Did I think I was in a bleedin' hotel"? and "Is that all I dragged him round for"?, it was at least 20 paces from his armchair, he informed me that the orderly on duty when we got our evening meal drew up the list. My attempt to thank him and to point out that nobody had seen fit to explain the system, was abruptly cut short by his slamming the door shut. I returned to my bag of goodies, took out the deck of cards and sat up at the table to pass the time playing patience. My ward mates by this time were all getting carried away watching The Gladiators, their number being added to by the appearance of the Holy One, who had decided to resurrect himself from his bed.

Meal time arrived and I saw the orderly, the same one that I had troubled earlier, to put my name down on the 'phone list. Actually, there wasn't a list, because as so few wanted to make a call, he could biro the names on the palm of his hand. A combination of not many people outside wishing to hear from them, plus more material things, such as tobacco, to spend their very limited funds on, kept the demand for the telephone extremely low among the residents of the hospital wing. I took full advantage of the situation when my turn came, following up the call to my wife with two quick ones to my daughter and youngest son. In prison, any little result has the effect of perking up the old spirit and I must confess to being quite pleased with myself not only for getting to make three calls, but also having a plastic bowl from the servery tucked away at the bottom of my goody bag, to take back to the spur.

Locked back in the ward, I settled myself down at the table again to play patience. The television had been removed, leaving One-lung reading his comics; Dave laid out on his bed with his earphones on, minus a radio; the Holy Man standing at the window, gazing up at the stars, and Adam pressed up against the door twitching, looking out for the arrival of the drug trolley.. The thought went through my mind that, having been admitted 24 hours previously with a suspected angina attack, nobody had taken my blood pressure, let alone see a doctor. Additionally, whilst it must be accepted that everyone should take responsibility to avoid practices detrimental to their health, I found it amazing that I was permitted to carry on smoking, irrespective of the affect on One Lung, laying two metres away. No hospital outside would have tolerated it, yet an institution designed to restrict didn't give a damn. Neither had any of my fellow patients been visited by a doctor, or indeed, anyone else with a medical qualification, for the same period. Later, I was to learn some inmates are lucky if they are monitored once a week, and that is only to see if they can be moved back to one of the spurs. The fact is, anyone claiming to be unwell in a prison environment, is automatically assumed to be making it up. It is the traditional reaction of both staff and administrators, including those specifically charged with health care, that becomes even more distorted in the paranoid world of Belmarsh. The case has since been documented of the IRA prisoner, Pat Kelly, incarcerated in the Double "A" unit during this time, who received no treatment for skin cancer, even though his symptoms and medical records had made the doctors aware of his condition months previously. Two other prisoners soon after, in the same unit, had their claims that excessive "bang-ups", lack of fresh air and exercise, poor diet plus unheated cells, were causing both physical and mental illnesses, rewarded by worse conditions in solitary confinement, with the acquiescence of doctors. It would appear that any dedicated doctor, adhering to the Hippocratic Oath they all take, who demonstrates a preparedness to "rock the boat" in the interest of his patient, do not have their contract renewed and the idle and incompetent know that the results of their neglect will be covered up by the security blanket. In the rare event of any examples seeing daylight, claimants would be rapidly bought off with a no-liability, out-of-court settlement: and if the almost impossible took place, whereby an inquiry was being called for, then it would be conducted internally; dragged out for as long as possible; the buck passed around until it disappeared, with the result being empty phrases, such as reviewing procedures. If a catastrophe occurred, with the inquiry going outside the "family" and some Home Office bureaucrat really fouling up by permitting it to be chaired by some lefty barrister, with the outcome actually criticising an official, then they would have conveniently retired months before on medical grounds, cushioned with a very lucrative financial package, and working as a consultant on penal affairs to some Third World regime.

The drug trolley arrived and the peace was shattered as soon as the orderly unlocked the door. Unlike the hefty woman orderly who had called with the morning trolley, this one was rather slim and completely lacked the stopping power of her colleague. Adam pushed straight past her to get at the selection, whilst the other orderly tried to hold him off. The first one was now blowing her whistle like a demented referee, that brought two screws running along the corridor, past windows that were now full of faces cheering and shouting. As a result of the struggle, the trolley had crashed back against the opposite wall, spilling little tubs of pills over the floor, many of which were being crushed to powder by the feet of the combatants. The reinforcements literally pounced on Adam, dragging him to the floor, and whilst three held him down, the fourth cuffed him. He was kept in that position whilst, having relocked our door, one of the orderlies tested an already prepared hypodermic syringe from the trolley and plunged it unceremoniously into his backside, giving him the full content. Whatever it was, it certainly worked, as within a couple of minutes he was out like a light. The door was unlocked again and whilst one orderly went for a dustpan and brush, the other one, with the two screws, carried Adam into the ward to dump him onto his bed, confirming once again he was completely knocked out before removing the handcuffs. My three remaining ward mates had their potions served up in double quick time and, as a follow-on to my previous thoughts, I took the opportunity to query when I was likely to see a doctor. Monday morning it would be, unless I became an emergency in the meantime.

Calm restored, I resumed playing cards, at the same time mentally weighing up the pros and cons of my present domicile compared with being on the spur. On balance, I thought, if I stayed too long where I was, it would end up with me trying to ambush the drug trolley. Time was dragging, which to me was the hard part. At least back in the cell you could have a chat, that helped to while away the hours, and when the doors were opened, go and socialise with some of the other inmates. When the cleaner, escorted by a screw, came round with the hot water for a cuppa, I decided to call it a day. A mug of tea and a read of my book would help me to doze off sufficiently, I hoped, that even the chants of the Holy One would fail to disturb me. As in an ordinary hospital, you don't get properly tired to have a deep sleep, but in Belmarsh that situation is off-set by a combination of whatever they put in the drinking water to reduce one's urges, and the effects of the central heating system. I was only disturbed once during the course of the night by a commotion in a ward down the corridor, that culminated in a posse of screws dragging three excitable inmates past my door, to spend the rest of the night elsewhere.

****

Chapter 8
Return To Partial Normality

I was wide awake at 7 a.m., and decided to spend the hour before breakfast having a shower and a shave. Adam still lay on the top of his bed, mumbling away to himself in the twilight zone, whilst the other three resembled green mounds under their blankets. Somewhere in the distance a metal gate crashed against the frame, accompanied by a screw yelling something in his football terrace voice, otherwise silence reigned. Flushing the toilet made me feel guilty as I thought the noise would wake the whole wing. When the time came to get our breakfast, it was only me and Dave that bothered, which enabled me to have extra scrambled egg, plus two shrivelled up rashers. I also learnt from one of the inmates on the hot-plate the cause of the commotion that had taken place. In prison, perverts, child molesters, rapists and suchlike, if they request it, are segregated for their own safety on what is referred to as the Nonce's Wing. This segregation continues to apply in the event of them being moved to the hospital wing, and the ward along the corridor is one reserved for them. What had happened during the early hours was a case of a gay triangle exploding. One had woken up to find his boyfriend sharing his bed with another, and had vented his wrath by urinating over both of them. The rumpus which ensued, as they

144

tried to scratch each other's eyes out, had brought the screws running and all three had been put in single cells to cool off and, in the case of two of them to dry off. On the way to the cells and when they got there, the jilted inmate had received quite a few additional wallops from the screws, having bitten one of them in the mêlée, and who was now sweating on the outcome of a blood test.

Straight after breakfast, the drug trolley appeared. Adam and the Holy One had to be shaken back to life, in order for their dosages to be administered, after which they both went back into orbit. From the cleaner who came to collect the breakfast utensils, I bartered two roll-ups for a mug refill of hot water, plus Saturday's newspaper. A read up of yesterday's news, and a crossword, would help to pass what promised to be a totally boring morning. When he returned, he brought a second mug for himself, as a chat with me would fill some of the time before he was due to dish out the mid-day meal. Nearly every prisoner wants to be a cleaner, for the reasons stated earlier, especially in a closed regime like Belmarsh. Very few want to be a cleaner in the hospital wing, due to the constant exposure to the unpredictable outbursts of the many drug addicts, and the increasing presence of Aids amongst them. Added to that is the regular mess caused by patients vomiting and urinating, both in their beds and on the floor; plus the frequent suicide attempts, a number of which are successful. The inmate who had bitten the screw had tried to top himself soon after being banged up. He had bitten open a vein in his wrist, but due to the taps in the plug-less wash basin being the type that shut themselves off, had been forced to resort to shoving his hand down the toilet pan. Whether it was the lack of dignity or the sight of his own blood, he ended up changing his mind after the first pint or so, and pressed the buzzer. Over yet another mug of tea each, my drinking companion, Eddie, explained that biting oneself was commonplace and there were prisoners that had had all their teeth removed, to stop them from chomping lumps out of their arms. Many of the occupants, he claimed, should be in secure mental institutions, but lack of places and red tape, kept them at Belmarsh. The most extreme case, which subsequently I heard others refer to, was the inmate who started off serving quite a modest sentence, less than a year, who was now unlikely ever to be released. Apparently, soon after starting his "bird", his mind flipped and he killed a fellow prisoner by ramming a biro into his ear, which resulted in his sentence being substantially increased. Regular assaults on both inmates and screws culminating in killing another prisoner the same way as the first, now had him serving life in solitary. A special cell had been constructed, much larger than the usual, that now constitutes his world. His food is served through a glorified letter box and he is taken out for one hour every three months for exercise, sharing the yard with a minimum of 10 screws, plus an assistant governor. Due to the lack of activity he is substantially over weight and it is hoped that the problem of what to do with him for the future will be resolved by him having a massive heart attack.

Listening to Eddie, and others afterwards, it is obvious that there are more sick minds than bodies in prison hospital wings, up and down the country. In high security prisons, such as Belmarsh, where the public spotlight is actively discouraged, such units are blanketed by additional secrecy where, after a while, people can actually disappear.

They are the Bermuda Triangles of mental health care in Britain today, where under-trained and over-stretched staff can only cope by keeping the patients strapped up, drugged up and banged up. I asked Eddie why he did a cleaner's job there, as such a function is not compulsory. His reply was he had taken up the proposition that had been put to him, which was, in return for spending 6 months in that job, he would receive an extra £2.00 per week and a transfer to a lower category prison nearer home, much sooner than he would otherwise. Our conversation was terminated by a screw shouting down the corridor that he was required at the hotplate. His reference to being moved nearer home sooner than would be customary, as part of a deal to suit the prison, stuck in my mind and made me more determined to pursue my own request vigorously.

I was faced with a bit of a dilemma. By ending up in the hospital wing, my prospects of a transfer nearer home had probably taken a nose-dive, whereas if I pushed it, I could end up worse off. My instincts, born of 22 years as an opposition councillor, told me I was a victim of sloppy management, backed up by bull-shit and threats, and it went completely against the grain for me to let them get away with it without a fight. As soon as I got back to the spur, for that is what I'd also decided, I would apply to see the governor again about my security category, at the same time writing to my M.P., the Board of Visitors, the Director General of Prisons, the Prisons' Ombudsman and anyone else I could think of. If it achieved nothing else, it would help pass the time and cause a fair bit of paperwork for the morons that pose as management. In the event of them retaliating by shunting me off in the opposite direction, I would have another angina attack, brought on by the shock and resultant stress, and refuse to move without a doctor holding my hand. The thought of having something to get my teeth into made me feel quite good.

Dinner came and went, and I helped myself to a second plastic bowl as a sort of going away present, then spent the rest of the afternoon reading practically everything, including the adverts, in the day old newspaper, with the crossword saved to last. Sunday tea was served at 4.30 pm., and I was able to make another 'phone call where, among other things, I was able to tell my wife of my intention of returning to the spur as soon as possible. I emphasised the reason as being OK., rather than my concern that if I remained too long I could wind up being certified, so as to put her mind at rest, as she had probably been worrying since my previous call. From the orderly escorting me back to the ward, I learnt that the doctor would see me some time in the morning, when my dual strategy would be first, to get myself medically discharged, and secondly, to enlist his support for a transfer, as the best way to avoid a recurrence. The television had been wheeled in during my absence for our two hour ration, so I joined Dave and One Lung to watch a documentary about Arctic animals mating in temperatures of 30° below freezing. They spent the whole programme trying to figure out how the animals could find it, let alone do anything with it. The set had been positioned against the window wall and towards the end of the film, my attention became distracted by what appeared to be gigantic fireflies darting about the darkened yard outside. Peering through the bars, I soon realised it was pieces of burning newspaper blowing around in the wind, after being dropped out of a window on the top floor. As each flaming sheet swirled around in the air currents, a high pitched squeal of delight could be heard, but the display ended after a short while, presumably due to no more newspaper or matches, or both.

Adam twitching at the door meant the drug trolley was on its way. The Holy One had materialised and was kneeling on his bed, rubbing his mouth with the back of his hand in anticipation. When it did arrived, accompanied by the same two from the previous evening, the skinny female orderly shouted through the door panel to Adam that she wasn't going to unlock the door until he was seated back on his bed. He showed no inclination to comply, until a screw she had called came pacing along the corridor, rattling his key chain. Obviously, to Adam, the orderly's white coat indicated something nice, whereas a miserable looking screw had less pleasant connotations. Whilst my companions were having their various nightcaps, a cleaner - not Eddie - came in to remove the TV set, returning with the jug of hot water.   I decided to retire to bed with my mug of tea and bury myself in a book, as the least painful way of spending the rest of the evening.   Now I had a plan of action, the morning couldn't come soon enough and, eventually, I dozed off against the backcloth of a bloke upstairs repeatedly calling for his Mother, whilst another couple kept shouting at him to belt up.

I was up, washed and shaved, ready for breakfast, with time to spare, so I started bagging some of my belongings up, ready to move out.   That event took place without mishap, except that toast was off the menu, due to the toaster catching alight, cremating two slices of bread inside.   Even the drug trolley got through its rounds peacefully.   Waiting for the doctor provided one last act of unreality that, in Belmarsh, especially in the medical wing, is so much of the norm, that you become conditioned to accept it. Adam, who for once seemed to be on the same wavelength as the majority of mankind, called across to ask if I fancied a game of chess, to which I agreed. We set up at the table and Adam studiously set the pieces on the board, with the white pieces nearest to himself.   There was no suggestion to decide who was going to lead off, it was going to be him, but seeing as it was his chess set, I let it go. The game commenced and after three or four moves, he took one of my pawns, clutching it tightly and giggling.   I responded by taking one of his, at which, without a word, he scooped all the pieces up, dumped them in the box, taking them and the board back to his bed, where he laid down to sulk.   That was it, game over, leaving me with one more reason to get back to the spur.

In my naiveté, I had presumed that a doctor would be doing a round of the wards, as they do in a real hospital, but that was not to be.   Keys rattled, the door opened, and the fat female orderly who had pinned Adam to the wall with her bosom, called me to follow her to the doctor's room.   Off we went along the corridor, through a couple of locked doors, ending up in a room which, according to the name-plate on the door, was the medical examination centre.   She recited my name and number from her clipboard at the doctor, an Asian man, who was seated behind a very large desk.   He, in turn, shuffled through some papers, extracted a sheet, then tested me to ensure I was the person that went with the name and number he had just been given.   Satisfaction being achieved on that count, he had a quick read of whatever notes had been made on my sheet, then asked what was wrong with me.   I recounted the symptoms of an angina attack, plus a reminder of blood pressure problems, ending up with the claim that I was OK now.   He queried what had provoked the attack, which gave me the opportunity to blame it on the stress caused by worrying about my wife and the difficulties for her to visit due to the distance, and her own health problems, ending up by asking him if he could do anything to relieve my anxiety, such as getting me transferred to Downsview.   He assured me that he would note on my sheet his support for such an application but, as I learnt later, he didn't do anything of the sort.   The medical examination was then terminated by his qualified opinion that I was fit to return to the spur, with the advice not to worry. The orderly was instructed to arrange my discharge and an escort back to the spur, with the comment, after checking his watch, that I should be back there before the mid-day meal. My own watch informed me that I had taken exactly 10 minutes of his time, without even a reading taken of my blood pressure. To qualify for that level of attention, I suppose one would have to collapse on the floor, preferably lapsing into a coma at the same time.

It would appear the staff were as keen to get rid of me as I was to go, seeing as the only word spoken to me on the way back to the ward was the instruction to bag up all my things straightaway. This I did, in the process giving the white cotton sheet an extra feel, as it would be the one of the few aspects of my stay I would miss. There was a temptation on my part to roll it up and shove it in my bag, like taking the hotel towels as holiday souvenirs, but the thought of what the consequences might be if caught, had it staying on the bed. Looking around, Adam still lay sulking on his bed; the Holy One was a mound under his blanket, so I just bade my farewells to Dave and One Lung, as a screw arrived to take me back to Houseblock Two. It was just as well I hadn't plundered their linen, as both myself and my plastic sack were thoroughly searched at the exit gate, where to my surprise, I was allowed to keep the two plastic bowls. Obviously they were not regarded as real booty. We then set off, plodding along corridors, around corners, through barred gates, eventually arriving at our destination, where I was duly booked back in, finally to drag my sack across the floor to Spur 2. It was all very quiet, due to most of the inmates being either at work, or banged up. Mo was over the Plug Shop, so after getting myself a mug of hot water for coffee, before the screw shut the cell door, I borrowed that day's newspaper from the desk, on the strength of a solemn promise to return it at lunch time. It sounds an odd thing to admit but I was glad to be back on the spur. By comparison to the hospital wing, it seemed almost normal. While my coffee cooled, I quickly unpacked and checked that Patel's goods seemed intact under my bed, then having rolled a fag, I settled down to have a read. Time soon passed until doors clanging, accompanied by a hubbub of voices, announced the workers' return. My cell mate, on entering, actually looked pleased to see me back and the next few minutes were taken up with "exchanging fives" with him, and others who insisted on welcoming me "home". Then it was line- up time to go to the hot-plate, sporting one of my newly acquired bowls, the other one having been given as a present to Mo.

It was pleasant having someone to chat with again and, over our meal, I was brought up to date with the spur news, in between recounting my experience of the medical wing, to which my companion repeatedly assured me I had done the right thing in getting out of. After lunch, Mo was called for work and whilst the door was opened, I took the opportunity of refilling my mug, at the same time asking the screw to witness the return of their newspaper, minus the crossword that my companion had torn out. I also stocked up with application forms for the afternoon ahead. Patel was in the line-up to leave the spur, looking very studious with his folder under his arm, and as a welcome back present, told me to help myself to a bag of crisps from his stock, which I intended to do anyway.

Back behind the door, I settled down to a writing session, commencing with an application to see the Governor, then one to see a probation officer, followed by a third to discuss my situation with someone from the Board of Visitors. With those completed, I moved on to write a letter home, mainly to reassure my wife I was OK, next a letter requesting the intervention of my MP and, finally, one to my solicitor to take the matter up with the Home Office. In the latter two, the main complaint was that my 5 co-defendants had been designated D categories, whilst I was a C. This meant additional restrictions, such as prohibited from working on the gardens, in an already highly restricted regime, that, added to the refusal to transfer me, effectively increased the severity of my sentence to the detriment of my health. On impulse, I then wrote an application to the Prison Medical Officer, requesting his opinion as to what measures could feasibly be taken to relieve the anxiety regarding my wife's health, in the event of me staying in Belmarsh as a C category prisoner. I never did get a reply, but if I had, it would probably be to recruit me to the nightly valium queue. By the time I had addressed the envelopes, writer's cramp had crept into my hand, so I decided to take up Patel's kind offer with the crisps. Sitting on the bed munching contentedly, feeling quite pleased with my efforts, I was abruptly disturbed by the spy-hole cover sliding back, to reveal a pair of eyes that could only be Mr B's. Keys rattled and he stood in the open doorway, regaling me with such pleasantries as "What are you doing back here so soon"? I replied by thanking him for his obvious concern, also the grapes I was sure he was on the verge of sending me, but which I could still enjoy whilst convalescing. His reply was totally negative, consisting as it did of a very crude reference to a lower part of the male anatomy. He was on letter delivery duties and as he handed me half a dozen envelopes, five of which clearly contained Xmas cards, I realised just how near the festive season was, and felt somewhat despondent at the thought of where I would be spending it. On my own again, I read the letter, which was from the solicitors bringing me up to date regarding my appeal against the severity of the sentence, then opened my cards, all of which included more letters. Due to all outgoing mail having to be put in unsealed envelopes so the censor can make sure they don't include details of escape plans or any adverse criticism of the catering, I was able to add a PS to my letter to the solicitor, informing him I had just received his. Next function was to extract a length of weave from my blanket, the way I had seen Danny do it, stringing it along the wall next to my bed, to hold my cards. As I gently positioned the last one, peace was shattered by the usual commotion announcing the return of my cell mate, along with most of my neighbours, affording me the opportunity of nipping over to the hot water machine.

Six o'clock came and dinner was served, with Patel asking if he could eat in our cell, partly to get away from his scrounging cell-mate, as well as wanting to delve in his bags of goodies under my bed. Mo didn't mind as he was able to liberally smother his tuna and sweetcorn with Patel's tomato ketchup. We chatted as we ate, with the main news from Patel being that our four co-defendants had been told their transfer to Ford Open was imminent, the effect being to stimulate him in his efforts to achieve the same. He had also been visited by his uncle at the weekend, who had informed him his solicitor had lodged his appeal against sentence and was very optimistic as to the outcome. Listening to him, he had obviously psyched himself up to the extent that not only would he be on the move shortly, but also that his sentence would be cut in half. Mo, who rarely gave an unsolicited opinion, advised him not to expect anything on either count, but that only earned him a dirty look. I realised he was trying to save Patel from having unrealistic hopes smashed to the ground, something he had probably seen many times before, even experienced himself, but like so many others in similar circumstances, Patel only wanted to hear that which suited him. There's a great similarity between prisons and hospitals, insofar as both are full of people who daily walk the thin line between keeping hope alive against the rising tide of unpalatable reality. Mo said no more and when Patel offered him a chocolate digestive from his canteen bag, he took 3 or 4 from the packet and went off to get on the pool table. The topic then moved on to how his Father was coping at the shop, which prompted me to suggest we stretched our legs around the spur. After sitting on the edge of the bed for half the afternoon writing, followed by eating my meal, I was definitely experiencing a square bum. The first thing I did was to hand my application forms in at the screws' desk, then the two of us headed upstairs, me with two burns already rolled in my pocket and my companion with two "tailor mades" in a packet, as our anti-scrounger measure.

It was a pleasant hour or so, chatting with people who, although only knowing them a short while, I felt had been mates for years. David was still running the 'phone list and in the process of arbitrating over how much time each three blokes could have, who were sharing a 20 minute 'phone card. We exchanged "fives" and moved on up to the top floor, where we could enjoy a smoke whilst looking out of the open landing window at the tower blocks and traffic in that part of Greenwich. Gopal, who rarely left his cell during association time, saw us standing there and invited us in to listen to an Indian music tape he was playing. Patel was all for it, but I declined, as I regarded myself as being more than sufficiently punished just by being there, so we parted company, with me walking on down the landing to visit the Irish brigade. The welcome was warm enough and room was made on one of the beds for me to sit down, but I quickly learned they were in a bad mood, and why. It appeared that Thomas, whose absence I'd noticed, had been visited by his Mother and sister, who had travelled from Ireland for the purpose, appearing at the prison gate first thing in the morning. Being a Monday, the visiting hall had not been particularly busy, yet although other meetings were permitted to run well over time, Thomas's had been terminated once the minimum half hour expired. He had quite naturally come away with the right hump and when he just happened to be the one selected for the random full body search, had completely lost his temper, resulting in a screw losing a couple of teeth. Now he was in solitary down at the isolation block, waiting to go before the Governor, with the likelihood of facing assault charges in court.

In the meantime, the screws had probably given him a pasting to be getting on with, all of which would be attributed to justified force to restrain him. To make matters worse, Thomas was a remand prisoner awaiting trial, and it would look bad for him to have further charges pending, especially ones involving violence. I suggested he lodged a complaint claiming discrimination, and for his Mother to take the matter up with the Irish embassy, or even the Foreign Affairs department in Dublin, but the consensus of the gathering was that officialdom, on both sides of the Irish Sea, would be a waste of time. The conversation was tending to go round in circles so, after a few more minutes, I expressed my genuine hope that he would be OK and took my leave, deciding in the short time left before lock-up to visit Harry, and obtain a couple of apples.

****

Belmarsh Bang-Up

Chapter 9

One Shitty Governor And A Frustrated Teacher

Xmas was looming and the effect was noticeable on the spur. Short-timers, such as myself, saw it as the main psychological barrier to get through, following which it would be downhill all the way. Those who had served a number of years and the coming Xmas was to be the last one before release, viewed it in a similar light; whereas those for whom it was going to be the first of many became noticeably quiet on the subject. Mo was under increasing pressure to complete drawings, especially those copied from family group photographs, with priority being given to screws who could enhance his private account. It was even being suggested to him that he could be left alone when inmates were called for work, in order to complete more orders, but as it would entail being locked in the cell, he declined. Greeting cards were available for purchase from the canteen, but were a pretty ropey selection at very inflated prices, which provided the opening for Benny, who was pursuing a computer course, to generate a little earner for himself. Amongst the equipment at the Education Block was the facility to run off photocopies, which he took full advantage of, producing a selection of seasonal pictures, complete with varied messages, that provided a substitute for cards at a far lower cost.

160

His asking price was one cigarette per copy, but quantities could be bartered for a range of items, such as "spliffs", sweets, tinned goods, etc., and for a small extra remuneration, plus a couple of days' notice, he would provide a personalised copy that included names, along with choice of wording.

A moonshine distillery was being set up, the operators consisting of two Peckham blokes on the top landing. Alcohol is forbidden in most prisons, especially high security ones, and the ban represents one of the more glaring hypocrisies of the penal system. Millions of pounds worth of drugs, particularly tranquillisers, are dished out quite freely every year; you can smoke until your lungs are like coal mines, provided you can afford to purchase cigarettes or tobacco from the canteen; a state of obesity can be readily achieved, potentially leading to a coronary, by stuffing yourself with the piles of bread and potatoes that confront you three times a day, and it is not unusual for many inmates to spend weeks cooped up in their cells for 20 hours a day, depriving them of both fresh air and adequate exercise, but for prisoners to have a can of beer at Xmas or to see the New Year in, is regarded as a threat to prison discipline that could even undermine the whole security apparatus. The Number One Governor, since retired, also viewed alcohol - even a minute intake - as contrary to his healthy eating programme, whilst studiously avoiding to touch any of the food that gets dished up himself. So the inevitable attempt to create a tipple takes place, although those involved know they risk substantial punishment if caught. Personally, I believe it is attempted as much for the satisfaction of putting one over the system, as it is to get tiddly. The practical problems entailed with the operation in a prison like Belmarsh are manifold. There is the difficulty in obtaining the ingredients; the lack of places to hide it during fermentation; the surprise cell spinning or the transfer at a few hours' notice. It was because of the almost insurmountable obstacles that encouraged the Peckham Pair to believe they would succeed. They reasoned that under the circumstances, the screws would not have the search for hooch rating a very high priority, and as the overall process generally lasted four to six days, any sniffing around would tend to occur during the week leading up to Xmas. Therefore, they were stirring the ingredients in a bucket during the middle of December, and by the end of the third week had filled four orange squash bottles, appropriately coloured to look like the contents printed on the labels. They had discreetly obtained the ingredients (see appendix for recipe), over a three week period, mainly through others so as to avoid attracting unwelcome attention, with the bucket subscribed by a cleaner. The eventual division of the booze was one bottle sold to the Irish brigade, one to the Afro's, the third shared during association time on Xmas Day among those who had assisted in the operation, with the last one polished off between themselves after bang-up time. It must have been quite potent stuff, as neither of them emerged from their cell until well after Boxing Day.

My applications were also generating some activity,

and over a three-day period I received visits from a Prison Visitor, a Probation Officer, plus was granted my second audience with the Assistant Governor. The latter turned out as much a waste of time as the first occasion, with him telling me they were waiting to hear from my solicitor regarding any previous convictions, before they could resolve my categorisation. In a distinctly patronising tone, he sought to assure me that my current C cat. status was only provisional, but when I stated that my solicitor had notified the prison nearly two weeks earlier, plus querying as to why I could not just as easily been provisionally made a D cat., he reverted to being a nasty little man. He snapped that anything from my solicitor would have to be confirmed by both the court and the police, and in response to my comments that it seemed a pointless exercise in view of his statement, to involve the solicitor in the first place, and couldn't the court and the police be telephoned to fax my record through, he almost snarled that I was not the only inmate to be dealt with. It was obvious to me that he had a real problem resulting, in all probability, from having been bullied at school, and was now one of those faceless little people in suburbia whose highlight of the week is to hide away in his little greenhouse to drool over the copy of Playboy magazine he keeps hidden under the bedding trays.

When he comes to work, though, his position makes him somebody. He has his own parking space, screws salute him and call him sir, he sits in an office five times the size of a cell that two men have to eat

163

and sleep in for months on end, and he most definitely resents any inmate having the audacity to challenge the bullshit he's been programmed to churn out. For my part, I felt I had nothing to lose, reminding him that whilst I fully appreciated I was not the only prisoner in the system, equally, I was only there regarding my situation, leaving others to pursue theirs as they saw fit. My reward for that observation was to be totally ignored, which prompted me to express the hope that my solicitor and MP would get the dual issues of my mis-categorisation and transfer request satisfactorily resolved through the Home Office and Prison Directorate, which as it turned out, they were unable to do. That evoked his final word on the subject, sarcastically declaring, in that case, I needn't be troubling him further, at the same time pressing the buzzer for the screw to take me back to the spur.

The Board of Visitors chap was as much use as a chocolate teapot, and repeated almost word for word what the Senior Officer and the Assistant Governor had already told me. When I responded to his view that my short sentence precluded a transfer, by identifying other inmates who had been moved against their wishes, some with as little as two weeks left to serve, he claimed it was because of the pressure for places at Belmarsh. My suggestion that they would have my bed if I was shunted to Downsview, drew the less than helpful comment that maybe the pressure for places there was even greater. He had called during lock-up time; therefore a screw had to let me out so we could talk privately in the association area, with the screw hovering just out of earshot. During our conversation, a Senior Officer from another houseblock appeared and was introduced to me by the Visitor, with the invitation to contact him, via an application form, if I felt I could use his help. I thanked them both for the kind offer and asked, in the event of not expediting a transfer, whether between them they might assist in rectifying my mis-categorisation. This they both undertook to do, then as we terminated the meeting, the S.O. did something that is completely against Home Office regulations. He shook hands, in front of witnesses, that included a couple of pairs of eyes peering out of cell door spy-holes, with an inmate. It was definitely a funny handshake. Looking back on the incident, one can only assume they were both aware I was still a serving councillor and had drawn the conclusion, wrongly, that I was a freemason. I was unable to return any recognition sign and, shortly after Xmas, when my appeal was turned down, thus terminating my councillor role, requests to see that S.O. went unanswered.

My recourse to the probation service seemed to show a more promising result, with the elderly gentleman undertaking to pursue both matters, at the same time as obtaining the doctor's alleged supporting notes. As the days passed by, though, with no report back on his efforts, plus seeing the frustration of other inmates who had sought help from that quarter, I am firmly convinced they indulge in the same winding-up mind games as the screws, either out of incompetence or laziness. After all, they know they literally have a captive audience who are not in a position to complain, and are likely to be transferred at any time; and anyway, who bothers to measure the cost effectiveness of the Probationers' Office? When screws abuse their position to wind inmates up, it is inexcusable, but for Probation Officers to bullshit and build up false hopes in prisoners, most of whom are not trying to "work the system", but have genuine problems, it is a betrayal of trust, especially when they are very often the only people to be turned to.

What is long overdue is for the Prison Inspectorate to adopt the theme of the film "Brubaker", where the new governor, played by Robert Redford, arrived as a convict to see what really went on, after a while announcing who he really was. It is a very safe bet that much of a report from a competent and honest plant inside Belmarsh, and probably most of the country's prisons, would soon be suppressed by government, under the usual hollow pretext as "not being in the national interest". When the Probation Officer visited me a second time, over a week later, he had obviously done a little homework on me as he was more interested in what I did as a Councillor, than anything else. He was visibly impressed when I mentioned the fact that, apart from other activities, I had served on the Housing Committee for 20 years, and he was full of questions about current changes in allocation policies as well as the ever increasing role of housing associations as providers of rented accommodation. It was not long before he was posing academic scenarios with regard to obtaining rented housing and I realised he was referring to actual cases he was supposed to be dealing with, minus the identities of the clients. I then decided to do what is incumbent on any prisoner to do, namely to exploit any situation that might show a result. Taking the bull by the horns, I offered to assist him and any of his colleagues whatever way I could, but not from inside a cell. I suggested, as they had the authority, that I be taken each time to their office whenever they thought I may "assist them in their enquiries", where my knowledge and experience could be utilised by two or three officers at the same time.

The benefits to myself of such a practice I refrained from spelling out, but were fairly obvious. In addition to having more time out of the cell, there would also be the inevitable cups of tea, hopefully accompanied by a few biscuits, the mental stimulation of being involved in some casework and, possibly, the use of one of their telephones for the occasional call home. He showed little enthusiasm for the suggestion, opining that breaches of client confidence could occur by me being in such close proximity to files. My response that, in prison, client confidence was non-existent due to all files being available for scrutiny on "security grounds"; that most inmates discussed such matters between themselves anyway; and that I was most unlikely to incur the wrath of the prisoners concerned by foolishly trumpeting to all and sundry intimate details of their personal problems, only served to generate a hollow protest on his part that their files were not available for scrutiny. An additional "reason" precluding such an arrangement was, he claimed, my C.cat. status, whereby a screw would have to stay with me whilst I was out of my cell, even though the Probation Office was secured inside the house-block. I reminded him that he had just voiced another reason to get me more properly categorised to a D status, adding that, in the meantime, I did not feel it to be right and proper, on principle, to condone such a blatant admin. cock-up by offering the benefit of my Council experience from the confinement of a prison cell.

He left soon after and that was the last I saw, or heard, from the Prison Probation Service to this day. It wasn't a totally fruitless occasion though, as I retrieved the very nice ball-point pen that he inadvertently left lying on Mo's bed.

I was still attending education classes, even though they were a complete farce. It was always a hit and miss affair when you arrived as to which class you ended up in, depending on such factors as whether or not the tutor had turned up, or the screws thought there were too many in one room and not enough in others. As in the rest of Belmarsh, they had an almost paranoid aversion to seeing too many inmates grouped together. On one occasion, I was directed to the Psychology class, which I thought was a novelty, seeing as I had actually listed it originally as a preferred subject, and what a strange experience that turned out to be. Nine of us sat round a very large table that took up nearly the whole room, with a white board set up on a stand positioned at one end. The woman tutor must have been extremely close to her

60th birthday and could only be described as mutton dressed as lamb. A red silk blouse, at least one size too small, with the buttons holding it together by a miracle, adorned the top half, marrying up with turquoise leggings so tight that hardly any blood could have flowed below the waistline. With the bleached hair, make-up that one would not expect to see outside a circus and hoops in her ears a budgie could have swung on, she was definitely dressed for an evening job around King's Cross. Her first words were to tell us we could dispense with calling her 'Miss', instead we were invited to address her as 'Samantha' and, to complete the friendly approach, we were asked to announce our first names. That done, she proceeded with the subject in hand, asking us in turn what we understood Psychology to be. Replies ranged from "finding out what makes people tick", "what turns you on", "getting inside someone's head", "dealing with nutters"; to "talking about things", "aint got a clue", a couple of "don't knows" and my own non-committal "not too sure". She claimed the "what makes us tick" was the closest, with our actions based on messages given out by the brain. These messages were formulated, she went on, by previously obtained knowledge and experiences that were stored in our memory bank and triggered by signals sent by our sensory equipment, i.e. our sight, hearing, touch and sense of smell. At this stage, with a couple already looking lost, she distributed large worksheets showing the human form, asking us to indicate the points of our sensory equipment, plus the location of the brain. A few minutes were allowed for this to be completed, then she moved round behind us to see the results. The first bloke she assisted by suggesting the brain was generally located somewhere in the head, but it was the third one that stimulated more than a point of debate.

Samantha disagreed that the genital area was part of the sensory equipment, at the same time querying why he had defined it as such. The inmate, a muscular chap in his late twenties, explained that whenever he is touched around those parts, a signal is soon passed to his brain, but teacher asserted that he doesn't exactly touch with it, to which he assured her he most definitely did when he was alone with his girlfriend. Muttered agreement emanated around the table, but Samantha was adamant. She sought to explain that it was the signals sent to the brain by the eyes seeing and the hands touching, that then sent the messages to the area referred to, culminating in an arousal. The bloke next to me chimed in at that point, to question as to how his mate, who was generally regarded as brain dead, never had any trouble getting a hard on. Samantha opined that maybe it was only the part of his brain responsible for that part of his body that functioned. Returning to the one who had prompted the debate, she leant across him to indicate on the drawing with little arrows, signals going one way and messages the other. It was noticeable how she pressed against him, with her breasts rubbing across the top of his shoulder, and doubtlessly influenced by the length of time he had been incarcerated, he was enjoying every minute. He prolonged the issue by stating that even with his eyes shut, and keeping his hands to himself, thus shutting off the emission of signals, as soon as contact was made down below, the reaction was the same. Could it be, he ventured, that his genitals had a mind of their own? No, she maintained, the genitals could not work in isolation from the brain, by now rubbing her hips against his body whilst continuing to lean over his shoulder. The bloke opposite declared that, according to his missus, his brains were in his bollocks anyway, to which I expected her to rebuke him for his language, but instead, she appeared to actually like that sort of talk. Men were luckier than women, she claimed, as they could experience arousal by either touching or just looking, whereas women almost exclusively depended on the touching. Men, she went on, almost with a note of regret in her voice, could obtain stimulation by just looking at pin-ups or watching a woman walking down the street, yet the same woman needed the feel of bodily contact to achieve a similar sensation. As if to oblige, the bloke she was draped over commenced to stroke her arm that, even with the rest of us looking on, didn't cause her to bat a false eyelash. It was as if the presence of an audience was a bonus. The thought occurred to me that all this had been started by one bloke's assertion that his genitals were part of his sensory equipment, but later learned Samantha performed like that anyway. After a few minutes she stood up and moved round the table to view the other sheets of paper, getting herself in nice and close with most of the pupils. She hardly paused at my chair, and two of the other older inmates, indicating she was not into middle-aged men, even though we were all at least six years her junior.

With an exaggerated wiggling of her backside, she returned to the head of the table to take us further into the mysteries of psychology, or at least her version of the subject. The bout of bodily contact had a marked effect on her, generating a note of excitement in her voice, accompanied by a distinct brightening of the eyes. Obviously being locked in a room with a number of men, with the majority young enough to be her sons, over which she exercised a degree of control, was a big turn on for her. It therefore came as no great surprise when she declared we would continue with the theme of sex as a motivator, seeing as love and lust, or a combination of the two, were major contributors to what made us tick. A bit of lust certainly did in her case. For the hour or so remaining of that education period, she invited the younger pupils to recount the various features that attracted them to different women, with particular emphasis placed on when, how and where, such relationships included the sex act.

A few of the lads were quite clearly exaggerating their prowess and successes in that area, but the more fanciful and physically questionable the claims were the more excited Samantha became. When one Afro recounted the time he spent the night at his girlfriend's home where, in between servicing her, padded in and out of her sister's and Mother's bedrooms to bestow his gift in full measure on them, Samantha literally quivered with an orgasm. One of my older colleagues dryly queried as to whether the family cat had been disappointed by being put out for the night, which provoked laughs and an assortment of lewd comments around the table. Teacher, though, was not amused, and warned him that if he was only going to mock the subject she would have him barred from future classes. The whole proceedings by now had become a complete joke, which encouraged me to contribute my two pennyworth. Keeping my face as straight as possible, I asked, in view of the previous comment, whether the sex act between different animal species should not only be regarded as normal, but actually encouraged. This brought forth the expected cries of "pervie" and "nonce", which were suppressed by Samantha who, having taken the bait, invited me to elaborate the point. I stressed that the concept held absolutely no attraction for myself, but went on to quote a fictitious article I had read recently which referred to cross-breeding animals, an example of which was the mating of horses and donkeys to produce mules. As humans were part of the animal kingdom, could we not be crossed with other species, with the mating part of the operation being physically performed, rather than with laboratory equipment. The room filled with noisy speculation as to how one would bonk with different animals, and Samantha, doubtlessly visualising a night of passion with a well strung orangutan, lapped it all up. Her rising passion was being ably assisted by the two inmates either side of her, who groped her vigorously below the waistline, where their actions would not be readily seen by any nosey screw peering through the door window. Any semblance of a lesson, Psychology or anything else, had totally evaporated, while teacher, keeping one hand on the table, had the other one clutching whatever the inmate on her right had inside his jogging bottoms. I felt very pleased with myself for having helped bring about a temporary release from our austere surroundings, and relieved in the knowledge that my fellow pupils recognised I was only joking about bonking animals, as any hint I may be that way inclined could make my enforced stay extremely unbearable. Screws yelling and keys rattling in locks, signalled the end of lessons, and we trooped out to join the line up for a rub down.

Samantha was clearly sorry to see us go and I'm certain two or three of the blokes would have been happy getting some detention from teacher, if only to test the belief that an old fiddle can still produce a good tune.

During this pre-Xmas period, my family pulled all the stops out to visit me at every opportunity, and the knowledge they were coping all right, especially my wife, was a great comfort. It was a few hours prior to one of these visits that I became, once again, a victim of what purports to be medical care at Belmarsh. I had managed to slice my upper lip with the disposable razor that one is compelled to use, generating a blood flow far out of proportion to the size of the cut, a result, no doubt, due to my daily intake of soluble aspirin to thin the blood. Mo hit the buzzer to summon a screw who, in turn, suggested I pressed my finger on the wound whilst he tried to get someone from the pharmacy. He returned about 20 minutes later with an orderly who, having diagnosed the problem as being a cut lip, prescribed a folded up piece of toilet paper be held firmly over it, until the bleeding stopped.   Then off he went, no doubt to write up his report as to how medical expertise had saved yet another prisoner from going to that penal colony in the sky.   Meanwhile, I sat at the sink accumulating little pieces of blood soaked toilet tissue, as every time I thought the cut had congealed, it was torn open again as I removed the swab.   This went on until we were unlocked for lunch, when Patel looked in to see what the visit earlier was all about. Seeing my predicament, he came up with one of his Mum's home-spun remedies, which was to wipe it dry, then quickly rub a piece of soap over the cut, before the bleeding started up again.   This I did, and it worked, although in order not to disturb the covering, I had to forego my meal and, more painfully, a mug of tea.   My visitors were very discreet though, declining to query why I had a portion of soap stuck to my top lip.   Maybe they thought it was some strange prison custom, or that finally the old man had flipped.   Before they departed, I explained what had happened, and they did seem somewhat relieved.

****

Chapter 10
Social Calls And The Xmas Day Quiz

Xmas in a high security prison such as Belmarsh generates a definite undercurrent of tension. Long serving inmates cross off yet another one behind bars, with the empty realisation of more to come, and can quickly flare up with those who keep twittering on about their imminent release.

Visits become more emotional, especially where young children are involved and some of the more unpleasant screws actually resort to any act of pettiness just to make it harder. Kids not permitted to sit on Dad's lap is the prevalent restriction, which is usually guaranteed to wind up the prisoner, plus start the children fretting and crying. Terminating the visit early on the grounds of others waiting, when the hall is only two-thirds full, is another common bit of nastiness, and then jumping on the prisoner if he protests. What a lovely Xmas treat that is for the kids, seeing Daddy being dragged away by half a dozen screws, while Mummy screams her head off. The only contented inmates during the festive season are the itinerants that engineered a short sentence for themselves. A lifestyle of scratching around, sleeping in doorways, becomes extra hard during the cold Winter months, so a few weeks with a dry bed, three meals a day, plus a bit of pocket money, does have a certain attraction. More than a few are actually prison regulars and are expert at gearing their criminal act, usually breaking a few shop windows or kicking a copper, to obtaining a custodial sufficient to take them through to the milder weather. One who got sentenced a few days after myself, told me that the magistrates originally sent him down for only three months, which meant that, with remission, he would be released at the end of January, whilst the temperature outside would still be freezing. To "improve" the situation, he promptly subjected the bench to a very ripe catalogue of verbal abuse and was rewarded with a further month for contempt of court, to which he thanked them for their generosity, and stressed his sincere hope they wouldn't take his outburst personally. With remission, he would now be tucked up until mid-February, at which time he would see how the weather was shaping and, if needs be, prolong his stay by seeking to lose some of his remission. The whole performance made perfect sense to me, but what a terrible indictment of society's neglect of this underclass, which is on the increase and covers the age spectrum from teenagers upwards.

Very few screws on the wings tried pissing inmates off with talk about the boozing and partying they would be indulging in, during the days and nights ahead. The overwhelming majority kept the whole matter low key and avoided including it in the usual mind games. Among the possible reasons for this approach, I believe, was the fact that, unlike at reception and the visiting hall, the screws were on a closer working relationship with the inmates, coupled with the reality that a prisoner, sufficiently wound up, is more likely to "kick-off" when not inhibited by having his family on the scene.

I was receiving quite a few cards that, as well as being very welcome, also served to emphasise where I would be spending the occasion. In order to display them all, I had to extract another length of weave from my blanket to rig up a second line over the bed. One of my Council colleagues thoughtfully sent me a copy of the Council minutes book and the minutes of the AGM of the Police Consultative Group, including the Divisional Commander's report, plus the latest edition of the police newspaper "The Job", to help me keep abreast of things. I read through them because, just like when on holiday abroad, in prison you will read anything printed in the English language. Once digested, though, the Council minutes compensated for the missing rubber foot under one corner of the television set and the other material quickly disappeared after being left out in the association area, no doubt enabling some inmate get through the tedium of a lengthy "bang-up" by reading how the crime rate in Epsom and Sutton is down one percent, and that the Met. is yet again seeking to recruit from the ethnic minorities.

Xmas morning dawned and as we queued up at the gate waiting to be despatched in sixes to the hotplate, I couldn't help noticing how many of the blokes were returning not just with their breakfast trays but also a card stuck in their mouths. Then I spotted the vicar hovering half way down the hall, clutching a wad of cards, and handing them out to blokes on their return journey.   He probably thought that catching inmates whilst their hands are full, and therefore having to stick them in their mouths, maintained the personal touch, rather than sliding the cards under doors during "bang-up".   The lack of any real feeling as to what he was doing, coupled with the opinion that, even though he was a resident vicar, he did sod all because he was never around where his flock was, irritated even a non-believer such as myself.   Subsequently, when it was my turn to be accosted and he held out the card in line with my teeth, I firmly, but quietly, so the nearby screw couldn't overhear, told him to stick it up his arse.   I quickly followed up, as a form of insurance, by wishing him Shalom, to make him think twice about reporting me, in case I registered a counter complaint as to how his action was offensive to my apparent Jewish faith.   The fact I had two curled up rashers stuck with my scrambled egg in the tray, was something I'd overlooked but it didn't matter anyway, as he'd immediately turned away to intercept the guy behind me.

We were having the weekend association format for that day, i.e. 9.30am to 11.30am with the second period being 2.30pm to 4.30pm.   This would allow most of the screws to get away earlier to hang their stockings up; leaving a skeleton staff to make sure Santa didn't get through the anti-helicopter cables and land in one of the exercise yards.   Once we were "opened up" and having dumped my tray on the floor outside the door, I decided to travel round the wing to wish some the chaps Merry Xmas. Up on the first landing it seemed as if half the population were in the telephone queue, where the organising had been delegated to another David, who looked and spoke like Frank Bruno, though just a shade smaller. He had worked out a formula whereby, in order to fit everyone in to the time available that day, those who insisted on making their call during the morning session would be restricted to five minutes, and those prepared to wait until the afternoon would have seven. To prevent one inmate going over time at the expense of another, he would tap them on the shoulder when they had a minute to go, followed up by a bigger tap when their time was up. I stayed a short while for a chat and to catch up on the latest gossip, some of which was quite juicy, as usual. It was always open season for even the wildest rumour regarding screws, with the latest including one who was being accused by an inmate, via his solicitor, for sexual molestation during a strip search, with the full details lacking as he was on another houseblock; and two others supposedly suspended after being caught at it in a store cupboard, her with her skirt up and him with his trousers down. Whatever the truth, or otherwise, of such tales, they were always going the rounds and proved distinctly more interesting than discussing the weather.

After a while I headed off to pay the Irish contingent a visit and to see how Thomas had fared. They were all clustered in a cell, but he was still missing, having been sentenced by the Deputy Governor to an extended stay in solitary. This would prevent any witnesses, apart from staff, as to his physical state, especially too many bruises that couldn't be claimed as having been self-inflicted. He was also facing an assault charge on the screw that had lost some teeth, but the charge was not being made official yet as that would mean his solicitor having access before all the swelling had gone down. The situation had cast a bit of a dark cloud over the Xmas spirit, but his countrymen were doing their best to alleviate it, having already polished off half the bottle of Belmarsh Beaujolais they had procured from the Peckham brewers. I was offered a taster which, out of politeness, I accepted, becoming rather warm as the liquid began marinating my chest cavity. With a voice that had suddenly developed a slight huskiness, I joined in the debate that was already under way, which boiled down to whether a Christian should spend Xmas Day in a church or a pub. It was a rather convoluted argument, with Semtex declaring that as Xmas was a time for celebration and consuming alcohol contributed to one's ability to be joyous, with most of such drink being located in the pub, then that was the place to be. Dermot begged to differ, claiming that whilst he enjoyed a drink as much as the next man, the inevitable drunkenness that resulted besmirched the whole essence of the Xmas message. John immediately chimed in with the opinion that Jesus would have been in favour of everyone taking a drop of the hard stuff to celebrate his birthday, seeing as he had converted the water into wine when He could just as easily turned it into orange juice or milk. That provoked Martin, who was tending to take Dermot's side on the issue, stating

181

that whilst there was nothing wrong in having a drink on the day, the Church was the only place for commemorating the spiritual aspect and it seemed wrong to only spend an hour there, yet think nothing of propping up a bar for three or four. Semtex challenged me for my views, to which I replied that the matter would be resolved if they installed a bar at the back of the church, then everyone could have a drink in between services and stay all day. My reward from Dermot was to be called an "Eejit" which, translated, amounts to being an idiot. Was I suggesting people could wander around the church with a pint in their hand and while I was at it, how about a couple of dart boards on the wall, alongside the pictures of the Stations of the Cross. I made it clear I was suggesting nothing of the sort. The drinking could be done in an adjoining room or hall and only between Masses, with the bar closing whilst a service was in progress. Warming to the theme, I suggested that it would also provide the church with some useful funds, putting it to him that it made more sense for a Christian establishment to have the profits from celebrating a Christian festival, than maybe a non-Christian publican or company. He retreated behind the opinion that if I was only able to spout such stupidity, then maybe I should take myself somewhere else and not be annoying sensible people such as himself. John and Semtex immediately rebuked him good naturedly for saying such a thing to a guest, on that of all days, claiming that he should make allowance for my English upbringing. He relented and with a grin, offered me a digestive biscuit, which I took, in return handing him the pre-rolled cigarette I had in my pocket. The subject was laid to rest and I stayed a little longer exchanging jokes against the background of one of Semtex's rebel songs cassettes, before taking my leave. It was quite pleasant wandering around the landings, exchanging little gripes and items of chit-chat with different inmates, most of whom I had previously only been on nodding terms with. There was a fair bit of activity around a couple of cells, where the look-outs, draped over the railings, tried not to make it too obvious they were doing anything other than having a quiet smoke, whilst idly watching the world go by underneath them. It was farcical, really, because the screws knew what was going on, but both they and the dealers seemed obliged to maintain the pretence of being the hunters and the hunted. Judging by the aroma, some of the goods were already being sampled. I made a point of calling in on Harry, who was immersed in a game of backgammon, from whom I received an orange as well as the usual apple, then David the Rasta.

David's cell was a double, and when I arrived, could only just get inside the door. In addition to himself, there were seven others squeezed in, including two white guys. He was in the process of lecturing one of them, plus a young black, who had got into a heated argument with each other the previous day over what TV channel to have on. The argument nearly became a punch-up, prevented only by other inmates hustling them away from each other, but some of the verbal exchanges had developed unpleasant racial overtones. David was stressing on

183

the two of them that their real enemy was the prison system, with most of their frustrations resulting from the petty, but suffocating, restrictions imposed by the Belmarsh regime.   Along with everyone else, they were victims of the mind games and wind-ups played by the overwhelming majority of staff, and that it was the same staff who got their buzz when prisoners took their anger and frustrations out on each other.   He emphasised that even if they didn't particularly like one another, prisoners were in the same boat, faced with much the same problems, and the only thing to do in order to cope was to try and get along with each other.   Faced with a mindless bureaucracy and too many sad screws working off their personal hang-ups, he continued, inmates had to stick together and, where possible, support one another, as every result obtained against the system was one up for every inmate.   His message, backed up with similar comments from the others, did appear to make some sense to the two he had been addressing because, after a little prompting, they actually shook hands and wished each other Merry Xmas.

David was a Cat.B. serving a long sentence for armed robbery, but it was his role as a leader and advocate of prisoners' rights, supported by an in-depth knowledge of the rule book, that had him viewed as a problem prisoner by the administration.   He knew he was a marked man, and shortly after Xmas was dragged off to solitary confinement, facing trumped up charges of "incitement to riot" and "actions detrimental to the maintenance of good order and discipline".   The charges were subsequently dropped, influenced no doubt, by the inability of the screws to find anyone that had felt incited, but he was transferred to Swaleside Prison anyway.

With the cell half emptied out, I accepted the offer to sit down, conscious that I had given away the one and only roll-up that had been in my pocket. I offered him the orange, accompanied by the little white lie that I had purchased it just for him the day before at the canteen. Thanking me for it, he gave me a burn, with the offer of some "whacky baccy" if I fancied it. I declined, settling instead for an ordinary smoke and a chat, until the homely tone of Mr B's yells, inviting us to line up for dinner, permeated the wing. As we assembled at the gate, he informed us that for those who were interested, he was going to hold a quiz during the afternoon association period. The first, second and third prizes, had been purchased for the occasion out of the Belmarsh Amenity Fund, consisting of a £4 'phone card, 20 cigarettes and a £2 'phone card, respectively. He was rewarded with a chorus of comments, mostly sarcastic and all unseasonal, but with his usual keen wit, replied with the offer that if it helped to make the participants feel comfortable, he would caution them before asking any questions.

I thought they did us proud for dinner, although the same old moans came from the same people that moaned every time. Apart from the vegetarians and Vegans, who had some strange looking pie, we each had half a chicken, chopped down the middle, topped up with potatoes, roasted or mashed; brussels and mixed veg. My tray was full to the brim, with my plastic hospital bowl holding a lump of pudding immersed in custard, crowned by a mince pie. My efforts to lose some weight were definitely put on hold that day. There were no holy men hovering as I made my way back from the servery. Presumably they had better places to celebrate the birth of their Christ, than in the company of the types who eventually accompanied Him on the Cross. Back in the cell, Mo had also decided to forego his healthy eating habit on this occasion, except for the token gesture in that direction when he gave me his mince pie. It never failed to impress me how silent the place became after lock-up time and, as I munched away, it was only the occasional slamming shut of a steel door somewhere or a couple of inmates holding a brief, shouted, conversation out of their windows, that prevented me from imagining everyone else had gone home. When we had finished eating, Mo went to work on one of his drawings, so I laid back on my bed to read a True Detective magazine I had borrowed from Stringfellow, he of the laundry vandalised designer track-suit. Within a few minutes, the combination of an over-filled stomach and the serenity of my surroundings had me drifting off into a very comfortable nap.

I was rudely wakened by Mo shouting out through the bars to Patel next door, telling him I was asleep. It gave me the right hump, as I was just reaching the climax of a terrific dream, where a gorgeous screwess had singled me out for a full body search. Hearing mumbled profanities and seeing my eyelids lifting, prompted my companion to yell that I was now

186

awake. Dragging myself into the sitting position, I glowered at the cause of being cheated out of what promised to be a very uplifting experience, to have him informing me that Patel wanted to ask me something. I told him "Stuff Patel. Tell him I've gone back to sleep", and proceeded to light the remains of a burn that lay on the table. We sat facing each other grinning while Patel kept calling out to me, waiting for his cell mate to get pissed off and threaten to strangle him. After a few minutes, we could hear the demand for him to belt up in the background, and silence reigned again. That was my cue to stand up, flick the last of my fag out the window then, with my face against the bars, shouting the query to Patel, "Did he want me?" Unsurprisingly, he did, but not for the purpose of asking whether I had enjoyed my dinner, or to invite me to help myself to a bag of crisps from his hoard under my bed. What he was after was my place in the 'phone queue, if I had one, for which, within reason, I could name my price. Ignoring the question, I reminded him that I had seen him on the 'phone that morning, to learn that the call had been to his Uncle's shop at Crystal Palace, where his wife was working, whereas he now wanted to ring his Dad to find out what their shop takings were. I told him I couldn't help him as I wasn't on the list until Boxing Day afternoon, when I had already arranged to call my wife. He then wanted to know whether any of those down during the coming association period would be inclined to trade their place, to which I shouted "How the hell would I know?!", but that I felt sure if he waved a Mars bar, plus 20 fags, around someone would oblige. He thought the addition of a Mars bar was going a bit over the top and would only include it as a last resort. That ended the window conversation and I returned to my bed and book, accompanied by Mo's assurance that he would get Patel on the 'phone that afternoon by splitting the 20 fags with David, with me having the Mars bar.   It seemed a very reasonable arrangement, making all concerned happy, except the poor sod at the end of the queue, who now wouldn't get to make his call.   When I voiced that unfortunate aspect, my cell-mate responded with the calculation that if David trimmed half a minute off the time for 12 blokes, then he would still fit everyone in, and even if one or two timed the duration of their own calls, they would not be over inclined to argue the point when he tapped them on the shoulder with his shovel-like hand.   In the event that is what happened, and as I chomped my Mars bar, it occurred to me that with Mo's ability to achieve an outcome where everyone is happy, any Chancellor with half a brain could do worse than enlist his help when drawing up the Budget.   To be strictly honest, though, not everyone was happy, but even Mo couldn't do anything about the shop takings being down on the previous year.

We were let out at 2.30 pm and as prisoners began moving around the spur,
Mr B yelled out for everybody's benefit that the quiz would be starting dead on
3 pm.   Paper for writing the answers on was available at the desk, but entrants had to provide their own pens or pencils.   I decided to enter, but in the

meantime would pay a visit to Don, whom I was given to understand was the only inmate on our spur with a nail clipper. It was one of the little oversights of a multi-million pound prison operation, catering for hundreds of prisoners at any one time, whereby no provision was made for cutting one's toenails. The presumption being, no doubt, that inmates could rip the nails off by hand, or for the very supple ones, bite them with their teeth. Possession of a nail clipper, and most definitely a pair of scissors, was a punishable offence. It was never too clear whether such implements were viewed as potential escape tools, a couple of life sentences should be sufficient to scrape a hole into the exercise yard, or as weapons. If the latter was required, then one would keep the top of the tin, purchased in the canteen and sliced off with the wall mounted opener, available to everyone near the servery. I would rather be attacked by someone brandishing a nail clipper, than the razor sharp, serrated, top of a tin can, but obviously some overpaid security advisors to the Home Office would beg to differ.

Anyway, Don, who was serving a lot of years, was the only one in possession, and it was available for hire in exchange for two cigarettes, the only condition being that you had to do your clipping in his cell. He was in residence when I called, along with three of his friends, reminiscing about previous Christmases in other jails and how they compared with Belmarsh. Mixed in with references to half the nicks in the South of England were also mutual acquaintances, and as I hovered in the doorway listening, it occurred to me that, collectively, these four had spent roughly 25 years behind bars, with a similar number in front of them.   Yet not one of them was anywhere near thirty years of age.   With apologies for disturbing the gathering, I explained the purpose of my visit, hastening to stress that in recognition of it being a public holiday, I was offering three burns.   We were in business but, as no-one fancied looking at my feet and as a precaution against a passing screw glancing in, my clipping had to be performed in the toilet cubicle.   I didn't mind that, although it was a bit cramped sitting on the pot with one foot up, with Don reminding me to catch the off-cuts to put down the pan, as he didn't want to be walking on them in his bare feet.   Inside the glorified upright coffin I chopped away quite leisurely, at the same time earwigging on their conversation, although I wanted to be finished in time for the quiz.   It appeared that the extent of Xmas celebrations depended on the individual prison governors, with our current one being right at the bottom of the list.   In one establishment they actually put up some decorations and, in another, every inmate was given an extra £2 to spend, although they lost a week's earnings due to the workshop being shut.   After sitting on the "throne" nearly 15 minutes, I was eventually hurried up by one of Don's company who was in need of it, so returning his clippers, at the same time accepting one of his peppermints, I went back downstairs to join the competition.

In spite of the derogatory remarks, about 30 were taking part, to some extent because there was nothing else to do, but mainly in the hope of winning something. Mr B emphasised there was to be no joint efforts and that the marking would be done by himself, and Mr W., another screw. Names were to be written at the top of the paper, with prison number optional, and answers were to be printed to assist the markers, as well as to save embarrassment for those who could not do joined-up writing.

I felt quite confident, as I had a very fair general knowledge, but by the fourth question I knew I would not be walking away with any prizes. The first one was, "In what year was the Brinks-Mat bullion robbery carried out?", followed by "How much did the robbers get away with?". Then followed the requirement to name two men murdered by the Kray Twins, and the value of the haul from the Great Train Robbery. The remaining 16 questions were in the same vein, except for one on football and another as to the name of the horse that won the last Grand National. Most of my fellow competitors seemed to have something to jot down in response to each question, and I seriously contemplated excusing myself to answer the call of nature and not return, in order to save face, but decided against doing so in case I got sussed out At the end of the contest, papers were handed in and the two screws began marking them against the list of answers, whilst inmates jostled around them trying to get some indication as to whether they were in the top three. It was noticeable that Mr B kept the prizes securely tucked inside his pocket, and equally noticeable was the fact that of the few spare pencils he'd furnished, none were returned. Eventually the marking was complete and the three winning sheets, along with the list of answers, were pinned on the spur notice board, whilst the three winners collected their prizes. The remaining returns stayed on the table, from where they were rapidly retrieved and double-checked. I collected mine and decided straightaway not to bother confirming my princely score of 2, slipping away to bin it, with the comfort of knowing I was only 16 correct answers behind the winner.

With the intellectual part of the proceedings over, I decided to make myself a mug of tea and take it up to the top landing where I knew Patel was visiting Gopal, to listen to his Indian music tapes. I didn't fancy the music but I reckoned there was a real possibility they would be munching either biscuits or sweets, or both. As it turned out, I never got to learn what may have been on offer as, on leaving my cell with the mug, I practically collided with a white guy about 30-ish, dressed in a blue and white bath robe, who was striding back to his cell. It was Tommy, the screws tea boy, whom we rarely saw as he spent all day down at their mess room and taking their teas and toast around the house-block, returning to his cell after the rest of us were banged up. Being Xmas Day he had finished early, as most screws intended to be away soon after our 4.30 pm lock-up time, with the remainder probably not wanting an inmate witnessing the odd can of beer being consumed whilst on duty. We exchanged pleasantries, culminating with his invitation to pop in for a chat, in the event of me not having any pressing engagements, to which I said I would, once I had filled my mug. Doubling back to shove baccy and tin into my pocket and with the mug filled, I went along to his cell, which was on the other side of Patel's from my own. His cell mate, Eric, who also worked down at the screws mess room, was laid back on his bed, his nose buried into a copy of Country Life. Stringfellow was also seated on the bed, having called to discuss an appeal they had lodged, with his expressed opinion regarding their legal representatives being distinctly uncomplimentary. All three of them were co-defendants, having been sentenced to terms ranging between 3 and 5 years, for being in possession of a lorry load of video films, plus a quantity of leather handbags, that didn't legally belong to them. I hesitated in the doorway, being uncertain whether an outsider would be welcome whilst they discussed such a matter, but the question was resolved by Tommy telling me to come in and sit down, as I was making the place look untidy. It appeared that Stringfellow was appealing against the length of his sentence, whereas Eric, although thinking his was also too harsh, had become resigned to it. Tommy thought that in his case, an appeal could result in his sentence being extended. This built-in possibility was designed to deter frivolous appeals and additional fees being claimed by lawyers, mainly from the Legal Aid fund, but in reality, also discouraged those whose case might be less than 100%. Their lawyers had advised that Stringfellow's appeal may be undermined if his two co-defendants didn't try to get their sentences also reduced. Tommy's argument was that their individual roles in the operation had differed, a fact that the judge had spelled out in his summing up, therefore it shouldn't matter one way or the other whether they all appealed or not. Stringfellow was still unconvinced, but Tommy closed the subject by stating that he would be talking to his Brief straight after the Xmas break, following which he should be in a position to say definitely what he would do.

Turning to his well stocked cupboard, he rummaged around and pulled out a box of Quality Street assorted chocolates, selecting a couple for himself then passing the remainder to the rest of us. Glancing around, I could not fail but be impressed with the way their cell was fitted out. Both cupboards were well stocked with groceries, with books and magazines neatly stacked on the shelves underneath. On one of the tables stood a radio/cassette player, with a box full of tapes alongside, the remainder being taken up with both men's toiletries, including expensive brands of shower gel and after-shaves. The second table had their jars of instant tea and coffee, plus two more with milk powder and sugar. Next to them was an ashtray, a packet of cigarettes and a plastic plate from the hospital wing, holding a selection of apples and oranges. On the floor between the beds lay a prison blanket, that functioned as a carpet, and by the door stood a little rubbish bucket that had already accumulated a collection of sweet wrappers and orange peel. The walls were partly decorated with pin-ups from the classier men's magazines, with a large section over each bed devoted to selections of family photographs, over which Xmas cards were suspended on the usual string lines. The tidiness and cleanliness of cells tended to reflect the habits of men, whether they were in prison or not; likewise, the contents also indicated their affluency on the outside. If they are generally skint before getting banged up, they will remain so for the duration, whereas those who have money that can be fed into their private accounts, will have cells looking like the one I was currently visiting. Since my release, I understand that the Home Secretary has severely restricted the amount of private money a prisoner can spend, as part of his effort to project a tough guy image at Tory Party conferences.

Stringfellow departed after sticking a couple of sweets in his pocket, to obtain a spliff to smoke that night, reminding me as he went out the door to drop his True Detective magazine back when I was finished reading it. This I promised to do, to have Tommy offering me access to his collection if I wanted any more. Whilst drinking my tea and offering baccy to my hosts, Tommy said he had heard all about my run-in with the Assistant Governor and, stressing it was none of his business, advised me to accept doing my time in Belmarsh. Soon after Xmas, he estimated, due to transfers and the screws habit of swapping people around periodically, there was bound to be some openings for new cleaners. At my age and doing a short sentence, I would be a likely candidate, especially as I hadn't got on the wrong side of Mr B. I replied that whilst I still wanted a move nearer home, for the sake of my visitors, I recognised that if I pressed too hard, I could end up somewhere further away still. He reckoned that was a real possibility as, in keeping with their sadistic mind games, the screws would deliberately send me in the opposite direction to the one I wished to go. Eric, having removed his earphones, chimed in to disagree with Tommy's view that all screws were automatically so bloody-minded. As I was very soon to realise, the subject was already a bone of contention between them, with me ending up fervently trying not to take sides. Eric, it transpired, lived at Chislehurst, and was seeking a move to a prison in the Kent area, for the same reason as I wanted Surrey. He had utilised his position working in the screws' mess room to sound them out regarding his prospects, with the result being a senior screw making him an offer that meant cleaning in the drug unit. Now not many inmates wanted to clean in the drug unit for two main reasons, namely, too many hours surrounded by junkies, many with AIDS and unpredictable; secondly, it meant moving to a single cell in the hospital block, away from mates and almost like being in solitary. The verbal deal was that if Eric would volunteer, because they couldn't force an inmate, to work there for three months, they would then facilitate a transfer to a Kent prison. He wanted to believe them, although he didn't fancy the drug unit, because he was so keen to get nearer home. Tommy, though, said they couldn't be trusted to keep their word but conceded that, in the event of him not taking up the offer, the screws could get cranky and take him off his current duties out of spite. That would then necessitate a cell change as they didn't have cleaners sharing with non-cleaners, because the cell door couldn't be left open for the additional times a cleaner was allowed out. Eric's mind was made up to give it a go and, I suspect, to avoid listening to what he didn't want to hear, decided to go and stretch his legs. Tommy wasn't finished with the subject though, and continued by stressing his indifference regarding the possibility of sharing with a stranger, as due to his rapport with the screws; he could see no problem in obtaining a move to a single cell. His main concern was that they would build up Eric's hopes, just to smash them down when the time came, and being his friend, he didn't want to see it happen. It was his firm belief they could only wind up prisoners and play their mind games once they were aware of a bloke's weakness, or knew there was something he really wanted. Their buzz came from the knowledge that, at a whim, they could facilitate or frustrate an inmate's hopes and wishes, and was one of the more overt abuses of authority that prisons such as Belmarsh were riddled with. What Tommy was highlighting is a truism that anyone serving a sentence would do well to bear in mind, namely, the less you want, the easier it will be. The system is designed to provide the minimum, so the closer an inmate can gear their requirements to that basic provision the better; and the scope for being messed about by the administration, or individuals within it, becomes substantially reduced. One can draw parallels with the outside world, where so many bring grief on themselves because they couldn't settle for a modest-sized house, one car, or a week away in a caravan, even though that was all they could really afford. I was more than happy listening to

Tommy's views on the matter, plus others that he digressed on to, whilst leaning back against the wall steadily chomping my way through his box of Quality Street. The thought occurred to me that, in the two-and-a- half weeks since my arrival, I had met some good blokes who, irrespective of how they might be regarded on the outside, had definitely helped me on the inside. I felt that in their company I would get through the coming weeks nicely, with the comfort of also believing once Xmas was out of the way, my wife would start perking up. The three toffees remaining in the box were spared by the plug being pulled on the TV, and Mr B bellowing that the evening meal was now available for those who wanted it. Thanking Tommy for his hospitality and with a couple of his True Detective magazines tucked under my arm, I strolled back to my cell, having remembered the lesson not to rush for the meal that precedes a bang-up.

Stepping through the doorway, I was confronted by the sight of Patel kneeling at the foot of my bed, raking around in his goody bag. Feeling sociable, I enquired how his Indian cultural session had gone up in Gopal's cell, but plunking sitars and blokes wailing were not items on his mind. What was though, consisted of a missing Mars bar which had definitely been there that morning. I told him I had eaten it, reminding him that it was part of the price he'd agreed to get him on the 'phone. His reply was that Mo had made the arrangement, settling for 20 Bensons, necessitating me to point out that he had agreed them, plus the Mars bar as a last resort, and as it was Xmas Day, I was in all probability not only his last, but only, resort. He mumbled something about being only obliged to pay Mo as he had done the business, to which I suggested that, in future, he should deal direct with Mo and not be waking me up. Our debate was cut short by a screw stopping at the door telling us to get our meal now or go without, but rather than end the day on a discordant note, I took the sting out of Patel's loss by offering to let him borrow Stringfellow's 'True Detective', provided he returned it to me first thing in the morning. He seemed reasonably happy with that, and I would be getting it back, which was more than could be said about his Mars bar. Any thoughts on my part, though, that I would be immersing myself in the copies borrowed from Tommy straight after I had eaten were quickly dispelled as, on returning with the tray, my cell-mate greeted me with a Jumbo Xmas Crossword that took up half the page of a newspaper. It wasn't 5 pm yet and I could see us still at it come Boxing Day, but there again, neither of us were going anywhere, were we?

****

Chapter 11
Seasonal Peace And Goodwill R.I.P.

The week between Xmas and New Year was marked by boredom. Education classes, along with the Plug Shop, were closed and, as a result of a sizeable number of staff enjoying an extended break, the gardening parties were not required. Even visits to the gym were severely curtailed as screws were not available to perform escort duties, and no one set foot in the exercise yard. The effect of everything practically grinding to a halt was blokes being kept locked in their cells up to 22 hours a day. "Bang-ups" for such lengthy periods are a regular feature of Belmarsh throughout the year for many prisoners, but very rarely are so many "banged-up" day after day, with the door only opening for the 2-hour association period; a visit, and to obtain a meal. No effort was made by the prison regime to alleviate the situation, even where they could. It was put to senior screws that as three of their number "sat in" on each of the three spurs during association time, they could introduce an additional hour period during the morning. By staggering it over a three hour period, it would only require 3 screws at any one time, instead of the usual 9, but they didn't want to know. For them it was easier to keep doors locked, and to mount a fire brigade type response when the inevitable flare-ups took place. And take place they did, with the frequency enhanced by the extreme diversity of prisoners. As previously mentioned, the spectrum ranged from blokes serving 2 or 3 weeks for motoring offences or non-payment of fines, through to those doing life for murder. Mixed in with these were about 20% being held on remand, who hadn't yet been found guilty of anything, or were awaiting sentencing. In the event of them being found not guilty, or receiving a non-custodial sentence, there is no compensation for the time spent in jail, where a year or so is quite common, unless they win a damages claim for false imprisonment, which happens with the same frequency as an eclipse of the sun.

The majority of long serving inmates, having mentally conditioned themselves to years of incarceration, (doing it in their head); just want to get through the days and nights with as little hassle as possible. Very often, if they share a cell, they have obtained a cell-mate who is also looking at a lot of time and with whom he can get on. Putting short term prisoners in together generally doesn't cause too much trouble; after all, they can discuss features of the outside world, not having been long away from it, plus their not too distant release back to it. It is when the two are shut away for lengthy periods together that creates the formula for friction, leading all too often to violence, with the short stay prisoner usually ending up the victim. Long sentence blokes will generally keep themselves and their cells clean and tidy. After all, it's going to be their home for quite a while. Steve, an armed robber, not only swept it out twice a day, he would also buff the floor to such an extent it resembled a mirror; likewise John, convicted of murder and arson, would wipe the walls down twice weekly, including the bars on the window and, ironically, rigorously enforced a non-smoking environment.   These two were fortunate in having single cells, but to lumber them, or others like them, with short stay inmates who can't be bothered, allowing the place to become a tip and smelling as bad as themselves, inevitably leads to confrontation. It is not uncommon, soon after opening up time, to see their bedding thrown out on the landing, compelling the screws to carry out a reallocation exercise.   Some have been prepared to go down the block (solitary), rather than share with scruffs.   Men looking at years before they will be considered for parole, with the accompanying loss of homes; businesses and careers, and a marriage break-up thrown in, can rapidly lose control after hours listening to a short term cell-mate twittering non-stop about fanciful get-rich schemes to be embarked upon when he is shortly released.   That is, provided he can fit them in between boozing and bonking. Likewise, having lost everything, his tolerance level can soon reach breaking point when "banged up" with some inadequate serving a few months for pushing pot, who's forever moaning because his girl friend has just had his Alsatian put down, due to it biting her new boyfriend.

In the event of these factors being insufficient to provoke a serious bust-up, we can throw in the scenario whereby the older prisoner just wants to relax and read a book, whereas the volatile youngster can't sit still and insists on having rap thumping out at maximum volume; where the flash Jack the Lad, barely out of his teens, keeps "blowing his own trumpet" as to how smart he is, and "Old Bill" only got him put away by "fitting him up"; or, having blown his meagre prison wages on cans of soft drinks and crisps, the short stay inmate becomes a burn scrounger, or worse still, starts helping himself uninvited.   In most cases the outcome results in ejected bedding, with the owner nursing a split lip and minus a couple of teeth that had been intact the day before.   The more serious altercations have screws running along landings in the middle of the night, in response to screams and shouts, with the end product being one inmate dragged down the block and the other to the hospital wing.   A lot of blood can get spilled when the long serving prisoner snaps, with permanent injury, even death, resulting for the one whose thoughtlessness pushed him over the edge. The administrators know it happens and why; the screws on the ground are aware in which cells the danger exists, as do many inmates, but not only do they fail to take preventative action, they quite merrily continue to create the conditions for more of the same.

The boredom, and the associated touchiness among prisoners, helped bring about the circumstances that gave the screws their pretext for jumping on David the Rasta.   It was midweek, during the two hour association period, with a dozen or so blokes sitting round the TV watching Star Trek.   One of the other inmates, in his early twenties and hyper-active at the best of times, decided it would be a laugh to keep running up to the set and changing the channel. The Trekkie addicts failed to see the funny side of his actions and as he did it for the fourth time, one of them leapt from his chair, grabbed him round the neck, dragging him to the ground. As they rolled around on the floor, David, who was standing chatting nearby, having delegated the running of the 'phone queue to the Bruno lookalike, moved in swiftly to break them up. Alarm bells were ringing as he, assisted by others, sought to separate the two combatants, but by the time they had achieved success, the spur was swarming with screws, plus dogs barking in the background. Not unexpectedly, the two central figures, now reduced to exchanging obscenities and hard looks, were hauled away to the block, the surprise for us came when they frog-marched David in the same direction. Our objections to his removal were shouted down by the screws ordering us all back into our cells, with the doors being rapidly slammed shut as soon as we were over the threshold. It was a typical over-kill reaction to a relatively minor incident, generating a lot of avoidable resentment amongst prisoners and culminating in at least two being put on report for "disobeying a lawful instruction". We were barely 20 minutes into association, having been banged-up since 8 pm. the previous evening, with some blokes still in their cells eating dinner. At least three men were hustled, dripping wet, out of the showers, and a dog handler, accompanied by a snarling Alsatian, was enlisted to disperse a very irate 'phone queue.

Within 5 or 6 minutes everyone was banged up, and the spur reverberated to the noise of steel doors being kicked and thumped, as the only way of expressing opposition to the screws' actions. Personally, I think most of the screws enjoyed such incidences, as it afforded the opportunity for a mass "wind up", at the same time demonstrating how tough they thought they were.

Eventually the noise subsided, with the peace being broken only by prisoners shouting to each other, mainly airing their disgust at what amounted to group punishment. The season of peace and goodwill soon died in Belmarsh, if it existed in the first place, which I seriously doubt. Mo had resumed work on one of his drawings, so I settled down on my bed to have a read, praying quietly to myself that all the recent excitement had put him off doing crosswords. Outside the door, we could hear screws clumping about shouting to each other, accompanied by the routine clanging of steel gates. After a while, even they quietened down. Half an hour had elapsed since our association had been so abruptly terminated and I thought that was it for the night until, accompanied by a resumption of yelling outside, the sound of keys rattling in locks could be heard. Then our door opened and a strange screw growled the invitation to "Get your water"! Out we went, to be confronted by a scene that was to say the least, designed to intimidate. One screw stayed by the cell door whilst another five stood imposingly between him and the water dispenser, less than 10 metres away. At least a further ten hovered around the area, whilst a dog handler circled within the spur and a second stood with his brute just outside the barred gate. Running true to form, the screws were letting only six inmates out at a time and as soon as two were re-locked up again, another two were let out. As we queued in front of the dispenser, one of the blokes asked a screw why David had been taken to the block, to be told in no uncertain terms to get his water, otherwise he could end up joining him. Another inmate had forgotten his plastic bottle for making a second cuppa later, and was told to get it quickly, but as he half ran back to the cell, his movements set the prowling Alsatian off barking. To encourage the beast in his efforts, a chorus of dog-type noises emanated from a number of those still locked up, resulting in the second animal joining in and the screws getting even rattier. When the bloke returned with his bottle, he was told to just fill his mug as he wasn't in a "bleeding hotel".

Behind a locked door again, I buried myself back in the magazine, whilst Mo worked away with his pencils. It was still only a few minutes past 7 pm., and I couldn't help thinking that our enforced extra early night was as a result of a minor fracas that was fairly commonplace in many pubs and clubs. If they all shut up shop every time one happened, they would only function for a few hours during the middle of the week. We were now faced with a 23-hour "bang up", only to be let out to obtain our breakfast and mid-day meal, unless we were called for a visit. To many members of the public, such group punishment may seem acceptable, but I would remind them that nearly

206

20% of those being punished were remand prisoners, awaiting trial and, as such, haven't even been found guilty of a crime yet.   The screws were happy, though, because now they were getting paid to put their feet up in front of the TV set in their mess room instead of having to watch us, and putting up with prisoners pestering them with questions.   We never saw David again, as he was kept in the block facing the previously mentioned charges.   The two that he'd accompanied there declined the offer of easier treatment in return for being witnesses against him, but he was "shipped out" nonetheless, to Swaleside Prison on the Isle of Sheppey, presumably in the hope that they would have greater success in "fitting him up".   Our reluctant witnesses returned to the wing after a couple of days, having received two weeks loss of wages; two weeks loss of canteen; and loss of association for the same period, which meant that apart from getting their meals, they could stay in their cells for a fortnight.

My own luck ran out that evening as well, due to Mo realising after a while that his efforts at attaining artistic perfection were being hampered by working solely under artificial lighting.   The latter part of the evening was spent scratching our heads, and other parts, over a bumper crossword, at the same time munching our way through a packet of Patel's cream crackers which I'd mentally noted to promise him would be replaced when next I got to the canteen.

It was during that same week that Patel fell victim to a penal system run by a computer and administered by robots.   The spur had been fed and watered and was settling down for the afternoon "bang up", with the usual grave-like silence descending on the place. Mo and I were laid back on our beds smoking, and quietly chatting about some of his hopes and plans that would follow his forthcoming release.   After all the years inside, no official help was on offer to assist his rehabilitation back into society, and in a little over a week he was faced with being put outside the front door, like an empty milk bottle, with just the balance of money saved, plus £45, to tide him over until he drew his first Giro cheque.   Minor details such as accommodation and a job were matters to be sorted out by himself, presumably as a result of officialdom calculating that, as so many unemployed slept rough, even with clean records, it would be a pointless exercise seeking to obtain such facilities for an ex-con.   Work carried out in this field by various voluntary agencies cannot be praised enough, but due to severe financial limitation, plus lack of access to prisoners pending release, their impact is minimal. This failure to actively assist released prisoners returning to the outside world inevitably fuels the cycle of re-offending, resulting in them being labelled, in Home Office jargon, as "recidivists", and to mere mortals, as repeat offenders.   I would no doubt be regarded as a mega-cynic if I suggested it suited the judicial system, along with the prison apparatus, to have a substantial number of "recidivists" supplementing the new faces that get captured.   Too many well paid jobs among the judiciary, the legal profession, and the prison industry, would be threatened, plus the vast area of lucrative supply contracts, if there was a significant and sustained drop in the volume of "clients".

Steel gates slamming and voices shouting, heralded that something was up. Keys rattling in the lock next door, followed by Patel's muffled protestations, had the two of us pressing our ears to the adjoining wall in an attempt to learn what was going on. The wall was too thick, though, and when we heard the door being slammed shut again we sat back on our beds, speculating as to what the visit could mean. It was common knowledge that, very soon after being sentenced, Patel had received a Home Office letter telling him he was being considered for deportation back to India, even though he had come to England over 11 years previously, with his parents, at the ripe old age of 10. The news had caused him, his wife and his family, great distress, and his solicitor had immediately taken up the issue, with the result, after nearly three weeks of legal representation, being a severe migraine derived from going round in circles on the bureaucratic carousel. Eventually, after nearly two months, the matter was dropped, with the authorities lamely claiming that the threat of deportation was automatic in the case of convicted people who had been born in another land but, in Patel's case, such action was not deemed appropriate. That was it. No further reasons given and most definitely no apology for the grief caused.

On that grey December afternoon, though, we could think of no other plausible explanation for his abrupt removal, and visualised him being taken in a sweat-box to Heathrow, and stuck on the first available flight to the sub-Continent.   Standing at the window with his face pressed to the bars, Mo shouted to Patel's cell-mate, in an attempt to learn what had actually been said to my hapless co-defendant, whilst I remained seated, absorbing the realisation that, in the event of him jetting off to sunnier climes, I was first in line to inherit his stash of goodies from under my bed.

My thoughts were broken by Mo urging me to join him at the window.   Peering out, there was Patel, marching along the path barely 30 metres away, most certainly not in the direction of Heathrow Airport. He was between two screws, handcuffed to one of them, with a third leading the way.   Behind him was a dog handler with the Alsatian looking distinctly keen to get at his backside, and they were all headed towards the Special Secure Unit, the prison within a prison.   The sight threw our speculation into complete disarray as there was absolutely no way he could be regarded as being eligible for shutting away inside that grim hole.   We sat back on our beds, having learnt nothing useful from Tony next door, eventually dropping our efforts to unravel the mystery.   Within the hour Patel was returned to his cell, but it wasn't until association time that the puzzle was resolved.   It would appear that a Frenchman, by the name of Batel, had been recently transferred to the Belmarsh SSU, who was also the subject of an extradition application by his homeland. On arrival, he had been inadvertently accommodated in one of the house-blocks and the mistake had only just been realised.   In most other establishments, such an oversight would have been rectified with little fuss, but in the paranoid world of Belmarsh, an occurrence of this kind had everyone from the No.1 Governor down, experiencing extremely soiled underpants.   Irrespective of the fact that they would have completely different prison numbers, being the first stage of identifying a prisoner, somebody in administration had confused Batel with Patel, an inmate who was on file as having been informed by the Home Office of deportation proceedings, and issued instructions for him to be moved to the SSU pronto.   He had actually been booked in, having received the compulsory strip search to ensure he did not have an anus full of contraband, when a screw on the receiving end of Patel's protestations sussed that his Croydon accent distinctly lacked a French flavour, and decided to confirm they had the right man.   The result was an extremely agitated Indian being frog-marched back to rejoin us, whilst the hit squad, complete with dog, rushed off to root out the real M'sieu Batel.

The remainder of the week dragged by, with each day feeling more like 44 hours instead of 24, the only other highlight being when Charlie, a long serving inmate, got booked for assaulting a screw with a tray of mixed veg.   He was a quiet bloke who, whilst being sociable enough, did not mix with the other inmates to any great extent, and had been working on the hot-plate since before my arrival.   The screw that ended up covered with our peas and carrots was a Welshman, Mr C., extremely disliked for his petty-mindedness and sarcasm, who was even ridiculed behind his back by his own colleagues. On this particular day, we learned subsequently, Charlie had received a letter from his wife informing him that she was severing their relationship, having met somebody new as a preferable option to spending a lot of years as a jail widow. "Dear John" letters are commonplace among long-timers, but even if half expected, still come as a blow when they arrive. As he stood, ladle in hand, behind the counter, his mind was definitely not concentrated on shovelling mixed veg. into metal trays, resulting in a slow-down in getting blokes back to their cells. Mr. C., in his capacity as Cleaning Officer, which includes the hotplate, starts flapping around, giving Charlie plenty of verbal, including the not very helpful suggestion that he tries getting a night's sleep instead of playing with himself. That did it. Before he had a chance to get out of the way, Charlie had grabbed the food container, emptying the contents over his head, at the same time casting doubt on his parentage in no uncertain terms. The deed done, and only pausing to rip his apron off to throw on the floor, Charlie marches out of the servery, heading back to his cell, leaving Mr C. scooping a large part of our dinner off his head and shoulders. He had taken no more than ten paces before whistles started blowing and alarm bells ringing, bringing forth screws from all corners of the building, and as we were hustled back to the spur, Charlie was being escorted to the block by three screws.

In line with the customary over-kill on such occasions, everyone was locked back in their cells, being let out again half an hour later to resume the feeding process, with Charlie's place having been filled by another inmate. Mr C. was nowhere to be seen, and the number of screws hovering around giving us their hard looks had been increased, with the inevitable dog handler also in attendance. When the bloke in front of me queried to whether the mixed veg. on offer was a fresh lot, he was rewarded with the knowledge that it wasn't, but the floor it had been scraped up from had been mopped that very morning. Charlie received two weeks in solitary for his outburst, with the accompanying loss of privileges such as wages, visits and letters, plus loss of two weeks' remission, adding a fortnight to the years ahead inside, before being shipped out to Wandsworth. That Victorian eyesore is designated as a discipline nick, which means the screws there are under instructions to give prisoners an extra hard time and is not a place to be for starting the coming New Year, or indeed any other time of the year.

****

Chapter 12

New Year; New Cell Mate & A New Job

We were into the first week of January and Mo was getting ready for release. Many prisoners on the verge of getting out develop the symptoms of what is known as being "gate-happy", whereby they become twitchy and blasé with the screws. Mo didn't get in that state, possibly due to having his work cut out to finish as many of his portraits as he could, during the few remaining days and nights before freedom. He spoke little about what he intended to do once out, probably because he wasn't too sure himself, which is a very common feature for inmates returning to the outside world, especially after long sentences. When a man is locked away for years, the result is to sever his links with not only his friends and acquaintances, but also very often to the break up of personal relationships and family ties. Marriages end in divorce; children that were toddlers when he went in are now young adults when he gets out, and even his home is no longer there.

He has become institutionalised and is expected to adapt, almost overnight, from an environment where he is fed, bedded, and does as he's told, to one where he has to fend for himself. Sterling work is carried out by a few charitable bodies, but for all their efforts, there are still hundreds of disorientated long sentence prisoners being let out with no more than one week's social security money and their train fare back to what was their home area. Once back on the streets, they join the thousands of others that have no job, no home, little money and even less hope, but with the additional burden of having a criminal record. Is it any wonder that so many re-offend? In many ways they are in the same boat as the thousands shoved out onto the streets, many prematurely, under the government's Care in the Community programme, with grossly inadequate provision made to enable them to cope, the only difference between them being that, unlike prisons, the long stay hospitals were rapidly sold off to private developers. One ironic exception to that process were the two long-stay mental hospitals at Belmont, in Surrey, that once emptied out, were demolished to make way for Highdown high security, and Downsview, prisons. There is also a similarity with demobbed long serving military personnel. Having spent years shouting and taking orders, spending most of their time wearing a uniform, their links severed with their pre-enlistment life, and having all material needs supplied by the tax payer, they very often find real difficulty in re-adapting to civilian life. A large number of them end up in prison, generally as screws, due to the work not only being well paid and secure, but also because it requires the minimum of adjustment. They can even carry on shouting at blokes who are only a couple of metres away.

In addition to completing as many portraits as

possible, Mo also checked whenever he was permitted to go to the canteen, that due payments were being made into his private account by his client screws.   He also continued to work out at the gym but, thankfully, had given up trying to get me to do likewise, which was just as well, as my "one-off" issue of singlet and shorts were now reduced to a couple of sodden balls under the sink, having functioned as floor cloths for the past three weeks.

During his last couple of evenings he spent time sorting through his accumulated possessions, pruning out what he no longer wanted, whilst carefully placing in the plastic prison sack those items for keeping.   In prison, especially maximum security ones, there is not much scope for hoarding, due mainly to so many items being prohibited and the need to travel light when being transferred, but I think even Mo was surprised at the assortment that had built up in his cupboard and under the bed. Tubes of toothpaste, toothbrushes, bars of soap, notepaper, envelopes, pens and pencils, books, various empty tins and pots, that may have come in handy for something, playing cards, assorted combs, postage stamps, boxes of matches, were just some of the selection spread over his bed.   Then we had some sweets and Polo's, teabags, containers half full of sugar, milk powder and marmalade, a few unopened tins of tuna, sweetcorn, and fruit cocktail, with even a packet of peanuts unearthed from the back of the cupboard that he thought he had eaten weeks before. On top of all that, there was the inevitable collection of letters, some going back years, photographs, plus assorted pictures and articles cut from magazines, and salted away.   After everything had been checked through, what he didn't want to keep was bequeathed to me or binned, the only exception being his store of pencils and unused card for portraits, which were donated to a couple of other artists on the wing.

The biggest concern regarding double cells is who you are going to end up sharing with.   I had no worry on that score, as Mr B. had already told me that Patel would be taking Mo's place, as his current cellmate, Tony, having just been made a cleaner, would be transferring to a single cell.   That arrangement suited me as I knew with Patel I wouldn't have to guard my belongings; if I ran short of some little luxury, his cupboard would be well stocked and he was not into crosswords.   Patel was also happy at the prospect of parting company with Tony, who was forever scrounging off him and had almost monopolised his Nintendo game, returning it whenever the batteries became run down.

It was during that first week of the year I noted a new bloke on our spur, who stood out because he wore prison uniform, embellished with a big yellow square on the back of the jacket, and stripes in the same colour down each leg.   I learnt that this denoted an inmate who was prone to escaping and, in prison language, was referred to as an "E-man", or being "on stripes".   When not locked in his cell, he was never allowed out of sight and had to be accompanied by a screw whenever he left the spur; in addition to which, he was also "on the book", meaning that a written record was kept of his movements, be it a shower, a visit, or just a trip to the pharmacy. He was confined in a single cell, presumably so as not to infect another inmate with his wandering tendencies. I could not help thinking that having put a prisoner into an unnatural environment, which is what prison is, the system then makes it a crime for him to do the most natural thing, namely seeking his freedom. In the event of an inmate running away from an "open" prison, it is quite understandable to transfer him, if and when recaptured, to a more secure establishment; but when the escape is achieved from high security prisons, in the face of very high walls topped with razor wire, an army of screws and a massive array of technology, then an award for achievement seems most appropriate, plus a few staff sackings for incompetence. The inmate, rather than punished, should be rewarded for their actions, because the Prison Service would reap the benefit from learning how he beat all the odds, therefore enabling them to prevent a repeat performance. Such a response would be similar to a company giving a bonus to an employee for a particularly worthy idea that they submitted through the suggestion box. To those who would claim that such a policy could actually encourage more escape attempts, I would remind that such inmates are confined in maximum security primarily because they are regarded as having a propensity to escape. For obvious reasons, prisoners serving short sentences, such as myself, or others like Mo, getting through their final few weeks, are not likely to engage in the formidable task of breaking out of a place such as Belmarsh, as well as risking the retribution that would swiftly follow if caught in the process, which only underlines the pointlessness of keeping us there at such additional expense in the first place.   A prime example of the bureaucratic   lunacy   that   poses   as   prison administration is the case of Patel, who from the outset had been designated the lowest security rating, namely a D category.   In his eventual capacity as an outdoor cleaner, which entailed sweeping up litter off the pathways around the houseblock, he was told to also clean it off the grassed areas, a function normally performed by the gardening party, as a visit was due to be made by some dignitary. Patel asked for the use of one of the rakes kept in the garden shed, but was refused on security grounds, as that would require a screw to stay with him to ensure he didn't dig a tunnel under the outer wall with it, or pole-vault over the top.   He was told to sweep the litter off the wet grass with his broom, which apparently wasn't regarded as suitable for pole-vaulting, or pick it up by hand.   A week later, having been transferred to Hollesley Bay Open Prison, he was driving all over the place on a tractor, and up and down the public road running through that establishment, without a screw in sight.

The Appeal Court judge turned out to be another one who had resisted being infected by the season of goodwill to all men. My appeal against the severity of my sentence, where a reduction by a couple of days would have permitted me to continue as a Councillor, had been rejected.   As part of my grounds of appeal were health reasons, it was a pity I had not been dealt with by the Appeal Court judge who had released Ernest Saunders, jailed for the multi-million pound Guinness fraud, on the grounds of alleged senile dementia, so he could return to wheeling and dealing in the City of London within weeks. I knew it had been a long shot because, in the event of me obtaining a result, it would mean the second judge implying that the first judge had gone over the top, as well as undermining his employer's wishes to make examples of us; but equally, I had to give it a go, not just for my own sake but also for my family, and all those that continued to support me.

During one of the association periods, I spent a few minutes having a look at the noticeboard. The mostly faded sheets contained various useful items of information, including a list of discontinued courses, a warning of catching something if tempted to feed the feral pigeons that grew fat outside the windows, a rule about inmates only sleeping one to a bed; a reminder not to take drugs unless dished out by the pharmacy, and a circular from the Governor urging all prisoners not to become one of the 80,000 plus disciplinary cases dealt with each year by the Prison Authorities. Hanging on by one drawing pin and half obscured, was a notice relating to the Personal Officer scheme. Momentarily, I thought this might be a screw who would ensure my laundry was done and run an iron over my shirts even pop down the shop for me. As I read on, it became obvious that wasn't the case. What it was though, was a situation whereby every prisoner gets allocated a specific screw, whose function is to assist them to settle in and help with any reasonable problem, plus give advice. The thinking behind the scheme was very laudable, as being sent to prison can be quite traumatic, especially for the first timer, and a helping hand in those early days can make the difference between a bloke coping, or trying to top himself. But like so many good ideas, it becomes meaningless if not put into practice and it occurred to that, having now been in the place a full month, not only had I not received a visit from my Personal Officer, I didn't even know who it was. I decided to find out who it may be, approached the desk where Mr. B. sat with two other screws, and put the question to him, whereupon he rang through to the Bubble. The reply came back naming one of the two screws seated alongside him who, in response to my query as to why he had not approached me, claimed it was because I seemed to be coping OK. A first-timer, facing the rigours of a maximum security prison, with a stay in the hospital wing, plus two interviews with an Assistant Governor clocked up, was, in his opinion, coping OK for the first four weeks. I refrained from asking him what would be regarded as not coping.

A regular feature of life in Belmarsh, as in other similar establishments, is the unannounced cell spin, when screws suddenly appear to turn everything upside down. These unwelcome visits usually result in prisoners being punished for very modest infringements of the rules. One lost a week's privileges for damaging prison property, having prised the shaving mirror off the wall in order to position it in a better light. Another received the same for breaking up a disposable razor, so as to utilise the blade for trimming his moustache. Any items over and above the official quota are taken back on these occasions, including towels, toothpaste and even toilet rolls.   Bedding is especially zeroed in on. Due to prison pillows not being much more than church kneeling pads, nearly everyone accumulates two or three for comfort, but as one is the allocation under Home Office rules, the extra ones get thrown out for returning to the stores.   The piece of chipboard, measuring one by one -and- a-half metres, that sits in brackets on the wall over each bed for the purpose of pinning up photographs and pictures, very often ends up under the mattress to compensate for the hammock effect of a prison bed.   That gets promptly removed and taken away, only to be returned if a new occupant pesters long enough for it. Wiring radios to cell lighting is also rife, and if caught, earns punishment for the inmate, including confiscation of his radio.   During these spins, light fittings get inspected for the signs of "wiring up" and, where detected, leads to an electrician replacing them. To demolish the usual defence by inmates that any tampering must have been carried out by a previous occupant, light fittings are frequently checked and confirmed as untouched when cell changes take place. When this practice goes wrong and the inmate ends up fusing all the cell lights along the landing, the screws usually indulge in a bit of group punishment by delaying any remedial work for a couple of days, on top of putting the culprit on report.   Other confiscations take place during cell spins, such as when screws arbitrarily decide that an inmate has above the permitted amount of tobacco, or too many 'phone cards, in his possession.   Following seizure, an application can be made for the return of such goods, but nobody bothers as they know it would be a waste of time.

The more unpleasant screw will go so far as to rip posters and other pictures off the wall, as they are regarded as an infringement of the rule prohibiting cell adorning, but such enthusiasm is usually reserved for pictures the screws know the prisoner is particularly fond of. Inmates deeply resent these cell spins as they know, just as the screws know, that they have little to do with security but are mainly intended to humiliate and remind the prisoner who's in charge. They are an integral part of prison management thinking, whereby control is maintained by not only locking up blokes for 80% of the day, but also by inflicting a whole range of dehumanising practices. Reading private letters; listening in to telephone calls; constant "rub down" searches, plus impromptu full body searches; regularly ferreting through personal belongings; peering through peep holes, having to explain to children on visits why Daddy has to wear a silly bib, are just a few examples of the extensive range employed. In addition to the spins, no Saturday morning would be complete if a screw didn't check the steel bars on the window, to make sure you haven't cut through them with your plastic cutlery.

Keeping men banged up for as long as 22 hours a day, and the constant efforts to degrade them, represent the harsher methods to exercise control. The softer method is the threat of losing remission, plus manipulating most long-serving prisoners' desire to have their security category reduced, thus enabling them to seek a transfer to a less rigid regime. This carrot and stick system is then effectively underpinned by the liberal doling out of tranquillisers, the amount of which, in a prison such as Belmarsh, would have a Colombian drugs baron drooling.

Now that I had settled down to prison routine and with a third of my sentence behind me, I thought I would treat myself to a haircut, not realising what a performance that would turn out to be. Before my hospital stay I had assumed, with a resident population numbering almost 800, there would be a barber available at certain times each week for whom you could put your name down for. Silly me!!! To have an outsider coming in trimming prisoners' locks would represent a serious security risk, plus necessitating a screw staying with him at all times, and another to escort blokes to and from their cells. On top of that, the barber would have to be cleared by the National Police Computer to make sure he didn't have a record; would have to be issued with an identity card; be prepared for a full body search both when entering and leaving, and sign the Official Secrets Act to prevent him recounting anything he saw or heard. This ritual would have to be duplicated for any substitutes required to cover in the event of the regular man, or indeed, woman, not being available. Then there would be the question of payment, as the possession of any amount of cash by an inmate is a serious offence. The prison administration would have to make payment, reimbursing themselves from the prisoner's wages, but that would involve work they are not wishing to make for themselves.   In order to have a trim-up, I had to find another inmate prepared to do it for me, who in turn, needed to obtain the battery-operated shears kept for the purpose in the Bubble.   This piece of equipment was only made available during Saturday morning association, for the 171 blokes on the three spurs in the houseblock, so there was no point in wanting anything too artistic.   As it turned out, I thought I'd had a result just by coming away with both ears intact.   Payment for this "service" consisted of either 12½ grammes of baccy or a £2 'phone card, with no expectation of a tip, with the operation itself carried out in the open area in front of the canteen. Being guided by the recommendation of others, I approached a young black bloke, who agreed to do the job on the coming Saturday.   He had a couple of others to cater for already, but seeing as I had precious little to cut, saw no problem fitting me in.   It was impressed on me to be ready when he called as there would be no time to hang about, as he could only have possession of the shears for half an hour.   In answer to my casual query regarding his hairdressing experience, I was less than elated to learn it solely consisted of trimming the cauliflowers as a kid, on his uncle's fruit and veg. stall.   His technique hadn't altered much since those days, although it took longer than expected due to the shears constantly packing up, only restarting after being whacked on the back of the chair.   I regarded myself as fortunate that the length of my sentence permitted me to confine it to a "one-off" experience.

225

A screw came for Mo at 7 a.m., to take him to the reception area where, after breakfast, he and his plastic sack would be searched.   He would then receive any monies owing to him, plus one week's Social Security payment to carry him over whilst he signed on, and sign his release form.   After that, he would be shown the door, having had every other screw shouting such pleasantries as "See you soon"!; Make sure you book early for next year!" and "Don't forget to recommend us to your friends!".   The whole process is timed to have discharged prisoners off the premises by 9 a.m., so the reception screws can then check out those being taken for Court appearances, and still have a couple of hours to put their feet up before having to book back in those being returned by the various Courts, plus any new faces.   At my insistence, Mo had woken me up to see him off and, although sorry to see him go, I felt that largely due to his help, I would be able to handle the two months I had to remain. Surprisingly, being a Monday morning, the screw was in a pleasant enough mood to allow me to nip out and get a mug of hot water for an early cuppa whilst Mo double checked that he had everything.   We exchanged "fives" and I wished him well, with similar farewell messages being shouted from neighbouring cells, then he was off and the door slammed shut on me.

It's amazing how a very modest sized room can suddenly feel big and empty, and I spent a large part of the time before being opened up for breakfast sitting on the edge of my bed, sipping tea, pondering

226

which one to occupy before Patel moved in. As it turned out, it was a pointless exercise because, for reasons not given, I ended up being moved in with Patel. I can only assume it was felt to be the quicker way, rather than have him transporting his mini grocery store in order to join me.

My name was still on the list for Education classes, although I had told Mr B. before Xmas I was no longer interested in going to them, as the whole set-up had become a farce. Thankfully, he had not pushed the official line that my name became deleted, with me re-allocated to other work, which would inevitably result in either being bored silly in the Plug Shop or trudging around with the Garden party, pushing a wheelbarrow in the middle of winter. By leaving my name on the Education list, I met the prison requirement of being allocated to doing something, at the same time continuing to qualify for the £4.50 weekly wage packet. In the event of him being on duty when my number came up for classes, or even if he wasn't, I would claim having either a headache, or a touch of the "runs", and be left alone. The tutors weren't bothered at my non-appearance as they were paid the same either way, and the screws cared even less, so long as they knew where I was. It was the best of situations where all involved were happy, especially myself, since I had amassed a substantial amount of interesting reading material. I was prepared to spend the rest of my sentence in this way, and had already commenced reducing my eating to compensate for the lack of physical exercise, as my weight was still greater than when I arrived. But even in a dreary hole such as Belmarsh, little surprises, like screws, can lurk around the corner.

Barely a week had elapsed since moving in with Patel and I was laid out on my bed reading, my cell-mate having gone to classes when, keys rattling, the door swung open to reveal Mr B.   He confirmed I was alone, then asked whether I might be interested in picking the litter up in the exercise yard.   It would not be too arduous he assured me, as the rubbish mainly consisted of empty milk cartons, plastic bottles, discarded food and newspapers, all having been thrown out of the windows by inmates.   It was a symbolic practice to show their contempt for the place, rather than utilise the buckets provided in each cell for the purpose, and eliminated the task of emptying them into the bigger bins that stood on each landing.   I would enjoy the perks of being a cleaner, particularly the substantial increase in time out of the cell.   The proposition was very attractive, except that we were still in the first half of January, and a very wet one at that.   In response to my querying as to how often I would have to venture out, he very bluntly declared he couldn't give a toss.   As far as he was concerned, it wasn't his rubbish and he most certainly didn't have to walk around in it, but suggested I used my 'loaf' in the matter.   The yard hadn't been cleaned up since well before Xmas, therefore his advice was to make an initial effort as soon as possible in order to clear up the accumulation, after which I could go out when I felt like it. Provided the powers that be saw me walking around with a broom two or three times a week, even if that was all I was doing with it, would be good enough. As it turned out, it was the one and only time my Cat.C rating worked in my favour. Having told Mr B. he had just got himself a new yard cleaner, he went on to explain the job was part of a broader function that included sweeping up around the outside of the House-block, but as a C Cat., that would require the accompaniment of a screw, none of whom were too keen on freezing their balls off just to watch me pushing a broom. His plan was to offer that part of the job to Patel who, as a D-Cat., could go out alone, whereas I could only work unattended in the yard, and he would arrange to have the £16.00 weekly wage split 50/50 between us. With us both redesignated as cleaners, our cell door could be left open during the extra time out, which would avoid the nuisance of having to lock it whilst I was out, or moving me to a single cell. Patel was so ecstatic when it was later put to him, especially as it would enable him to ring the shop every day, that in the two months following, it never occurred to him that he was sweeping three times the area I was, or that my litter emanated from each side of the two spurs flanking the yard, whereas his not only came out of the windows on the other two sides, but also from both sides of the third spur. It wouldn't have mattered even if he had realised, as Mr B's job offer was most definitely made on a take it or leave it basis, and I never felt the inclination to mar his joy. The pathways outside Houseblock 2 could not have ended up cleaner, even if someone went over them with a vacuum cleaner, thanks to Patel's daily efforts; following which, he would use up 'phone-cards at

229

almost the same rate as I drank mugs of tea.

The day following Mr B's proposal was overcast, but dry, so I decided to make a start on the yard, and as I lined up at the gate for breakfast, informed him of my intention. He told me that Patel could do the same and that our cell door would be unlocked along with the others, but we were to hang about until the work parties, along with the students, had been sent on their way. Eating our breakfasts, we were both actually looking forward to our new functions, for my part because it meant getting some fresh air, whereas Patel was drooling at the thought of lots of time on the telephone. Nine o'clock came and keys rattled in our lock, whereupon we were both straight out and across to the water dispenser, replenishing our mugs. We sat ourselves down, mugs on the floor between our feet, to enjoy a smoke while surveying the activity both around us and over our heads. Screws were working their way along the rows of doors, unlocking some to let out the occupants, whilst shouting to others through the observation panel that they were not required. In many cases, one inmate would be called out and the other one told to stay put, which resulted in loud protests filling the air until the door was slammed shut again.

Prisoners who were listed for working in the Plug Shop tended to be the most aggrieved if not required, as they were paid on a piece-work basis, which meant no wages for that day. It was another little Belmarsh irony, where everyone had to work, even though most days there was nothing for them to do. Watching blokes lining up on the first floor landing to receive the rub down as they passed through the gate, reminded me of a particular scene from Snow White and the Seven Dwarfs, prompting me to shout a couple of 'Hi-Ho's' to them. The replies were very colourful and a descending apple was only prevented from bouncing off my head due to the anti-suicide mesh covering the ground floor. On this particular occasion, the rub-downs were being carried out by a not unattractive female screw, leading one bloke - after she had frisked him - to claim that he needed to return to his cell for something he'd forgotten. Having done no more than slip back into the queue, when he appeared again at the gate she declined to realise his objective with another going over, loudly declaring she couldn't feel anything tucked away the first time. Somewhat disgruntled, he made his way to the second line-up, where a male screw was carrying out yet another rub-down, prior to the blokes leaving the house-block. Eventually, after approximately 20 minutes of organised confusion, calm was restored, with the only inmates loose on the spur, apart from ourselves, being one collecting up the breakfast trays for returning to the hot-plate, and another slowly pushing a broom along the top landing.

Then it was our turn and we were sent to the Bubble to locate Mr N., the current Cleaning Officer, who would kit us out for the task ahead. Of course, he wasn't there and we were advised to seek him in the cleaning store-room, adjacent to the hot-plate. Tramping down the iron stairs to the ground floor, we were intercepted by a screw coming up, who

231

immediately informed us that inmates were not permitted to use them and couldn't we read the sign. I confessed to having not seen any sign, whereupon he pointed to the bottom of the steps where a small plastic plaque had been stuck on the wall.   It was tempting to query how one was expected to read it from the top step, but didn't wish to jeopardise our new postings, and although we were no more than 10 steps from the bottom, at his insistence, we tramped back to the top.   The ones we were obliged to use were 20 metres away on the other side of the landing, so we clattered down them and headed towards the cleaning store, carefully avoiding two blokes who were cheerfully drowning the ground floor with their mops and buckets. He wasn't there either.   Who was there though, behind the hot-plate, was a Mike Tyson look-alike, washing the metal trays in a tank of soapy water with a toilet brush.   I asked him if he'd seen the elusive Mr N., to be told that he'd just gone upstairs to the Bubble for his early elevenses.   Back we went with me almost doing a somersault on the wet surface the two mops had created, up the permitted stairs and along the landing to the Bubble. Inside were four screws lounging around, all clutching mugs of tea and even with the door shut, you could hear one of them recounting yet another sexual conquest, although it wasn't too clear whether it was with a man or a woman.

As the word implies, the Bubble consisted of windows all the way round, giving a clear view in any direction, and we were seen approaching as soon as we reached the top of the stairway.   Our presence outside the door, though, was studiously ignored until we had knocked a couple of times, and even then it wasn't opened until the nearest screw had downed the contents of his mug.   We had located Mr N., who turned out to be the screw we had met earlier on the forbidden stairs and who now commenced to moan because he had to take us back downstairs to be kitted out.   Before doing so, he checked that Mr B. had entered our new functions on the computer, then rang him to confirm we were who we said we were, and on receiving affirmation, gave us a red armband each. He stressed we must not venture outside without wearing them and that they must be handed back in at the Bubble each time we finished; failure to do so being regarded as a serious breach of prison discipline.   Then it was back to the store-room, using separate stairs en route, and gingerly stepping across the ground floor that the buckets and mops duo had succeeded in turning into a lethal skid patch.   They were in the process of manhandling a buffer into position and, as Mr N passed by, asked if he could give them a towel to place under the machine, as it would give a better shine to the surface.   They had to settle for a half torn bed sheet that immediately twisted itself round the buffer heads when one switched on, totally jamming it.   Whilst they struggled to release the heads, Patel and myself were each issued a pair of rubber gloves, a broom, a dustpan and brush plus a handful of black sacks, all to be retained in our cell so as not to be forever troubling whoever happened to be the Cleaning Screw.   The kitting out thus completed, Patel was let out of the houseblock and I was released into the yard, on each occasion Mr N. notifying the outside security patrols, via his mobile, of the fact.

With the door slammed shut behind me, it was great to breathe in the crisp winter air after the dry staleness of the spur. I was not completely alone, as a flock of pigeons that had been gorging themselves on bread and rock cakes until being disturbed by my arrival, now sat thoroughly disgruntled along the overhead cables, watching me as intensely as any screws. The far end of the yard was catching some watery sunlight, so I decided to stroll up to that part and smoke one of my pre-rolled fags, before commencing my task. I spent a pleasant few minutes leaning on the wire, with the sunshine on my face, only looking up to observe an aircraft descending onto the runway of the nearby City Airport. As I watched it, I also noticed that, in turn, I was being studied by a dog handler standing about 50 metres away, near the entrance into the S.S.U. Feeling sociable, I called over 'good morning' accompanied by half a wave, receiving for my effort a total blank, but at least the Alsatian growled, which I took as a cue to start work. Most of the rubbish was concentrated along the two sides underneath the windows, with just a scattering of newspapers blown against the perimeter wire, so the plan of action was to sweep the mess into a pile, prior to scooping it into the sack, finishing off by picking the paper up by hand. I donned the rubber gloves and commenced to push the big wooden broom, whereupon the head promptly dropped off. Sticking it back on and banging the other end of the handle on the ground to hopefully wedge it tighter, I

234

tried again, but on the first push the two halves parted company once more. That was it, and I spent the next half an hour walking round with the sack, scooping up soggy meals' residue with the dustpan, topping it up with the paper. For the rest of my stay that was how I kept the yard in Houseblock 2 clean, as the screws expressed helplessness regarding how the broom head could be kept attached. The only usage it enjoyed for almost two months was when other inmates borrowed it to sweep out their cells. Patel's broom was held together by having a big nail driven through it, but it appeared that no one was available to do mine until, coincidentally, a maintenance man took on the job a couple of days before my release. Of course, if it had been fixed sooner, the screws would have been deprived of the sight of me going out to sweep the yard with a dustpan and brush, but I didn't mind, the extra bending provided some much needed exercise.

The yard was cleaned up with the best part of an hour still to go before the mid-day meal, so I decided to stay out a while longer. Lighting up another fag, I returned to the wire fence, to bask in the sun and watch the regular arrival of descending aircraft. Without making it obvious, I had noticed the dog handler watching me periodically, but I put that down to anything - even the sight of me - serving to break the monotony of walking round and round the grey walls of the S.S.U. Even though the whole area was festooned with surveillance cameras, plus the latest in sensory equipment, with those inside being locked away more securely than gold bars in Fort Knox, the

235

Governor still insisted on a screw walking round in circles with a dog, 24 hours a day.

Reaching the fence I spotted Patel round a corner of the houseblock, darting about on the grass, picking up litter and shoving it into his sack. He stopped and came over when I called, telling me about the bollocking he'd received from one of the dog patrols. As he was pulling on his rubber gloves, a gust of wind had blown his sacks across the open ground, with them eventually ending up against the inside of the main wall. Naturally he went after them, but before actually reaching them, a dog handler bellowed out for him to stop where he was. Upon explaining what had happened, he was abruptly told to keep hold of them in future, and although he could retrieve them this time, if he ventured off his defined area again he would be put on report and automatically taken off cleaning duties. Before letting him resume work, the screw even confirmed his number on the mobile, and this was an inmate with the lowest security rating bestowed by the Prison Service who, as mentioned previously, would be driving a tractor in and out the gates of an open nick eight weeks later.

During the whole time we'd been chatting, my own friendly neighbourhood dog handler had stood watching us, so we decided to go back inside, wash up and have a cuppa before lunch was served. It turned out to be almost as hard to get back in as it had been to get out, and I spent nearly ten minutes kicking the door in order to attract a screw's attention or,

236

more correctly, to attract one who could be bothered to unlock the door. Once inside, I dumped the sack of rubbish as instructed, next to the hot-plate, then went upstairs to the Bubble to return the armband. The screw who took it also informed me I was to see Mr N. in the store-room, as he wanted a word in my ear.

This I did, and managed to make him lose count of the latest delivery of toilet rolls. The word he wished to have was that, although I need not worry about it, the dog handler had radioed through his concern that I appeared to have been taking too much interest in the yard fence. My reply that an extremely fit monkey would have trouble getting over the fence, especially with rolls of razor wire strung along the top, only served to irritate him. I was told, in no uncertain terms, that I'd be a prize prat to lose a cushy little number, just because I couldn't use my loaf by remembering rule No. 1., which was, don't make waves for the screws. The picture was clearly painted, so I apologised for any trouble he'd been caused and assured him that, in future, my loaf would be fully used. I then left him to get myself a cuppa, whilst he returned to counting the toilet rolls again.

*   *   *   *   *   *

237

Chapter 13

Burglars Break In And A Hot Plate Flare Up

Becoming a cleaner opened up whole new horizons for me. It was lovely picking my times to go outside, which was most days when it wasn't raining, and after picking up the litter, plus scooping up the soggy bits, which took no more than 20 minutes, would spend an hour or so chatting through the windows with some of the blokes in the ground floor cells. Having learned my lesson, I kept a wary eye out for the dog patrols, and would activate the broom handle I always kept hold of when one hove into view. I banked on them being too far away to notice there was no head on it. Inevitably inmates me asked to pass on messages, which I did, but declined to convey any items, conscious as I was that screws could view me from any number of windows, including those in nearby buildings. Additionally, every square metre of open ground in Belmarsh, the yards included, was covered by at least one camera. To be caught passing a spliff would not only cost me my job, but also extend my stay in the place. Whether or not I ventured forth on any given day, I also enjoyed the extra time out of the cell, which was the main perk of the job. We were unlocked at 9am and not relocked back in until 11.30am. For the afternoon, it was

2.30pm and 4.30pm respectively, followed by the routine association time of 6pm until 8pm. At weekends, we were out for the same times as everyone else, but then half the cleaners stayed unlocked between 6pm and 8pm on Saturdays, with the other half on Sundays. The 'phone queue became a thing of the past, and my expenditure on 'phonecards quadrupled due to me ringing up people almost for the sake of it. Another welcome privilege was, when out, no longer being confined on the spur, which enabled me to study my surroundings more fully, plus the people in it. I was able to get to know more of the other inmates, and some of the screws, which proved invaluable when, after my release, I decided to write this book.

A focal point of the houseblock was the canteen, or shop, situated on the ground floor halfway between our spur and the hotplate. It was in full view of those screws positioned on two of the three spurs, with the added security of having the permanently manned Bubble directly above it. The area around the canteen was totally visible to screws moving around the landings above, and an inmate seen loitering would rapidly be challenged as to what they were up to. The buzz that went round the spurs, therefore, when it got burgled, was tremendous. A door had been forced, and almost the complete stock of cigarettes, tobacco and phonecards removed, with the deed only coming to light when a screw opened up for the afternoon trade.

I was outside in the yard, chatting to a bloke in the

adjoining spur through his window, when the discovery was made. Alarm bells were ringing, screws yelling, and it turned out to be the only time I didn't need to kick the door to get back inside, as two actually came out insisting I returned to my cell immediately. They were so keen to get me back behind a locked door that one took charge of the half filled sack, whilst the other carried my pan and brush, plus the broom handle, as he escorted me inside. It was a hectic scene of activity that confronted me, with screws rushing blokes back to their cells and slamming the doors, a couple of dog handlers making their presence known, plus the Deputy Governor involved in a heated discussion with three senior screws, all of whom looked as if they wished they were on leave. For a moment I thought there must have been a mass break-out, but all I received for my query as to what it was all about was a very abrupt opinion that I would be better off not knowing. It was serious enough, though, for the screw to deny me getting some hot water to make my afternoon cuppa. The cell door had no sooner shut than it re-opened to let Patel in, who then told me about the break-in. His main worry, and one I subscribed to, was that all the cleaners, because of their extra scope for movement around the houseblock, would be prime suspects. He thought that the prison mentality would dictate us all being sacked and replaced, with the resultant loss of our perks, especially access to the telephone. All I could suggest was we waited to see what happened, and hope it didn't come to that. Then I realised that in their haste to bang us up, the screws had left us with the all-important armbands which, under any circumstances, let alone the present one, were the last things we wanted to be caught with in the cell. I pressed the buzzer that activated a red light outside as well as registering in the Bubble, and on my fourth attempt was rewarded with a pair of eyes squinting through the observation panel. The sight of Patel waving two armbands soon had our door unlocked, whereupon an extremely pissed-off screw snatched hold of them, at the same time bollocking us for having them. Our explanation was completely ignored but we knew the matter wouldn't go any further, as no screw would want to explain why they were not taken off us after we had been called back in and physically escorted to the cell. Their individual and collective priority for the immediate future was to cover themselves when faced with the inevitable question as to how the canteen was burgled, literally under their noses.

Like naughty children, we were all kept confined for the remainder of the afternoon, with the deathly hush that always descended on the place during such occasions only disturbed by the sound of a maintenance man repairing one damaged canteen door. The association period that followed our evening meal was cancelled, partly as an exercise in group punishment, and to prevent any plunder being distributed around the houseblock. One inside cleaner, not Patel or myself, as we were designated outside cleaners, was let out to collect up the meal trays and return them to the hotplate, all the while shadowed by a screw. Those who needed to visit the Pharmacy for an evening "fix" were escorted there and back on an individual basis.   As it turned out, much of the goods had already been spread about by the burglars, free of charge, the main purpose of the exercise being to shaft the system.   They knew they would have to get rid of the goodies as quickly as possible, and for the short while before the alarm went off, there wasn't an inmate out of their cell who didn't have pockets bulging with packs of cigarettes and tobacco.   Every cell on the spur, not ours, where the   perpetrators   resided,   had   a   quantity   of 'phonecards slipped under the door.   Our regret was that we were both outdoors at the time.

Having association cancelled made it a long evening and there could not have been a cell where speculation wasn't rife as to whom may have done it, or how the administration would retaliate.   At the very least, we would all suffer the loss, for a time, of any shopping facilities.   When our door was unlocked to fill mugs for a night-time cuppa, the same as the weekend routine, we noticed it was a second screw carrying the jug.   They were definitely keeping all prisoners under wraps.   The two screws at our door were distinctly grumpier than usual, probably due to having had their shafting by inmates topped up with a roasting from the Governor, then being told to trudge around the landings to ensure those same inmates got their hot, bedtime drink.   Thinking along the lines of what I'd be inclined to do in their position, I declined to have my mug filled.   Much as I fancied a drink of tea, I didn't want to chance they'd wee-ed in the jug, so I settled for one of Patel's cans of soft drinks instead.   We spent most of the evening playing cards, deciding about 11pm to turn it in and go to bed. It was when I opened our window to throw out some empty cans plus the contents of an ash tray, for my companion to sweep up the next day, that I nearly had a heart attack. Before I could stick my hand through the bars, up popped a dog handler's face, to leave me in no doubt that any such dumping would get us both nicked, and to keep the bloody window shut. So as not to undermine the treat that awaited us all in the morning, dog handlers were to prowl around outside of the houseblock all night and into the next day, to ensure nothing was unloaded out of the cells and to identify those that did. No doubt they blamed us for the fact it rained the whole time, but then, like a policeman's, a screw's lot is not supposed to be a happy one.

The new day dawned and we were unlocked for breakfast at the usual time, but as we congregated at the gate to be despatched to the hotplate in sixes, there were definitely more screws to be seen hanging around. Many were strangers to us, no doubt having been drafted in from other parts of the prison and their purpose became clear when, on returning with our meals, we were informed there would be no work parties or classes that day. They were going to spin every cell in the houseblock, all 117 of them, and woe betide anyone who was found to possess more than the regulation maximum of 50 grammes of baccy, 200 cigarettes, or £4 in 'phonecards. Patel and I felt most unhappy with that bit of information as we exceeded those levels on all counts, and though purchased legitimately, we were without receipts to prove it as the canteen never issued them. Our meal became dominated by the debate as to what to do about it. Glancing outside, the sight of screws prowling around, stooping every so often to retrieve discarded booty, ruled out that option. We tried wrapping some cigarettes and baccy in toilet paper to flush down the pan, but even after a couple of pulls, shredded leaf kept floating on the surface. To avoid them being spotted by screws, who would interpret our efforts as an admission of guilt, we had to skim bits off the top of the water with Patel's spoon. Short of eating the stuff, we had no alternative but to take our chances, accepting that, at the very least, our surplus stock would be confiscated.

Time crawled by as we lay on our beds, chain smoking. In the distance, on one of the other spurs, doors banged and screws shouted, with dogs joining in every so often to keep an atmosphere of tension alive. It proved impossible to try and concentrate reading a book or even play cards, and Patel's radio got turned off as we found the constant twittering of the DJ more irritating than usual. If it was intended by the screws to make inmates sweat, they had certainly succeeded with the occupants of Cell 3, Spur 2, Houseblock 2.

It was very near lunch-time when we heard the activity getting close to us. We were almost looking forward to our door being opened as, with the window having to be kept shut, continual puffing had created a cloud layer over the beds. Then it was our turn and whilst one screw told us to step outside for a "rub down", another entered the cell to turn it upside down. Our next door neighbours were also being done, likewise two cells on the landing above, and it was noticeable that none of the screws involved were regulars on our houseblock. Three of them we recognised from the Visiting Hall and one out of the Education Wing. We speculated afterwards whether the "regulars" preferred it that way as they had to live with us when it was over, or was it due to the Governor not fully trusting them to do the business.

The screw in our cell must have had a terrible hang-up from childhood days of being made to forever tidy his bedroom, as he ploughed through it with the finesse of a deranged bull. Having first lifted our beds up to look underneath, he then tipped the bedding over, including both mattresses. Our two extra pillows came flying out the door, followed by spare towels, all destined to be returned to the stores. Next the contents of our cupboards were dumped on the upturned mattresses, at which point he got excited at the discovery of our surplus goodies, waving them triumphantly to his companion. A yell brought another screw hurrying over armed with a clip-board, on which he wrote our names and numbers, followed by a recording of what was being confiscated. Our signatures were required before they bagged up our property, and we were told to expect a visit to the Governor's office.

Patel and I had become two thoroughly pissed-off prisoners as, with the door slammed shut on us, we half-heartedly set about straightening up our cell, speculating whilst doing so, what sort of punishment we might be looking at. Much would depend on whether it was accepted we had only exceeded the regulation amount permitted, and not some proceeds from the burglary. Either way, it looked as if our cleaning careers could be over and the perks that went with it. When we were let out to get our lunches, even my appetite was at a low ebb, aggravated by the sight of what appeared to be a load of vomit spread over some cardboard, that the screw adamantly claimed was a pizza. The alternative spam fritter resembled what a dog leaves on the pavement, after someone has stepped on it. I settled for some potato and mixed veg., drowned in gravy, followed by a slab of jelly, with the regular rock cake perched on top. Patel couldn't face any of it, and the sole occupant of his tray was a rock cake I had asked him to collect for me to eat later. His lunch that day was a Mars bar, followed by a bag of crisps, from the mini-store over his bed.

We were all kept locked up for the afternoon and time really dragged, made worse due to my cell-mate continually bemoaning the anticipated loss of our jobs so soon after getting them. During the short space of time available whilst getting our lunches, we had obtained some idea of the results of the recent mass "cell-spinning". Quite a few of our neighbours had been put on report like ourselves, in many instances for rather trivial misdemeanours, such as defacing prison property by sticking pictures on the wall with toothpaste, having a blanket covering the window and, in the case of one of the pencil artists, possessing

246

a number of drawings depicting screws performing extremely lewd acts with each other. He was being threatened with a charge of "actions prejudicial to the maintenance of good order and discipline". Initially I was surprised as to how few had been caught with some "puff", but on reflection realised most inmates with any experience would have "sussed" the previous evening what lay in store, and had spent the night totally "spaced out" having smoked their stock up. One bloke, calculating the increased value that would occur for the following few days, flattened a quantity in the bottom of his socks, before pulling them on. Unfortunately for him, his cell-mate started to get stroppy with the screws during their "spin", leading to a dog handler rushing over as back-up and his secret being exposed by the Alsatian vigorously sniffing round his feet.

The association period was reinstated after our 6pm meal and became dominated by inmates voicing their grievances to each other regarding the recent upheavals. Out of the 57 blokes our spur, it seemed that at least a third had been put on report for various infringements of the rules, mostly quite trivial as already mentioned. Semtex intended to complain to the Commission for Racial Equality, having had his Irish republican posters ripped off the wall and torn up, whereas other inmates had just been told to removed their collections, mainly pin-ups. Don was on report due to the screws unearthing his much valued nail clippers, whilst an Afro on the top floor was listed to explain his collection of metal meal trays. It would appear that as his window overlooked the exercise yard, he took great pleasure in launching a couple through the bars in the middle of the night, taking great care that their trajectory had them landing away from the immediate vicinity under his cell. The crash as they hit the tarmac would start the dogs barking in their nearby compound, and have handlers running around shining their torches into every dark corner.

Someone suggested he told the Governor that he was just being helpful, ensuring the outside security staff were "on the ball", but whatever the outcome, I am sure those in ground floor cells underneath him were not sorry he'd been caught. The big news though, was that four cleaners from one of the other spurs were booked for the break-in and had been marched off to the isolation block, pending formal charges. No one really believed they would appear in court as the Prison Service could well do without the embarrassing publicity, which explains why it was subsequently dealt with strictly internally. They ended up losing plenty of remission, being transferred to Wandsworth for a hard time, and probably blew any chances of becoming cleaners again for the remainder of their penal careers.

Due to such a large number of prisoners on Governor's report, we estimated 50 to 60 for the three spurs, minor offences were being dealt with by the Principal Officer, who was senior screw in the Houseblock. In the event of not being agreeable with his decision, you could insist on having the matter referred to the Deputy Governor who, being the miserable sod that he was, would undoubtedly increase any punishment just for taking up his time. The P.O. was already in the process of having blokes brought to his office, and it was during the latter part of association that Patel and I heard our names being yelled out.   Off we trudged, under escort, relieved that we would soon be put out of our misery one way or the other, and telling ourselves that during our one previous encounter, as new arrivals, he had seemed quite a reasonable bloke.   Once in his office, we were subjected to a short lecture regarding the accumulation of too many goodies and how it could leave us open to harassment by those who had nothing, thus creating the potential for trouble.   A note had obviously been made about the well stocked shelves in Patel's cupboard, as the P.O. pointedly reminded him that, as with all other inmates, he was in Belmarsh on a full board basis, not self-catering. In the case of possessing above the permitted amounts of cigarettes, baccy and 'phonecards, he went on, which were recognised as prison currency, we were inviting suspicions as to what we might be dealing in, more so having recently acquired the relative freedom of movement enjoyed by cleaners.   He claimed to accept our protestations they were all purchases from the canteen and that neither of us had any intention to deal in anything, but nonetheless, they were to be confiscated.   We were to be permitted to continue our cleaning duties, but with the warning that, in future, would be liable to unannounced searches when out of our cell, plus regular spins of the cell itself. That was it, and although the P.O. had commenced shuffling some paperwork about, we didn't realise he

249

had finished with us until the escorting screw demanded to know what we were waiting for. Returning to the spur, both of us knew that, under the circumstances, we'd had a result, marred only by the thought that our genuine purchases would be utilised towards restocking the canteen.

Over the following couple of days, what passes as normality returned to Belmarsh. Work parties and Education resumed, and Patel and I made a point of looking like the busiest cleaners the place had seen. Keeping the yard tidy was a piece of cake, as I was out there almost on a daily basis, and the amount of rubbish accumulated barely filled half a sack. I used to call up to blokes' windows asking them to keep throwing out their crap as I was worried I might be working myself out of a job. One took me literally and only just missed me with a lump of what should have been flushed down the toilet, that he had loosely wrapped in a piece of tissue. On one occasion, having finished my task and wondering who may be "at home" in a ground floor cell to have a chat with, a voice called across from one such cell on my spur. It was a young lad, 20 years of age as it turned out, who had moved in barely a week previously and was in need of a light. Having first lit my own roll-up, I offered him the burning match, only to be asked whether I had a spare burn for him to light, as he only had dust left in the pack. To his credit and before I had time to reply, he did very generously offer to go "two's", e.g., share the one I was already smoking. I let him have it and dug out the second one of the three I always kept pre-rolled in my pocket, lighting it from the first in order to save matches.   This was Tom who, he later told me, was a not very successful burglar from Plumstead, and had just seen his fifth Xmas behind bars, having spent the better part of his teenage years in and out of Feltham Young Offenders Institution for varying lengths of time.   Leaning on his window sill, I noticed through the bars that he possessed a sizeable collection of books, including one of my favourite authors for a spot of light reading, the American crime fiction writer, Ed McBain.   In response to my remark about having nothing to read, Tom invited me to give him a look-in during association, when I would be welcome to sort one or two out.   Chatting on, I also learnt he could see his Mum and Dad's tower block flat about half a mile away from the top landing window, and that every week day, just before the 8pm "bang up", he would be up there watching them turning the front room light on and off, three or four times, to let him know they were thinking of him.   We had finished our cigarettes and were in the process of going "two's" with my last one, when I noticed a dog handler hovering ominously on the other side of the wire so, deciding not to give him any excuse to get on his mobile, I told Tom I'd see him later, and walked back to give the door a good kicking to gain re-entry.

Back on the spur, I washed my hands, changed out of my boots back into the gym shoes that were ideal for indoor wear, then went along to Tom's cell to continue our conversation through his door.   The red light was on outside, which meant he had pressed the call button for a screw, so I shouted through the narrow gap around the door frame, asking what the

251

matter was.   Due to the thickness of the door, shouting was our only way to communicate, even though he was only on the other side, and he replied the same way telling me he'd been waiting nearly an hour for a screw to take him to the Bubble to make a 'phone call.   He had told a senior screw earlier that morning he wanted to speak to a named C.I.D. officer, based at a local station, regarding some unsolved burglaries.   Apparently it was not uncommon for convicted criminals, especially burglars, to contact police officers, usually the ones who had helped put them inside, admitting additional crimes in return for immunity from any charges being laid against them, provided of course such confessions didn't relate to something really heavy, like rape or murder.   Both sides benefited from the arrangement; the inmate had a day out at police expense, starting with a café breakfast of their choice, then a tour round scenes of unsolved break-ins, followed by a pub lunch; after that, another little tour, culminating very often with a short home visit.   The price would be owning up to jobs he had done and even some he hadn't, so when eventually released, he had the comfort of knowing there was no danger of a "gate arrest" to face new charges.   For their part, the police could show improvements in the sensitive area of burglary clear-up rates; the Commissioner and various politicians could pat themselves on the back during their media interviews; and the public be duly impressed that the boys in blue were making headway in the war against the slags who kept ransacking their homes and businesses.   It's a classic case of everybody being happy except, of course, the victim.

I pondered afterwards as to whether the victim of a burglary he thought remained unsolved, was subsequently told it now featured in the clear-up statistics, or would that be running the risk of him demanding to know what was happening to the perpetrator.   A screw coming up behind me, rattling his keys and muttering about inmates being a bloody nuisance, terminated our conversation, and whilst Tom was chaperoned to make his 'phone call, I went seeking that day's official issue to the spur of one newspaper.

After the mid-day meal, I had a call almost straightaway to go on a visit.   My daughter and two friends were waiting in the visiting hall, which really helped to brighten up my day.   The usual commotion reigned, with screws prowling around regarding the visitors as criminals, cowing the elderly and intimidating the children.   One little boy, no more than six years old and obviously with a lot more nerve than most, ran over to a screw to give him a good kick in the leg, telling him it was for not letting his Dad go home.   His Mother went to retrieve him, and was told that if she couldn't control him, their visit would be terminated.   A couple of other inmates seated nearby took full advantage of the temporary distraction and quickly swallowed more than their tea. The news from home was good, the general feeling being that with Xmas out of the way and almost half my mandatory sentence completed, it would now be downhill all the way.   My wife was coping OK., which was the main thing, aided by a combination of support from our children and friends, plus me

253

ringing up for a natter every other day. Being Winter and a pig of a journey from Sutton, I had stressed that visits could be cut right back, especially as I now had such ready access to a telephone, but the point was disregarded because all concerned felt they would be letting me down. Like all situations of great difficulty, you certainly find out who are real family and friends when you are in prison. The news about the break-in at the canteen gave my visitors a good chuckle, and as I was telling them, it dawned on me that the screws would be painfully aware of the tale being recounted at every visit during the following days, which would explain them being more sour than usual.

When I returned to the houseblock, I bumped into Tommy, the screws tea-boy. Incidentally, to this day, I haven't figured out why so many inmates had Mums who liked the name Thomas. He invited me into the screws messroom, under the guise of us admiring the contents of their fish tank, to tell me the latest big news item. It would appear that some of the blokes had identified the one who had informed on the canteen burglars, and in order to avoid the inevitable retribution, the "grass" had applied to be placed under Rule 43 and removed to the segregation wing for his own safety. In a small minority of cases, Rule 43 is imposed on some inmates and they are segregated for the good of other prisoners, but overwhelmingly it is utilised for sex offenders and bent policemen, where they need to be kept apart for their own safety. The use of informers by prison staff takes place in all prisons and is a vital element in maintaining control, but the price that would be paid by such "grasses" if found out, far outweighs any rewards obtained. After all, if they received too many perks, suspicion would soon surround them and undermine their value to the screws.   Tommy had an additional piece of information that involved me personally, which was why, he explained, he'd been keeping an eye out for my return.   It would appear that as the cleaner who had sought sanctuary under Rule 43 functioned on the hot-plate, a vacancy now existed and Tommy had overheard Mr C., still the Cleaning Officer, suggesting to Mr B. that I filled it.   I pondered that one, whilst Tommy took a lump of the screws Cheddar from the 'fridge, sliced me off a nice portion, and wrapped it in a serviette for me to slip in my pocket.   Suddenly a screw walked in, and I quickly made a complimentary remark about the contents of the fish tank.   Pausing just long enough to count them, he bluntly told me to do myself a favour and get out, and to stay out.   With the cheese wedged down in my pocket, I promptly headed back to the spur, and the waiting Mr B.

Tommy's forewarning presented me with a bit of a problem.   A job on the hot-plate was much sought after, as it enabled one to have the pick of the menu, but it also entailed a lot of washing up.   I was also very happy keeping the yard tidy, enjoying the fresh air and reaping the same perks for a much easier workload.   The real problem was that, if I refused the former, the screws might get petulant and take me off the latter.   I need not have bothered even thinking about it, as Mr B. told me I was now a member of the food shovelling squad. My query regarding the yard cleaning was met with the considered opinion that, as he'd so impressed everyone with his performance during the past few days, Patel could have it added to his current working area. Any further discussion was stifled by Mr B. telling me I'd better show my face, as the evening meal was due to be served within half an hour.

As previously mentioned, the hot-plate always has the potential for trouble, where the inmates serving are routinely accused of holding back the choicer items for themselves and skimping on the amounts made available for others. This explains why the job is rarely filled by those of a nervous disposition and on my arrival, the four waiting for me to complete the line-up all looked like bouncers in doctors' coats. It had already been decided my function would be to shovel slabs of rhubarb crumble out of big metal trays, with an implement that resembled an army trenching tool. I had barely donned a white coat when the first six "customers" arrived, so I vigorously started hacking away at the layer of crumble, which would have been ideal for surfacing a motorway. Eventually breaking through, I excavated a lump to put on the first bloke's tray, only to find that the component underneath had the adhesive qualities of glue, necessitating me to force it off the serving spade by hand. I had barely got it on the tray before Big Reg drowned it with a ladle of custard, whilst I commenced to dig out another portion.

We had served about thirty inmates when a

particularly mouthy bloke, in his early twenties, turned up. The meat dish consisted of spam fritters with the edges curled up, and chicken for those on a pork free diet. Motormouth insisted he was pork free and demanded chicken, which Mr C. allowed because he couldn't confirm the matter one way or the other, on his computer print-out. Not being content with his result, Motormouth then launched into a load of verbal as to how we were all stuffing ourselves silly with the better food, at the same time pushing the crap onto everyone else. Having helped himself to extra chips, he moved his tray in front of me, at the same time telling me to shove my offering up my arse. I ignored his suggestion, mainly because I was still battling to get it out of the tray, when Big Reg, whose movements seemed to be automatic, emptied a load of custard over his chicken. The effect was immediate and as I stepped back, being conscious of how close I was to the obvious target for his tray, Motormouth was throwing a wobbly, whilst Big Reg, now holding the ladle like a club, protested that he had moved his tray after he'd started pouring. Motormouth could not have been very popular on his spur as, instead of any sympathy, the other inmates almost pissed themselves laughing, whilst Mr C. and the other screw on hot-plate duty grabbed hold of his arms, giving him the choice of getting back to his cell with the tray, or without it. He went with it, at the same time threatening Big Reg with a colourful variety of retributions, with the other screw accompanying him in case he took it into his head to double back and carry some of it out.

257

At the end of the session and as we tucked into the pieces of roast chicken which had been put away earlier, Mr C. came over to tell me that, in his opinion, I was not suitable for working on the hot-plate. He had observed that, instead of getting the regulation 24 portions from each tray, I had managed no more than 14. My defence that no one had told me, and we were still throwing nearly three tray-fulls down the waste disposal unit, was not deemed relevant. After less than an hour, a budding career in catering had come to an abrupt end and my services were no longer required. I was permitted to remain long enough to munch my way through my share of chicken, followed by a generous lump of crumble, and helped down with two bowlfuls of Big Reg's custard, before having to return to the spur. On arriving, Mr B., who had already been notified of the situation, called me over to tell me that due to my redundant status, I might as well go back to keeping the yard tidy, which suited me fine. The whole episode did me a big favour as, once the word got around I had lost a highly coveted job due to giving the blokes extra large portions of a popular dish, I was regarded throughout the houseblock as one of the chaps. A bigger bonus, though, was that Fitz, the Mike Tyson lookalike, who tended to dominate the hot-plate, from then on ensured I could pick whatever I wanted to eat without the usual hassle. It was a lovely situation, but not very helpful in the ongoing battle to keep my weight in some sort of order.

Association time was nearly over, and I spotted Tom making his way up the stairs to watch Mum flashing the front room lights on and off. Calling up to him, I reminded him of his earlier offer to lend me a couple of Ed McBain books. He shouted back to go in his cell and help myself. I did just that, but after selecting two, I couldn't help noticing his inventive efforts at DIY "home" improvements. In addition to having "tiled" round the hand basin with used-up 'phone cards, he had also used toothpaste to stick two "single servings" cereal boxes above it, one to hold his toothbrush and razor, and the other his plastic cutlery set. A paper tissue box, similarly "glued" on the wall alongside his bed, contained letters, and with some cleverly folded cardboard, he had even made three small shelves capable of holding lightweight items such as matches and pens. The remainder of that wall was dominated by a very large poster of Charlton Athletic football team. In answer to my query, on his return, as to how his fittings had survived the recent cell spins, he explained that apart from the tiling around the basin, they had been taken down prior to the screws arriving. He had been before the P.O. regarding the tiling, to be fined two pounds for defacing his cell and ordered to remove it. The fact they were still in place was because he hadn't got round to it yet.

A screw yelling for everyone to get their water, signalled that association was over, so agreeing to continue our chat the next day, I departed clutching his books. All in all, it had been a good day and I couldn't wait to get stuck into one of them as a nice change from trying to win some matches off Patel at cards, which I very rarely succeeded in doing.

Chapter 14

Cell Classes And A Posting To The Special Secure Unit

The days following my reinstatement as a yard cleaner passed quite amiably, although I realised it was only a combination of my relative freedom of movement, no shortage of blokes to natter with, ready access to a telephone and plenty of books to borrow, that prevented the usual tedium of enclosed prison life boring me silly.

Incidences on the spur, even tragic ones, were regarded as a welcome break in the monotony. When the E. man finally got pissed off having a screw walking everywhere with him, and almost knocked him senseless with a head butt, everyone was full of it, except the screw of course, and possibly the E. man, who was dragged off to solitary for a good thumping prior to being shipped to Wandsworth. One of the Irish contingent became very indignant with a female screw who had taken it on herself to walk into the shower room at random, and demonstrated his annoyance by repeatedly approaching her on any flimsy pretext, as naked as the day he was born. We were never too sure who enjoyed the performance the most, but it was eventually terminated by Mr B. blowing down his ear, and the screwess conveniently moving to another

261

spur.   A bloke on the top landing, in a single cell, decided to end it all after learning that his wife had gone abroad with her replacement lover, and their three kids were now in council care.   He had knelt in front of the toilet, lacerated his wrists with the blade extracted from a disposable razor, and rammed his hands as far round the 'S' bend as they would go. After a while, he evidently had a change of mind but was unable to dislodge himself from the pan and it was his neighbours, woken by his yells, who summoned a screw.   They in turn, having no success in dragging him out of the 'S' bend, had to call up a maintenance man to smash the pot and shut off the water supply.   He disappeared to the medical wing where, we later learned, he made a full recovery and was receiving psychiatric help, which most believed would guarantee him doing it again.   One inmate, having realised the tea whitening powder was flammable, decided to pack an empty drinking chocolate container full of the stuff.   His plan was to ignite it in the middle of the night, drop it out of the window, hoping that the expected bang would have security running round in circles looking for a breach in the outer wall.   Unfortunately for him, the paper fuse burned down too fast and the whole lot went up in a flash whilst he was still holding it. He was lucky to get away with some medium degree burns, severely singed eyebrows and a smouldering head of hair.   The Governor took a very dim view of the whole affair and, after deducting a load of remission, giving him a couple of weeks in solitary plus cancelling all privileges, including wages, for a month, told him he should be thankful not to be facing a charge of attempted arson. Events such as these, plus lesser ones, all helped in the daily fight against boredom, although even minor occurrences could generate the typical Belmarsh "over-kill" reaction. Ray was sitting down in the association area minding his own business, tucking into the contents of his meal tray, when a young inmate just to annoy him, hurried past, pinching some chips in the process. Ray instinctively picked up his slab of jelly and hurled it at the retreating offender's head, which he just missed, with the missile landing instead between a screw's shoulder blades where, having clung to his crispy white shirt for a couple of seconds, it then fell with a plop onto the floor. A night in solitary was Ray's "reward", and when he returned the next day he was faced with the loss of all privileges, including wages and association, for one week, for assaulting a prison officer. In reality, he would be confined to his cell 24 hours a day for the week, only allowed out to get meals, which then had to be eaten in the cell. His record would show an assault being carried out by him, which would go down like a lead balloon with the parole board, who would not be made aware that it had been perpetrated with a misdirected slab of jelly.

During association times, and as a reflection on there being precious little else to do, another welcome escape from boredom were the ad hoc discussion groups that took place in some of the cells. On occasions they almost assumed the status of education classes. Subjects varied but, in the main, revolved around the workings of the legal system or how to carry out criminal activities more efficiently. With regard to the latter, I obtained within a modest length of time a basic knowledge of the drug scene, including how to "cut" the pure thing and what to mix it with. I also learned of the relative safety factors regarding potential targets when planning an armed robbery, for example, building societies appear to carry a higher risk rating than bookmakers. CCTV was an unwelcome development, but not regarded as an actual deterrent, especially if the perceived haul was big enough. Most participants at that particular "seminar" felt cameras would pose a greater danger if they were manned, whereby a person monitoring could summon the cavalry before any robbers had even left the premises, and if the outside was also covered, exposed faces of accomplices, plus details of any transport, could be picked up by the camera's eye. Yet another class taught me the pit-falls of burgling residential, as opposed to commercial, property. These boiled down to partly the unknown factor as to whether or not there was much of value to steal and, equally important, the possibility of confronting an occupant either fit enough to capture you, or so frail they suffered a heart attack, leaving you looking at a likely manslaughter charge. Some discussions went over my head, such as those ones dealing with the intricacies of modern alarm systems, and how to get round the latest anti-theft devices being built into new vehicles. The subject of firearms provoked heated debates, with a surprisingly large number being against carrying them, let alone using them. Their reasoning was devoid of any tender feelings, but based simply on the heavier sentence to be expected if captured "tooled up", plus the highly probable outcome if confronted by an armed police unit, with one or two trigger happy members among their number. All in all, these sessions were infinitely more interesting than the official Education classes, although I did wonder from time to time, with all this apparent knowledge and expertise, coupled with their foolproof scams and frauds, how come they were all behind bars. Had they underestimated the police; overestimated their own abilities; fallen foul of the unexpected, such as the getaway car conking out; or just being clever with the benefit of hindsight?

The debates revolving around the legal system I found generally more absorbing, mainly because I could chime in with my two pennyworth along with everyone else. Sometimes the topic was a specific case, when a remand prisoner awaiting trial would have the assembled "experts" telling him what he should, and should not, do. Mostly they dealt with the workings of the courts, the police, and the legal profession. The police, as an organisation, whilst not very high in the popularity stakes, were not regarded with the degree of hostility I would have expected. One bloke, I recall, referred to them as a necessary evil. Extreme contempt was expressed about individual coppers though, mainly where they had given families an especially hard time when carrying out their searches and arrests; or subsequently added to the list of charges, then lied in court to obtain not only additional convictions, but also longer sentences. Solicitors and barristers were

265

either thought very highly of, especially when they had achieved results against all the odds, but denigrated, probably unfairly, if they failed in the face of similar odds. High profile barristers, such as Michael Mansfield, and solicitors like Gareth Pierce, due to their achievements in cases as famous as the Guildford Four, the Birmingham Six, and others, generated supreme praise, but due to their high fees, the consensus opinion was that barristers certainly disproved the saying that crime does not pay. Judges and, to a slightly lesser extent, magistrates, evoked total scorn and animosity, not because of the role they performed but due to their having been drawn almost exclusively from the middle and upper classes. Unlike most other areas of our class-ridden society, the total domination of the judiciary by the upper crust is so blatant that even the most naive defendant can see they are from a different world. One black guy, who had obviously studied the subject, pointed out on one occasion the additional racial dimension whereby black people, whilst being over-represented as suspects, defendants and inmates, were completely absent from positions as High Court judges, Justices' Clerks, police officers above the rank of Superintendent, and Chief Probation Officers. The operation of the "Old School Tie" network and probably Freemasonry, was also a sore point, and when convictions are overturned on appeal after judges have misdirected juries, or make outrageous comments whilst summing up rape cases, yet are allowed to continue sitting in judgement, demolished yet further any vestige of respect towards them. One wit, I remember, gave his opinion that any bloke who

266

enjoyed dressing up in a wig and black silk stockings, has got to be very suspect.

Juries were universally regarded as essential, both to counter-balance the class bias of the bench and as a means of affording the vast majority of defendants any prospect of a fair hearing. A substantial number of inmates claimed they would rather run the risk of a bigger sentence, if convicted, in a Crown court, in front of a jury, than be dealt with by middle class magistrates with middle class prejudices. Maybe this explains why the periodic attacks on the jury system, going so far as to dispense with them altogether, never emanated from working class organisations, or individuals. Indeed, the consensus opinion was for expanding the jury role to include them in the function of sentencing, as a counter to the all too frequent pendulum swings between harshness and leniency that is a feature of the present set-up. This issue of gross inconsistencies in the levels of sentences meted out was always guaranteed to generate passionate criticism, with a seemingly endless list of examples being quoted. One example, current at the time, was where individuals with previously clean records, some of them elderly, were receiving prison terms for not paying the Poll Tax; yet a Hull landlord, found guilty of the manslaughter of a tenant due to a faulty gas fire, obtained a suspended sentence of 18 months. The class bias of the system was also highlighted with examples such as the substantial numbers of women jailed in Holloway for not having a TV licence, yet the Marquis of Blandford, routinely convicted on drug offences, has yet to taste porridge anywhere near the extent that some of my Belmarsh neighbours were tasting it, for a much lower involvement. Another related to the 30-year sentences meted out to working class blokes for robbing a mail train of £2.5M. back in the '60's, yet a member of the nobility, a mate of Prince Charles, gets 5 years for swindling £4.5M. with an insurance scam. One Rasta, I recall, added a further dimension at one such discussion group, by highlighting how the State exerts tremendous influence on the legal system to protect its enforcement machinery. He referred to not only how, after serving less than two years of a life sentence for murder, Private Lee Clegg returned to his regiment to be immediately promoted, but also how few prosecutions, let alone convictions, occur following unlawful killings by the police. They were extremely interesting sessions, permeated not by any self pity, but by a deep resentment of a corrupt system, whose track record made it abundantly clear that the overwhelming majority of people were not equal in the eyes of the law. I could agree with almost everything I heard on these occasions, and when the corruption and hypocrisy of the judicial system became the theme, as it regularly did, would add my own contribution.

It went down very well when I pointed out that Michael Howard, the Home Secretary, was still in place and spouting about law and order, yet had more court judgements against him, including from the European Court, than any other Government Minister in history. I would follow my assertion by claiming this situation not to be surprising, as the party, and currently the government, of which he was a senior figure, were more than happy to accept very big sums of money as gifts from some very dubious sources, such as Asil Nadir, the financier who fled abroad just as the Serious Fraud Office were putting the finishing touches to their case against him. The Tories keep a very tight lid on the identities of many of the donors who put millions of pounds into their funds, some of whom are believed to include arms dealers, Chinese businessmen, even a Bosnian Serb warlord, none of them noted for their charitable instincts; yet the same Tories go berserk when it is suggested their extreme secrecy could be covering up bribes for past favours and others to come. It gave me a warm feeling adding this new horizon to the debates, especially as I knew some inmates would follow the usual tendency to repeat them in the future as their own products, both in Belmarsh and when transferred elsewhere. Maybe, just maybe, I had made a minute contribution towards moving prisons beyond their traditional roles as Universities of Crime into becoming centres of social and political debate, leading to some inmates, when released, participating in the much needed struggle for a better run society. At the very least, I have provided another aspect of our rotten system for them to talk about during association.

The achievement one morning, of a pigeon perched on an anti-helicopter cable, to land a little white mess on my head, coupled with some raindrops starting to fall, prompted me to call it a day with my yard cleaning. Following the usual good kicking of the door, I was readmitted into the building by none other than Mr. B., who informed me that if I was agreeable, my services were much needed elsewhere. The floor and showers in the Special Secure Unit, apparently, were in desperate need of a thorough mopping, and the task could only be carried out by a cleaner from one of the houseblocks for security reasons. What he didn't point out was that they were in such a state due to the deliberate Home Office policy of making life as unpleasant as possible for the inmates there, and were only cleaned up if a VIP, such as an Irish T.D. (Member of Parliament) was due to visit, following pressure in that country regarding the appalling conditions imposed on IRA prisoners incarcerated there.

The princely sum of £2 was on offer but I said I would do it anyway, for two reasons that I kept to myself. Firstly, I was curious to see the inside of that dreary monstrosity, having looked at the outside on an almost daily basis, and secondly, I didn't want to refuse Mr B. personally, for I regarded him as having done me a fair bit of good. Having obtained my agreement, Mr B. suggested I made myself a cup of tea as I wouldn't get one over in the Unit, also to empty out my pockets of literally everything, whilst he went upstairs to the "Bubble" to notify them and arrange my escort. He was gone long enough for me to finish a cigarette and for my tea to cool down sufficiently to drink before returning, not just with another screw, but also a dog handler complete with German Shepherd that looked as if nothing would give it greater pleasure than to bury its fangs into my bum.   Obviously it was felt that, at 52 years of age, well overweight, with five weeks to go, I might overcome a screw half my age and a bloody sight fitter, scale a 20-odd metre wall, wriggle through a couple of rolls of razor wire, leap down the other side and leg it into the wilds of Woolwich.   Once outside the door, the dog handler radioed our position to his control, and then made a second call to the Unit informing them we were on our way, and off we went to complete the two minute walk in complete silence, with me being more than happy for him to keep between me and his dog.

On arrival, our presence was announced through an intercom and the door electronically opened, that once we were inside, immediately re-locked itself.   It reminded me of the Starship Enterprise in Star Trek. A camera scanned us whilst we stood there, then an unseen hand released the inner door which operated the same way as the first, permitting us to pass through, where another screw waited to receive us. Without so much as a 'hello', he straightaway took us into a side office for a senior screw to check my details, enter my arrival in a log book and formally release the dog handler from his heavy responsibility of minding me, whereupon he departed back through the two-door system.   Standing there gazing around, the thought went through my mind that I hadn't been given the routine rub down, then first screw finally spoke, telling me to get undressed and to put my clothes on a nearby chair.   Such an instruction, coupled with him pulling on a pair of rubber gloves, left me in no doubt as to his intention, and I

271

straightaway told him no way. That had the senior screw quickly turning round on his chair, telling me in no uncertain terms how it was an offence to disobey a lawful command, to which I replied that I was there voluntarily and wouldn't have been if I'd been told the job entailed the degradation of a strip search, including my arse being probed for drugs. Neither of them appeared too impressed with my point of view and the first screw, now flexing his fingers inside the gloves like a concert pianist, showed his keen powers of observation by stating I was here now so therefore we might as well get it over with. I was still having none of it and told them I wanted to be taken back to the houseblock because, even if they forcibly strip searched me, it would be a pointless exercise as they couldn't force me to push a mop around on what was, after all, a voluntary function. The first screw now turned really snotty, probably sensing that the opportunity to stick his finger up my bum was slipping away, and sarcastically asked how long I'd been a lawyer. Thankfully though, his superior was able to think more rationally, suggesting as a compromise that I undressed down to my underpants and left it at that, to which, after going through the motions of thinking about it, I agreed. Quickly disrobing, I repeated the comment I had made at the court, as to how my Mum had warned me about blokes wanting me to take off my clothes, but it met with the same sour response, with the first screw looking distinctly cheated as he peeled off the surgical gloves. I stood there almost in all my glory as he checked through my clothing, whilst his superior impressed on me not only that I mustn't speak to any inmate, but to totally blank any who may attempt talking to me.   As it turned out, any effort at conversation would have been almost impossible, due to all the occupants being "banged up" for their usual 23 hours a day.

Dressed again, the one with the bum fetish took me out of the office and across to a nearby cupboard, from which, after unlocking it with a flourish of his keys, he handed me the cleaning implements.   I was to sweep the central area, plus a couple of short corridors off it, then mop it all over.   The buffing machine had packed up so I was spared that chore, but as I would still be holding the mop, I could continue straightaway to slop it around the shower room.   My finale would be to wipe around the hand basins and the bath.   With the screw keeping close by, as he did all the while I was in the place, I made my way to the farthest point in order to work back towards the main door.   It was like walking through a gigantic tomb, or one of those American-style mortuaries, where all the bodies are tucked away in large filing cabinets embedded in the wall.   I don't know whether I had turned up during a particularly quiet period, but apart from hearing an occasional cough, a muffled voice calling to the bloke next door, or an en-suite toilet being flushed, you wouldn't realise that within a few metres there were about forty men buried away.   The whole atmosphere was both eerie and claustrophobic.

My main problem with the sweeping up was finding something to sweep, and by the time I had covered about a third of the floor area, was pushing a grand total of two dog-ends and four matchsticks along, with a broomhead almost a metre wide. The scarcity reflected on how little the area was utilised, rather than any house-proud tendencies on the part of the inmates. Moving along in front of the cell doors, when the screw got extra close to me, curiosity compelled me to take a quick look at some of the detail cards on display outside each one. The length of sentences those prisoners were serving, to my mind, just added to the sense of unreality permeating the unit, and for the blokes themselves, doing so much of it in almost solitary conditions, must make them feel like the Prisoner of Zenda. Later that day, when once again sprawled on my bed, I tried to get my head round the concept of spending 25 to 30 years in such conditions, and in some cases, the rest of my natural life, but found it impossible. No doubt, many of those personally serving such sentences fully deserved them, whilst others may have not, but either way, spending so many years locked away in a massive lump of concrete, mostly by yourself, must be the nearest one can get to being dead without actually dying. Some of the names on the door cards indicated an international element among the inhabitants, whilst various Irish ones confirmed what I had been told weeks before, namely, that more than a few IRA prisoners were regularly incarcerated in the Belmarsh SSU.

Eventually, I reached the main door, indeed the only door as far as I could see, having accumulated enough litter to just about fill a cigarette packet, which was duly scooped up and deposited in a black sack.

274

Having checked their broom and dustpan back into the cupboard, the screw then shadowed me as I wheeled the mop and bucket to the far end. From behind two or three cell doors muffled voices called as I passed by, but a combination of extra thick steel doors, plus rattley wheels on the mop bucket, drowned out any clarity. Another typical Belmarsh "over the top" measure was also noticeable, whereby every shutter was closed over the observation windows in the doors, presumably in case either I, or one of the inmates, were able to lip-read. Just what a threat to security was perceived in the event of me saying "hello", or some of the prisoners watching me slopping a mop around, completely eluded me; but with such obsessional thinking, it occurred to me that probably each card on the doors had been switched around prior to my arrival, in case I memorised - for some unknown reason - which cells Smith or Jones occupied.

In addition to my chaperone, a couple of other screws appeared from time to time, carrying sheets of paper in and out of the office, to confirm their contents with the senior screw. They all shared a common expression of absolute boredom which, I suppose, was inevitable, working in such a depressing environment. Not many jobs can be on a par with being locked in a building every working day to watch paint dry, but at least they can get away from it at the end of their shift, and the pay for keeping all the doors locked is very good. With two-thirds of the floor nicely wet, the senior screw emerged from his office to tell me to finish up, and that he had arranged for me to be escorted back to the houseblock, without giving any reason for terminating my services so abruptly. Within five minutes, the mop and bucket were being securely locked back in the cupboard, and in response to my query as to whether I would still be paid the full £2.00 even though I hadn't touched the shower unit, was left in no doubt by my chaperone that if it was left up to him, "I'd get fuck-all"! Resisting the temptation to ask if he had ever considered a career in industrial relations, I followed him to the front door to await the arrival of one man and his dog. Our timing was perfect, as he came through the outer door, we got to the inner one, which suited me fine because I felt the sooner I was out of the Unit and back to the relative normality in the houseblock, the better. On our way, I saw the reason for prematurely ending my cleaning operation, in the form of a mini-bus full of visitors passing us on the roadway. The occupants were mostly women and children and as we stood on one side to give way, I took the liberty of waving at a couple of young faces peering out the windows. This action on my part immediately provoked an ominous growl from the German Shepherd, whose training probably taught it to regard an upraised arm as a sign of aggression, or else it was just naturally sour like its handler.

Watching the 'bus driving past with its passengers effectively under escort as myself, brought home to me comments I had heard during previous weeks regarding the aggravation people visiting friends and relatives in the Unit were subjected to. Belmarsh, as a prison, is distinctly visitor unfriendly at the best of times, as I have outlined earlier, but for those visiting the Double A category inmates, their ordeal reaches nightmare proportions. For starters, each individual had to obtain Home Office clearance to qualify for a Visiting Order, which entailed lengthy checks into their pedigree. No scope existed for an appeal in the event of refusal, which was highly likely if the applicant had a previous conviction and, in many instances, no reasons were given anyway. Having cleared that bureaucratic minefield, applications for visits had to be made well in advance, usually a number of weeks, only to find on arrival, the prisoner had been moved days earlier to another prison, at the opposite end of the country. This practice is called "ghosting", whereby the prisoner receives no forewarning, and no one outside the prison service is notified for security reasons. It is a practice routinely carried out with IRA prisoners especially, and the impact on their loved ones - very often including young children - after a weary and costly journey from Ireland, can only be scarcely imagined by those of us who have not experienced it. None of the sentences which have put men in places such as Belmarsh included a recommendation that the State should inflict avoidable misery on their families, and when an inmate is 'ghosted', a short note to their expected visitor, telling them no more than not to call that day because he is no longer there, would not undermine the need for security. Having turned up at the main gate, and subject to the prisoner being on the premises, visitors for the Unit are immediately segregated from the rest, taken to separate rooms where, after having their papers thoroughly

277

scrutinised, are then put through the gross indignity of a full strip search. There are no exceptions made for age and therefore elderly grandparents, along with young children, are equally subjected to this obnoxious practice, which many decent people regard as nothing short of legalised rape. Having reduced the kids to tears and clinging terrified to their mothers, with all the adults being treated like criminals, the screws then hustle them onto mini-buses to be transported, under guard, to the Unit. By this stage, having restored some composure, a first time visitor probably feels the worst is behind them, where others know that is not the case. On arrival, there is the welcoming delegation of dog handlers waiting by the door, with their Alsatians eyeing the passengers alighting in the same way as lions studied the unlucky Christians in the Roman Coliseum. Once inside, their identities and papers are checked again, with the screws making a meal out of non-existent discrepancies, following which, they are shepherded into the visiting room.

Very often they sit there waiting for up to a quarter of an hour whilst prisoners are fetched from cells less than fifty metres away, which gives the uninitiated time to fathom out the purpose of a thick Perspex screen that cuts them off from where the inmate will be seated. This is the 'closed visit', which is used generally where a prisoner has a record for obtaining drugs from their visitors, and prevents any bodily contact taking place, but is imposed routinely within the Unit. The pain inflicted by denying a kiss and cuddle with a loved one, or having to tell a young child that Daddy, sitting a metre away, cannot pick them up and hold them, must make old-fashioned tortures such as pulling out fingernails and teeth with pliers, look like a piece of cake. It is no wonder that some prisoners, particularly among the Irish contingent, regularly refuse to have visits, in protest at the torment generated by such inhumane conditions.

Deposited safe and sound again inside the houseblock, I left my escort radioing through to the Bubble, all of 15 metres away, that his mission had been completed, and slipped onto the end of a queue waiting to obtain their goodies from the canteen. None of the half dozen blokes in front of me looked familiar, which was due partly to them being from another spur and a reflection on the turnover of faces generally. The one at the head of the queue was engaged in the usual argument as to how much money should be in his wages and private account, receiving in return the stock reply that if it's not on the computer, then he hasn't got it. He must have been a newcomer, as he was trying to explain to the civilian employed to run the canteen why her computer print-out must be wrong, but he would soon learn she was as hard as granite with a built-in cut-out switch when confronted with any criticism of her computer. As the bloke became more agitated and raised his voice whilst condemning "poxy computers", the obligatory screw at the end of the counter heaved himself off the wall to give him two options - namely, to take what the print-out says he can afford, or go without. I knew for certain he was a newcomer when he asked

279

for credit, to be told he had more chance of getting struck by lightning indoors. He settled for the first option, which meant a sort out on the counter between what items to take and those to leave behind, with Mrs Granite repeating the prices, reminding him after each item what balance he had left. I'm not sure whether it reflected a spark of kindness deep down inside her or just pure sarcasm, but whilst seeking to round his total up to the nearest penny, she cut a 12½ gramme pack of tobacco in half with a pair of scissors, he was invited to choose which half to take. When the same disagreement commenced with the next bloke, I decided I'd rather make myself a cup of tea back on the spur and have a smoke. There was nothing I needed straightaway and one of my perks was regular access, unlike the vast majority who could only go if a screw felt inclined to let them.

Ms. O was seated at the desk when I got to the spur gate, who studiously continued reading the cartoon page in our newspaper issue, rather than respond to my request to be let in. She had recently transferred to Belmarsh from Court duties and already enjoyed a reputation for being petty minded and spiteful, which generated contempt amongst the inmates and, I am convinced, even some of her fellow screws. From day one, she had made it very obvious that not only did she not fancy men, she actually despised them and took every opportunity to make their lives difficult, although making sure a couple of her male colleagues were always nearby before indulging herself. A screw was escorting two blokes along the landing over my head so, in a voice loud enough for them to hear, being potential witnesses in the event of the situation escalating, I made it perfectly clear to Ms. O that if she didn't open the gate, I would be forced to urinate on the highly polished floor. That did the trick and the gate was unlocked, to the accompaniment of a sneering remark that at my age, control over certain functions does become difficult to exercise. My immediate reply as to how it was the sight of her that caused me to lose control over my lower parts was not at all well received, and with a slam of the gate, causing it to rebound open to hit her arm, she reminded me that being disrespectful to an officer could have me put on report. Pointing out that she had started the discussion regarding the controlling of one's bodily parts, I realised the best thing for me to do was to end the conversation, because being the one wearing the uniform, she must win or, more precisely, couldn't be seen to lose. Taking advantage of the short pause whilst she re-locked the door, I started walking towards my cell, remembering as I did that, with Patel out litter picking; it would be locked as a precaution against some of our more dubious neighbours. That meant I would have to go through the agony of asking her to open it up for me, with the inevitable snide comments which I would have to try and ignore. But I was to be spared such an ordeal by Mr. B., clattering down the iron stairs from the landing above, yelling that he wanted a word with me. Seeing as there was no love lost between the two screws, Ms. O. held back, trying to look macho, whilst I stood wondering what little treat he had lined me up for now. His long legs soon carried him down to the ground floor, whereupon he wanted to know how I had got on over in the Unit. I asked him whether he wanted a reply for the record or the truth, and when he chose the latter, told him it was crap. He responded by declaring he was getting the feeling I was not too impressed, and would possibly not be over keen to pop across there twice a week for the remainder of my stay. I left him in no doubt that his feeling regarding my lack of enthusiasm was right on target and that no way would I go back there, especially with one of his mates waiting to probe my arse each time. He reckoned I might get to like it, to which I suggested he sent one of the nonces as they would probably regard it as ample payment for the job, and could he be so kind as to unlock my cell. With a flourish of his keys the door was opened, and he went off muttering as to how there was no pleasing some people. I finally got my mug of tea and rolled a burn, but never received my £2, which goes to show that not all the con-men in Belmarsh are banged up.

****

Chapter 16

Good Screws; Bad Screws And The Majority

I was now into my final month and had started counting off the days, thinking about the little pleasures I would soon be returning to, such as drinking tea from a china mug, that had been brewed in a teapot; watching TV after 8 pm; sleeping between cotton sheets with the door open and, of course, the main one of being back with my family. Due to the journey and the hassle on arrival, I had told them not to bother too much about visiting, especially as I could telephone home daily. The need for visits greatly reduces the nearer one comes to release, although there were blokes going out before me still having them up to the end, because they were banged-up 22 hours every day and couldn't get on the telephone. My suggestion to the Principal Officer in charge of the houseblock that it would take some pressure off the visiting hall if they were let out to make a call each day, was rejected on the spurious grounds that it would tie a screw down censoring their conversations. The overwhelming majority of inmates that would have been affected were C and D categories who, had they been confined in a more appropriate prison, would have had more than enough access to telephones, without the perceived need for an eavesdropper.

Patel was running hot and cold as my release date loomed on the horizon, between joy because it meant the halfway mark in his sentence and gloom, as it brought the uncertainty into focus regarding who, or what, might replace me as his cell mate. If it was someone who just wanted to get spaced out on spliffs, they would be poor company to pass the long bang-up periods with, especially at week-ends, but in the event of them being short on spending money, then his well-stocked cupboard would become extremely vulnerable. His only options were to either push for a single cell as a cleaner, or to find someone he could get along with, or more to the point, could bear his irritating know-all attitude, to move in after I went. I knew the matter was worrying him but only realised the full extent when, one night, I awoke to hear him mumbling a prayer for help to the picture of one of his gods, that adorned on his cupboard door. It was tempting to suggest he tried the one our Asian co-defendant spoke to, just before the sentences were dished out, but I refrained, instead pointing out he'd be better off talking to Mr B. Patel did so the following morning, to be told that a lot could happen between then and me going home, as Belmarsh was full of little surprises. I'm not sure whether Mr. B. put his mind at rest, but if there were any further approaches to the picture stuck on the door with toothpaste, I certainly slept through them.

Having relative freedom to move around within the houseblock served to increase my appreciation of the waste of public money that exists in Belmarsh, and no doubt, is repeated elsewhere. My awareness was probably sharpened by my previous local council involvement, where each year we were faced with public expenditure cuts, inevitably hitting vital functions such as Social Services and Education. Such waste, along with the systematic mistreatment of many inmates, will continue whilst the Prison Service can hide behind their wall of "security requirements", with individual Governors only having to deal with the occasional, generally pre-arranged, H M Inspectorate visit and some carefully vetted, but ineffective, B.O.V.'s.

There is the minor waste of purchasing table-tennis tables that spend their whole existence stacked against a wall, to the provision of a large central hall, presumably for dining and recreational purposes, which is never used. A library, stocked and staffed, but inaccessible unless you make a bloody nuisance of yourself, very often ending up on report rather than among the bookshelves; the well-equipped gym, utilised for about 20 hours a week, or squash courts that see even less usage - and then only if a screw can be bothered to locate the racquets. £150M. of taxpayers' money was originally spent in building this penal Fort Knox, plus much more since on the constant upgrading of security features, so the Prison Service can half fill it with low category inmates, some serving as little as a month for motoring offences or non-payment of fines. Instead of using the large area of land within the perimeter wall for building accommodation, they pack men into four houseblocks like sardines, creating instead grassed areas which would be the envy of any holiday camp

285

whilst keeping blokes banged-up most of the time, with just a mere handful escorted out occasionally to tidy up these areas.   One feature I found very disturbing was the total lack, as far as inmates were concerned, of any plan in the event of a major fire, especially if it took place at night.   Doubtless the screws knew what they would do, but with over 800 prisoners securely locked up, many of them officially drugged and a skeleton staff on duty, I had the distinct impression of a tragedy waiting to happen.   For a fairly new construction there was still plenty of material to burn, and with all the windows shut, especially during cold times of the year, the whole place would soon fill with smoke.   I queried the matter with a screw, who claimed that although the steel doors would get hot, they couldn't burn, and they would have us out before we cooked.   I must confess to not feeling very comforted, as I couldn't quite visualise many screws risking their own lives, battling through the smoke and flames in order to unlock our doors and lead us to safety.   I suspect it would be just a far greater equivalent of a sweat-box colliding with something, where the inmate's chances prove a lot slimmer than the screws.

Harry's earlier contention, when I was pushing for a transfer to an open nick, that Belmarsh provided a relatively hassle-free environment, was very valid. With so much time spent banged-up, a vulnerable inmate was safe from any bullying, unless it was from their cell-mate, and when opened up, the scope was severely limited, as you weren't able to go anywhere unless the screws could keep an eye on you.

Obviously, for a determined assailant some opportunities did exist, such as if the target stayed in his cell during association with their door open, or walked down the stairs in front of someone he had upset, but generally, the ability to routinely bully or give a bloke a good kicking, was only enjoyed by the screws. There are occasions though, when all the bang-up and surveillance becomes meaningless and that is if the aggressor is a "nutter", either naturally or drug-induced, or just simply doesn't give a damn about any consequences. The inevitable stint in solitary and loss of remission, plus a few thumps from some screws, becomes a price worth paying provided he has been able to give the subject of his grievance a bloody good hammering.

Racism as an issue never openly raised its ugly head, although it would be extremely naive to believe that a substantial number of screws and inmates, both black and white, didn't have their prejudices. Like birds of a feather, some prisoners of mutual origins tended to congregate together, such as the Irish and Afro-Caribbean's, but never to the exclusion of others. The apparent harmony was due to a recognition that they were all in the same boat facing a common enemy in the form of both screws and the prison system. In the event of individual inmates, usually among the younger ones, acting in such a way as to fracture the harmony, their efforts would be rapidly subdued following some extremely clear advice regarding their future prospects. At the very least they would be ostracised, and if that didn't get them

287

to tone down, then a few good thumps would shut them up or have them clamouring for a move elsewhere.   With regards to the screws and the Prison Service as a whole, they operated a distinct policy of equality, whereby all inmates were afforded the same degree of contempt and subjected to a uniform pattern of dehumanising treatment.   As a group, Irish prisoners were most inclined to be on the receiving end of overt racism from the screws, particularly following some major action by the IRA. On those occasions, even totally non-political Irish blokes serving time for run-of-the-mill offences, such as burglary or drug dealing, would receive harsher treatment from the screws, many of whom having become hyped up from reading some lurid media report with their breakfasts.   The relationship between the two was never good at the best of times, largely due to the constant flow of witty piss-taking many Irish inmates excelled at, coupled with an insistence by some to keep playing tapes of rebel songs, very often joining in at the tops of their voices. Ripping Semtex's republican posters down during the recent mass cell spinning, whilst leaving others untouched, exemplified the biased attitude of many screws that is reflected throughout the system, probably explaining why he never even received a reply to his complaint.

The worst screw of all hailed from the North of Ireland, complete with his Orange bigotry, who demonstrated an acute identity problem. He resented the Irish inmates referring to him as a Brit., went ballistic when others called him a Mick, insisting all the time that he was an Ulsterman. Whatever he was, he proved to be a right bastard who never missed an opportunity to cause misery for the Irish contingent.

Roving around the three spurs, much of the time passing messages from one locked cell to another, wallowing still in the role as the bloke who got sacked for giving out too much crumble, enabled me to get on chatting terms with many fellow residents. This not only broke up much of the boredom for me, and hopefully, some of them, but also increased the sense of unreality that had been with me since day one. There was Stan, scratching his head to find a way of thwarting an imminent move to Hollesley Bay, near Ipswich, although due for release in a fortnight. He lived with his old Mum not far away in Peckham, who visited him with the aid of her bus pass, two or three times a week, and he was worried she would try trekking through the wilds of Norfolk, so as not to let him down. Two Portuguese blokes who didn't know more than ten words of English between them, were each banged up for the normal 21 hours every day with an Englishman. Instead of four inmates being able to converse, we had them trying to communicate in sign language and drawing endless pictures on bits of paper. One prisoner, who must have been a Health and Safety rep. in a previous existence, had a fetish for jumping from upper landings onto the anti-suicide netting that covered the ground floor. He claimed he was helping the prison by ensuring it did the job in the event of a serious attempt being made. Constant warnings not to do it were ignored, so they carted him off to the medical wing for psychiatric observations, never to be seen again. Ron was serving 12 years for three stabbings, one of them fatal, with nobody on the outside; which had led him into the practice of using his weekly prison issue letter for writing to various public figures, such as the Pope, the Queen, the Prime Minister, etc. Very often, after picking the litter up in the yard, I would give him a game of draughts through his cell window, provided the dog handler wasn't watching me, which eventually led to him feeling he could confide in me as to what he'd been doing. Stressing that his letters contained no obscenities, or pleading to review his case, but were confined to social small talk such as asking how they and their families were keeping, he was very suspicious as to why he was receiving no replies. Even an application to see the censor in order to check they were being sent out had been ignored, which prompted him to request an audience with the Assistant Governor. That had taken place, where he had been informed they were not being despatched, and if he persisted in the practice, his privilege of a weekly free letter would be withdrawn. Ron took great exception to the news, arguing that nowhere in Prison Regulations did it state who you couldn't write to, and in the absence of any complaints from the recipients, which was understandable as they weren't receiving anything, the A.G. was well out of order. Their meeting had been terminated by the A.G. telling Ron that until he gave an undertaking to only use the facility in a proper manner, weekly letter issue would be stopped whereupon two screws promptly marched him back to his cell. A question of principle was at stake, whereby in addition to the obnoxious censorship of prisoners' mail, staff were dictating who could be written to, and my draughts opponent was determined not to back down. He intended writing to the Prisons' Ombudsman, the purpose for which I ended up donating stationery and postage stamp.

Of equal interest as the inmates from an observer's position, were the screws. Watching them at close quarters, it dawned on me that although there are tens of thousands of them, they remain as much hidden from public view as the inmates. Apart from those few Prison Service officials who actually visit prisons, their work is only seen, and very rarely appreciated, by those they keep confined. There is not much difference between being a screw or a zoo-keeper, except the latter can pose in front of the public when their captives are being fed. With few exceptions they are disliked intensely by prisoners, more so even than those that captured them or the judge who put them away, not just because they are locking them up on a daily basis, but mainly as a result of the mind games and petty acts of nastiness they inflict on them and their visitors. Very often situations become personal, whereby a particular screw will continually "home in" on an individual to make his life a misery, and a clash of wills develops with the screw holding all the trump cards. It never failed to amaze me how petty incidents could escalate in such circumstances. Gary, a happy go lucky thief from Bermondsey had expressed very loudly to those around him that, in his opinion, Ms. O. was a dyke. He was probably right, but nevertheless, she got the right hump and commenced to show it. During the days following he was never required for work, thus having more "bang ups" and no wages; his cell always seemed the last to be opened up at meal times; the canteen had always just closed as she remembered he'd requested to visit it earlier in the day; and a cell mate he got on with was moved to another houseblock, to be replaced with one we all knew Gary didn't like. It finally came to a head one evening at the end of association. Gary was sitting on his bed chatting with a couple of mates when Ms. O. passed the door, telling them to get their mugs filled, which generated a response of bollocks. It was almost custom and practice to drag out the time around the water dispenser, with most playing the gentleman by inviting everyone else to go in front of them, to delay their bang-up for an extra 10 to 15 minutes. Gary held back in his cell, determined to be the last one to fill up, then sauntering back to show his contempt for authority in general, and Ms. O. in particular. Unfortunately for him, she must has sussed his intentions, and hovered out of view near his door waiting for the return of his cell-mate. As soon as he was back inside, she promptly stepped forward, slammed the door shut, and moved off to join her two colleagues chasing up the loiterers. Almost immediately, the noise of Gary kicking his door echoed around the spur, with his muffled shouts barely audible in the background, all of which were totally ignored by the three screws. What did attract them though, was the tinkle of falling glass when Gary graduated to using a chair, one leg of which succeeded in shattering the observation panel. Reinforcements were speedily brought up,

292

culminating in seven screws steaming into his cell to drag him out cursing and struggling, to spend a night in the solitary block. He never returned, and was shipped out in a sweat box a few days later to savour the hospitality of HMP Wandsworth, a high price to pay for not keeping his mouth shut about Ms. O's probable sexual orientation.

To further my understanding, I put myself out to obtain views from both the more experienced inmates, and the handful of prison officers who could bother themselves to talk to me. The general consensus of the former was that, with very few exceptions, such as Ms. B., who I will refer to again shortly, all the screws were crap compared with those at other prisons. This was not because staff at Belmarsh were fundamentally different but due to them reflecting both the muddled management of the place, and having no scope to develop the practical working relationships achievable in the more settled atmosphere of a long term prison. Inmates, in their opinion, were literally numbers in a book, to be treated with varying degrees of contempt and, due to their continuous clamour for information; toilet paper; trips to the canteen, etc., nothing more than a bloody great nuisance.

All prisoners, irrespective of length of sentence or offences, are subject to whatever is deemed as the appropriate conditions of incarceration. That is why different categories of prisons exist. In Belmarsh, the whole concept is turned upside down, whereby lifers; remand prisoners awaiting trial; blokes doing a few weeks for not having paid fines, some in for a fortnight because they didn't buy a TV licence; convicted drug barons and armed robbers, all get jumbled up together. Additionally, the endless flow of blokes both coming and going; after 3 months, there were only 9 inmates out of 57 who had been on the spur longer than me, made the place feel like a penal Charing Cross. In such circumstances, coupled with a sloppy management, can it be any wonder so many screws were confused as to what was expected of them, and saw their function as no more than a never-ending cycle of unlocking and relocking doors? I have already referred to the unpleasant, and financially costly, feature of putting very low category prisoners in a maximum security gaol; one example being Reg, doing two weeks of a four week sentence for getting captured viewing his unlicensed TV, in which time he received 21 hours daily bang-up, plus three full strip searches; but the inevitable effect on the screws working in such a bizarre environment should also be recognised. Obviously I cannot comment on that aspect in any depth, and feel that an appropriate body should examine it, but it must be a safe assumption any screw working in an establishment where all the inmates share a similar security category can adjust himself accordingly; whereas in Belmarsh he/she can be faced with two prisoners, one worrying himself sick as to whether the neighbours are feeding his cat during the couple of weeks he's inside, and the other one doing so many years he's got nothing to lose by breaking a chair over his/her head. Most seem to handle the situation by switching off to the endless stream of requests, whilst keeping as many as possible banged up for the maximum period of time. In the event of that approach not working they apply for a transfer, like Mr W., who was like a child on Xmas morning when his posting to HMP Maidstone came through.

Ms B., was not only different, she was unique. As one of the women recruited into the Prison Service as a measure, supposedly, to constrain the excessively aggressive tendencies among many of their male colleagues, she stood out for more reasons than just being very plump. In a world of indifference and confusion, Ms B. was a beacon of caring humanity who would always put herself out to assist an inmate, had a smile rather than a scowl, and never indulged in the incessant "mind games" played by so many at the expense of prisoners. Some made the mistake of interpreting her kindness as softness, but on those occasions where liberties were being taken she would soon crack down on the offender, leaving them in no doubt as to their grave error of judgement. For her efforts she paid quite a high personal price, as inevitably she became the target for so many with requests and problems, thus adding considerably to her workload, and amongst her fellow screws, an object of derision, with any promotion prospect not enhanced in the eyes of a macho management. Her uniqueness lay in an extremely rare attitude she had generated among most inmates on the spur, highlighted after one young new arrival had given her some abusive lip. During the following association period he received a visit in his cell from some of the blokes, when he was told to apologise to Ms B., and in order to get along with his new neighbours, to make sure it didn't happen again. He did, and it didn't. The men's approach to the newcomer was not based on any thoughts of sentimentality or chivalry; such luxuries are non-existent in prison, but solely on a practical appreciation of Ms B's value to them. They didn't want to risk her turning sour and becoming like the other screws. There is no doubt in my mind that if she was ever assaulted by an inmate, he would have to be moved off the spur to avoid the battering dished out by other screws being complemented with more thumps from some of the inmates. The Prison Service would do well to actively recruit and encourage more screws like Ms B.

Mr. W., not the one that couldn't get to Maidstone quickly enough, but an Afro-Caribbean with bulging muscles and an infectious laugh, was another one who stood out from the crowd. His very unorthodox style, whereby he would challenge inmates to a game of pool in which they stood to win a Mars bar, or the humorous arguments he constantly instigated, cleverly masked the fact that he missed nothing taking place around him. Physically, he had little to fear from most prisoners, yet possessed a wonderful ability to defuse a tense situation with a funny remark, whereas another screw would be threatening dire consequences and summoning reinforcements. Many blokes distrusted him, regarding his overt friendliness as a ploy to glean information from the unwary and maybe they were right, but as far as I was concerned, his great sense of humour coupled with a deep resounding laugh, injected a cheerfulness into an otherwise dreary existence.   Even his "party piece" of walking round the landings after our night-time bang up rendering a very good impersonation of Louis Armstrong singing "We have all the time in the world", never failed to have me smiling and nearly everyone else kicking hell out of their locked doors. In the same way as Ms B., prisons could do with more screws like Mr W.

The extent of any conversations with screws as part of my research was extremely limited for five reasons, which were: the limited time left before my release; they didn't wish to talk with me; it was not wise on my part to be seen chatting too much with them; if one stood still long enough, any conversation would soon be interrupted by another inmate airing a grievance or raising a problem; and a recognition that any probing question I might ask could be interpreted to suggest I was fishing for exploitable weaknesses, generating a reaction which could end up with me becoming a redundant yard cleaner.   There also existed the danger that a screw, thinking I had nothing better to do than pester them with pointless questions, would find a job for me, thus interfering with my wanderings around the houseblock.   Nevertheless, I could not avoid the conclusion that the manner in which a screw performs, and their attitude to prisoners, relates very much to the reasons for which they enrolled in the prison system to start with. Minus a few exceptions, such as those who failed to get in the police force, screws originate from three main sources and even though they all the wear the same uniform, the differences still show through.

Firstly, we have men and women, either unemployed or faced with the likelihood anytime, who see in the Prison Service the good salary and job security that up to then had always eluded them. They come from a whole range of backgrounds, manual and white collar, skilled and unskilled; predominately motivated by seeking the means to provide for families, pay mortgages and enjoy a decent standard of living. If they are young enough and don't get totally disillusioned by much of the routine violence and management stupidity, once inside may even start to cultivate ambitions for promotions. The major ingredient they bring into prison life is a fairly open mind that enables them, at least initially, to regard most prisoners as human beings and to deal with them accordingly. I suspect Ms B. would rank among their number.

The negative side of this category is they are prone to becoming lazy screws, viewing each shift just a period to get through as easily as possible, and the moment it is over being one of the first out of the gate. Not all turn out that way, but those which do are the ones who avoid getting involved with inmates' requests, and if they do, fail to follow through with their undertakings, not with any malicious intent but because they can't be bothered, which has the same winding up effect on prisoners as if the neglect was deliberate. These are also the screws that keep blokes banged up rather than permit them to exercise, as to do so would entail them standing around in the corner of a draughty yard to oversee the proceedings,

298

whereas it is more comfortable sitting indoors with a mug of tea.

Secondly, there are those with a military background, predominantly from the Army, due to ex-soldiers generally enjoying less useful qualifications for civilian life than their counterparts from the Navy and Air Force. Statistics show ex-soldiers being unemployed a lot longer than civilians, almost twice the average and, as mentioned earlier, after years of mental and physical conditioning, giving and obeying orders, discharge must prove quite a culture shock. The Prison Service is tailor made for them, with minimum variations on their previous theme making the transition a fairly smooth one, and from the administration's standpoint, they are ideal material due to having regimented backgrounds. With their propensity towards developing a camaraderie, which includes closing ranks against outsiders, they are useful staff to be involved in an external inquiry regarding a prisoner's sudden death. As screws they very readily adopt an elitist attitude towards those without a military pedigree, which manifests itself blatantly whilst dealing with prisoners, when they almost welcome the opportunity to indulge in brutality. As the backbones of the Mufti-squads, (Maximum Use of Force to Intimidate), and the first to race around when the alarm bells ring, wading in to baton anyone unfortunate enough to get in their way. Being fair though, they do make a positive contribution in a sloppily run place such as Belmarsh, injecting some semblance of order and consistency, plus maintaining standards of cleanliness which would shame most hospitals. It was more by accident than design that the existence of ex-military screws did me a favour. Mr N. who, as he told me later, was an ex-Guardsman and still looked the part, had answered my plea to be let back in from the yard. As he unlocked the door, I realised I had left the broom handle leaning against the wire over in the far corner, and went to retrieve it. My ankle was playing up due to a touch of arthritis that I have suffered with for years, and as I returned with a distinct limp, it was to the accompaniment of Mr. N. yelling for me to "Move it"!, as he had better things to do than watching me shuffling about. Light-heartedly I responded by telling him that that was no way to treat an old war veteran, who was suffering the consequences of doing his bit for Queen and Country, having risked his life in the line of duty. The reaction to my bullshit was amazing, and I was caught completely off guard when he asked me, in a voice reduced by at least two octaves, what outfit I had served in. Now the truth was I had served in nothing at all, unless a couple of years in the Boy Scouts as a kid counted, but having shot my mouth off, rapidly decided I had to follow it through in case he thought I was having a dig at his background. One of my brothers-in-law had been a regular in the Royal Engineers, so I based my extended bullshit on his career, going further to claim service back in the late 1950's in Cyprus, when the natives were shooting at us. Mr. N. seemed quite impressed, forgetting temporarily that he was supposed to have better things to do, which encouraged me to get carried away, claiming my limp to be due to a piece of shrapnel from a land mine exploding nearby that scattered pieces of a couple of less fortunate comrades all over the island. He was sufficiently impressed to hold the door open for me, whilst I privately offered up a prayer of thanks that he hadn't asked to see my non-existent war wound, not forgetting at the same time to accentuate the limp. Once inside, he forgot momentarily that he was a screw at Belmarsh and offered me a cigarette, which I accepted, whilst he regaled me with his Gulf War involvement, where he was choked by the action almost being over by the time he got there. The main result of all this crap was when, as we parted company, he told me that he was the Cleaning Officer for the coming week and therefore if I wanted anything from the stores, to just give him a shout. He was as good as his word, and for the remainder of my stay I had the pick of the bedding, plus enough toilet rolls to wipe every arse on our spur.

The third main source of enlistment are those who actually chose, at an early age, to embark on a career in locking people up. It is true to say that some of the first two groups, having joined, then decide to elevate their employment from being just a job into a career. Mr. B. was one of these, but in their cases it happened only after their previous ambitions either failed or were terminated. In this category we are talking about people who couldn't join quickly enough once their school days were over, very often influenced by already having parents, or other relatives, in the Service. Within their number are those whose motives for choosing such a career should effectively exclude them.   There will be the ex-playground bully, who has realised most other forms of adult employment severely inhibits their scope to continue such unpleasant tendencies and, ironically, their victims are also attracted to apply due to the opportunities afforded to work off old frustrations, plus loss of any self-esteem, from behind the protection of a screw's uniform. For the duration of each shift at least, the sense of being somebody with an authority denied them on the outside, appeals greatly to the otherwise nonentities of society, the stereotyped, hen-pecked husband, and now, with the recruitment of more women into male prisons, many who just hate men will lick their lips at the almost limitless opportunities to make them suffer, in many instances as a result of having been sexually abused as youngsters.   As a group, including those lacking any unsavoury hang-ups, this career intake contribute substantially to the dehumanising process of prison life whereby, at best, they seek to maintain a cold detachment in which every inmate is literally just a number, and at worst, generate unnecessary tensions with their continual acts of petty vindictiveness.

In an imperfect world there is obviously a need for some people to be screws, just as there are inmates who should never be let loose again on society, and many staff strive to carry out their duties with both efficiency and consideration.   The main issues needing to be constantly kept uppermost are recruitment screening procedures; training; controls, and clear leadership, especially, as with the police and other enforcement agencies, they are vested with so much power over people, many very vulnerable, and all enjoying precious few protective rights.

****

Chapter 16
Bums Rush To The exit Gate

I was now counting the hours, all 72 of them, that were left before my release. On the following Monday, at 7am, my door would be opened up and I would be taken to reception, fed, booked out, then shown the door. As I started my count-down, the spur resembled a departure lounge at Gatwick Airport, with blokes milling around clutching plastic sacks filled with their possessions, whilst screws ran back and forth checking and double-checking names and numbers. A third of our spur were being shipped out to Hollesley Bay, an open prison near Ipswich, to make room for higher category inmates being moved from Houseblock 4. It was all part of the Home Office decision to downgrade HMP Parkhurst from its top security rating, due to a number of embarrassing escapes, moving their A cats. into Houseblock 4 once they had spent pots of money installing yet more security equipment. It was often a boast from some of the screws that nobody had ever escaped from Belmarsh, but seeing as blokes were banged up most of the time, watched during exercise and association, and escorted whenever they left the houseblock, I often wondered just how great their achievement was. When one considered the closed regime already in existence, backed up with a vast array of sophisticated surveillance equipment, it became impossible to imagine what could be left to spend so much money on. Maybe they were going to manacle prisoners against the walls like in medieval dungeons; or just brick up their cell doors as if they were lots of little pharaohs, leaving just a small hole to feed them through. Whatever they were doing though, the knock-on effect was that all of a sudden more appropriate places were available for low category inmates, many of whom had been told for months they weren't going anywhere.

Patel numbered among the contingent soon departing to sample some bracing North Sea air, relieved that all his worries regarding unknown cell mates were now over, a relief slightly marred by the knowledge he would now be sharing a hut with nineteen others. His happiness became further reduced with the realisation he was moving a further hundred miles from home, and in order to cheer him up, I pointed out that once he starts working eight hours a day on the farm with an invigorating Scandinavian wind whistling up his trouser leg, he would soon get the colour back into his cheeks as, during the past months, he had been looking distinctly beige. Many of the blokes being shipped out I had become particularly friendly with, and whilst I was pleased for them moving to an 'open', knew I would miss their company during my final weekend. Some having less than a month to serve didn't want to go, because on release, they would have to travel all the way back to London, whereas from Belmarsh they could be home within half an hour on a bus; but as the move was to suit the Home Office, their protests were ignored.   Remembering how I had been told that almost three months didn't justify the paperwork to move me, made me determined to pursue their refusal, plus the associated mis-categorisation, even after my release.

Mr. B. had already invited me to pick which one of the single cells being vacated I wished to move into, and to have my things packed ready for transferring once the commotion died down. This I did, and was surprised as to how much had accumulated in a relatively short space of time, without even trying. In prison, possessions such as letters that represent a direct link with friends and loved ones on the outside are treasured, therefore very rarely get binned for the duration of a prisoner's sentence; but in addition to such items, my hoard of books, toilet rolls, toothpaste, magazines, assorted bowls and containers, plus other sundry articles, surprised even me.   My recently acquired "old soldier" relationship with Mr N., the screw in charge of the stores, resulted in me having enough bedding and towels for three other inmates. This was duly stacked on the bed, along with my collection of food supplements such as a tin of milk powder, apples, hard boiled eggs and polos; enhanced by opened bottles of tomato ketchup, orange squash and Ribena, plus two tins of fruit and a packet of cream crackers Patel had to leave behind.   That done, I went out to have a final chat with some of the blokes who were leaving, and to marvel at the performance entailed in moving twenty inmates, with screws running back to the Bubble every couple of minutes to confirm whether so-and-so was supposed to be going or not. Much of their stress was self-inflicted, resulting from their security mania, whereby having opened a double cell to let one out, another screw, seeing only one bloke remaining, would promptly slam the door shut. A few minutes later they would realise that the inmate cheerfully nattering with the departees, having taken the opportunity of nipping out to fill his mug at the hot water dispenser, should be behind the door, and the one who was, should be in the line-up. Then there were those who wanted to get back into their cells to retrieve overlooked items, some of whom were only asking to wind the screws up, and when they eventually refused, arguments erupted with those inmates whose requests were genuine.

I had just about completed bidding my farewells, shaking hands and wishing blokes good luck who, whatever their sins on the outside, had been good company during the past weeks, when the exodus began. With a flourish of keys a screw unlocked the steel gate and the travellers filed through dragging their plastic sacks, pausing to receive the obligatory rub down search, then continuing along the first floor landing, past the Bubble, to the exit gate. Watching the procession, it came as little surprise to see that the Belmarsh security mania had gone into its usual overdrive, with at least ten screws accompanying the transfers, presumably until everyone was on board the waiting transport. Considering they were all low category inmates, going to an 'open' where there was one screw to about forty prisoners, some of whom would be released within the month, I couldn't help visualising the scenario in which a group of top security categories were being moved. As a minimum, all leave would be cancelled, police and Army units would saturate the area, sealing off every road within a mile radius, with a squadron of RAF fighters constantly circling overhead.

When they were all gone, I ambled back to my cell to gather up my belongings. The place suddenly felt empty, and I realised that the joy of seeing out my last weekend would be coupled with a sense of loneliness. Even Tom had been moved to a neighbouring spur for winding up Mr B. through an act of youthful stupidity. They were both Charlton Athletic supporters and Mr. B. had shown great interest in the team poster, complete with players' signatures, that Tom had stuck on the wall over his bed. In order to have a laugh at his expense Tom removed the poster, and in full view of other inmates, asked Mr.B. if he would like to have it, as he had sent off to the Club for another one. Now no screw could afford to be seen accepting a gift from a prisoner, yet it was obvious to all that Mr. B. wanted to say yes, but before he could respond either way, Tom, with a malicious grin on his face, tore it to shreds in front of him. Tom and a few others had their laugh, but he paid dearly for it the next day. Immediately after breakfast he was moved in with a very unstable Geordie on the next spur, who was not only built like an ox, but smelt like one as well.

Once I had moved my worldly goods into my new abode, I decided to sit outside the door with a mug of tea and a burn, and watch some new faces arriving. It was not that I would know any of them, but motivated solely by a combination of curiosity, and would be potentially the only live entertainment available. Screws shouting and doors slamming heralded the appearance of the first half dozen, the maximum number of inmates deemed desirable to be off a spur as a group, which explained the substantial flapping earlier when twenty had to be taken to their waiting transport. Dragging their sacks, none of them looked very happy at being uprooted just to live in another houseblock, as the only move the overwhelming majority of inmates want is the one that takes them out of Belmarsh. No sooner had they entered the spur when another six were marshalled in to join them, and the inevitable arguments began, aimed at the screw with a clipboard. Some blokes had been cell-mates in Houseblock 4 and wished to remain together, which would seem to be no great problem as there were a number of empty doubles, but what they were up against was the Belmarsh way of doing things, whereby logic and common-sense were completely alien. Transfers and allocations were carried out on the scratch-card system, in which a prisoner's number is married up with one over a cell door, and the computer record amended accordingly. With various protesting voices getting louder and more heated, delaying the priority objective of getting inmates behind locked doors, the P.O. saw the need to put in a rare appearance. A dozen prisoners arguing the toss was bad enough, but with more on the way to swell their numbers, could develop into a situation compelling him to call up the riot squad, and be an admission that both he and his staff were incapable of carrying out an apparently straight-forward function. Most blokes were standing firm on the issue, and ignoring orders to get into their allotted cells, but to my surprise, instead of resorting to the usual heavy-handed response of nicking them, the P.O. adopted a conciliatory approach that even had some screws looking puzzled. Singling out the more vociferous protesters, he acceded to their demands, with the clipboard screw painfully making appropriate amendments on his print-out sheet. That defused the situation, coupled with the P.O.'s promise whereby any other requests to change an allocation would be favourably considered, and the group disappeared through various doors which were promptly slammed shut behind them. Nobody on either side was under any illusion of his promise being kept, or that those whose name and number now appeared written in ink on the print-out would not be singled out at a later date to receive retribution for their stroppiness. For the moment, they could savour their little victory, but in the never-ending conflict that is prison life, everyone knows the people in uniform cannot afford to lose.

I was now alone drinking my tea, a captive audience whilst some pissed-off screws were having their ears bent by the P.O. for allowing the confrontation to get started in the first place. A couple of sour looks in my direction had me deciding I would be better off being some place else. With the weather dry and a bit of sunshine breaking through, an obvious place was the yard, where I would make my last foray as the official litter picker-upper. Boots and jumper on, I headed up to the Bubble for the required red arm-band, arriving simultaneously as the next six transfers. They were more disgruntled than the previous lot, but the screws had learnt their lesson. These blokes were to be taken to the spur one at a time, accompanied by two screws with another couple waiting for them, where they would be faced with the choice of either walking into their new cell or being thrown in. Expressing profound regrets for being a bloody nuisance, I obtained the vital arm-band and headed downstairs to find a screw who would be kind enough to let me out into the yard. That was easier said than done as all the ones I could see were either involved in moving blokes around, or sitting at the desks on each spur guarding rows of locked doors. Looking down the central area towards the hot-plate, I could see Reg, who had drowned the mouthy sod's chicken with custard, washing a stack of metal trays, so I ambled along to join him, both for a chat and to keep out of the way. As I approached, I noticed too late that the adjacent storeroom door was open, with the ex-soldier screw who regarded me as a kindred spirit, busily sorting out towels and bedding for the new arrivals. My mind was racing as he asked what I was up to, because I immediately saw the danger of being rowed in to performing a door-to-door linen delivery service, which the screws would have deemed preferable to having to escort complaining inmates back and forth on an individual basis. No way did I fancy tramping up and down the stairs, when I could be out in the sunlight having a smoke and chatting through a couple of windows. I quickly told him that the officers in the Bubble had told me to locate him, to let me out into the yard. His description of his colleagues was as flowery as that frequently expressed by prisoners, coupled with a rather obvious claim that he only had one pair of hands, but then his well disciplined instincts took over and, grumbling all the way, he strode off ahead of me to unlock the yard door.

Once outside, I headed to the far end where any sunshine wasn't obscured by the building, lit up a burn and leant back on the perimeter wire. The tranquility was only broken by one or two blokes shouting lewd comments from the upper windows, to which I replied with an appropriate obscene gesture, emphasised with the aid of my broom handle, but it was all done in fun. Gazing around, I felt for a fleeting moment that I would actually miss it, but quickly cancelled such thoughts. Surely I couldn't become institutionalised in three months? Judging by the amount of litter, I reckoned it would take me about ten minutes to have it cleared up, so I decided to make a start and afterwards resume my standing-up spot of sunbathing. In the event of the sun going behind a cloud, I could always see who was "at home" on the ground floor to have a natter with.

Making myself busy, the clean-up was soon completed and as I tied a knot in the black sack I heard Joe, an Irish bloke about my age, calling me from a nearby window. He had arrived just over a week previously, to commence a five-year sentence for running a thriving business supplying building plant and machinery, whereby you told him what you wanted, and within days his little firm would acquire it from a construction site when the rightful owners weren't looking. We had played a few games of chess, which proved quite agonising affairs, as neither of us were any good at it, made worse due to the set being a little pocket variety where you almost needed a magnifying glass to tell a pawn from a bishop. He wanted to know if I fancied a game to pass a bit of time, and whilst I was not too keen, seeing as the sun still shone on the top end of the yard, I said OK., as I appreciated the boredom he was probably suffering through being banged up so long on his own. Any attempt at a serious game was further inhibited by the box containing a built-in board having to be precariously balanced on the narrow ledge between two window bars, so we were both looking from the sides, with me having an additional handicap of a bar obscuring half the board. After about five moves apiece, with Joe moving the board back and forth each time to give me an overview, we gave it up as a dead loss, settling instead to just having a chat, an activity we were both definitely more expert at. He had a wealth of humorous stories derived from a very active life spent ducking and diving, and in his company it was easy to forget we were both stuck in a maximum security prison, which probably contributed to me ignoring a dog handler who paused every few minutes in his patrolling on the other side of the fence. Whether he saw a security risk in the situation, or simply resented two blokes enjoying themselves, is anyone's guess, but just as I was

313

finishing my second burn a screw stuck his head out the door to call me back inside, plainly in response to the dog handler having put a call through to the Bubble. Telling Joe I would see him later, I headed back inside, feeling mildly cheated because my last effort in the yard hadn't been ceremoniously rounded off by giving the door an extra kicking.

Throughout my final weekend, I made a point of seeing all the blokes that were left who had helped me during my stay with their friendship. Having a free run of the houseblock enabled me to visit those on other spurs, even though they were banged-up, and undoubtedly due to the good offices of Mr. B., my door remained unlocked when the weekend cleaners' rota stated it shouldn't be. Tom was thoroughly pissed off, regretting I'm sure, having wound Mr. B. up over the Charlton F.C. poster, so I gave him my surplus goodies, retaining only what I needed to see me through until Monday morning. Tommy the tea boy featured high on my list for a visit, not only for having become a friend, but more especially as I recognised the risk he had taken when giving me a lump of the screws' cheese. From an outsider's view, his action may appear really petty, but in a highly restricted world, where any job affording relatively large privileges is rare and much sought after, you do not chance losing it just to give a semi-stranger a treat. Harry insisted I took a couple more apples from his constantly stocked fruit bowl, and I made a point of thanking Fitz for ensuring I could pick from whatever had been on offer at the hot-plate. Later, when banged up on my own, I pondered the situation

314

whereby I was saying my farewells with a touch of sadness to blokes who, up to three months' previously, I would have studiously avoided. With the exception of nonces, the causes of a bloke being inside are a non-issue, yet they were still armed robbers, drug pushers, burglars and such like. Friendship between such diverse inmates as murderers and TV licence defaulters; bank robbers and council tax non-payers, could only evolve in a place such as Belmarsh, where all are faced with a common enemy in the form of a grossly aggressive regime, implemented by a mindless bureaucracy. Having said that though, there were still some I had socialised with, who I would certainly think twice about before inviting round for tea on Sunday.

On my going out list I included both Mr. B. and Ms. B., who were living proof that even in a maximum security jail, screws could do their job effectively most of the time without being unnecessarily heavy-handed, or giving blokes a regular kicking. Mr. B. was off duty for the weekend, returning early Monday morning, but I was able to have a pleasant chat for a few minutes with Ms. B., which included not only thanking her for being human, but also receiving her assurance to pass similar thanks on to Mr. B. in the event of me missing him before I departed. Screws like them tread a difficult path between liberty-taking inmates, and sneering colleagues and superiors, with both sides regarding their methods as a sign of weakness; but for their own sakes as people, as well as future prisoners in their charge in the future, I hope

315

they don't give up and become dehumanised pigs like so many wearing the same uniform.

Monday morning dawned, with me dressed, packed and ready to go long before my door was due to be unlocked at 7am. Sitting on the bed in my overcoat, which had hung over three beds in as many months on one of the few coat-hangers available that Mo had obtained for me, a feeling of unreality returned. I knew I would soon be going home having been away for a time, but it was that concept of time which kept fluctuating. One moment it felt I'd been there for ages, the next for no time at all, as if it had all been a bad dream from which I was in the process of waking. Yet it couldn't have been a dream because I was now wide awake looking at real bars on the window, waiting for a bloody great steel door to be unlocked. The mild bout of disorientation I was having probably resulted from being on my own, whereas chatting with a cell-mate would have kept the old grey matter focused, but even so, I couldn't help thinking if I was like that after such a relatively short time, mostly spent in company, how must it be for those released after many years from the isolated conditions of the Special Secure Unit. The other contributing factor encouraging a bit of mental wandering was the uncanny silence of the place. More than a thousand inmates and screws were on the premises, yet I could very easily imagine everyone having been evacuated except me.

The tranquility became shattered in the regulation manner at precisely one minute to seven. Keys rattling in a lock was swiftly followed by the steel gate crashing back against a wall, much to the joy of those still sleeping. Boots clumping in my direction had me up on my feet ready for the off. No ex-con ever forgets the sound of a cell door slamming shut, likewise the sound of a key opening it, and on this occasion it resembled sweet music. Mr. B. stood to one side as I dragged my sack out, reminding me not to forget anything. I was pretty sure I hadn't, but just in case, let go of the sack and popped back in to check. Within seconds I was back out to witness Mr. B. with my sack in his hand, already halfway up the stairs leading to the first landing, calling for me to get a move on. Now no screw carries an inmates belongings, unless it's to join them for a long stay in the isolation block, followed by being shipped out, so it was no surprise when he received some funny looks from other screws. He gave it as his opinion that it would take me half an hour to drag it up the stairs, whereas he just wanted to get rid of me as quickly as possible, but no-one was really convinced. We parted company at the Bubble where, whilst I was being rubbed down and another screw checked the contents of my sack, I apologised for not being able to tip him as I only had travellers' cheques, but wished him well for the future. Another screw then took charge of me for the walk to reception which, in prison, also doubles as the departure lounge, where straight after having my breakfast in the adjoining dining room; I would be formally discharged from their establishment.

The routine with discharges was to feed them, pay

317

any monies due, return confiscated property and get them booked out; prior to assembling others for court appearances, and generally, everything ran quite smoothly.   That was until some great mind in administration decided those for court appearances could be despatched more promptly if they had breakfast at reception, rather than hassle them to eat up on time in their cells.   Waiting patiently with two others also going out, for the servery to function, we were blissfully unaware of the new thinking until a door crashed open and our number suddenly swelled to more than thirty.   Any semblance of a queue completely evaporated in the absence of the control exercised in a houseblock, and by the time I had loaded my tray I realised the seating arrangement equated to two chairs for every three diners. My two options of either leaning against a wall or sitting on the floor didn't appeal to me, so I took a second metal tray and placed it across the top of a nearby litter bin, as a means of taking the weight of my feet.   I was still unable to even contemplate putting a prison sausage in my mouth, settling instead for a helping of porridge, which I continued to enjoy, followed by two slices of bread to mop up a very generous double scooping of baked beans. A mug of tea sat on the floor at my feet to wash the whole lot down. I had barely started on the porridge when I heard my name being called, and in response to my waving spoon, a screw came over to present me with the need to make a decision.   It appeared that within a few minutes they would begin processing the court appearances, and as they took priority, it could be more than an hour before us three discharges got dealt with, or alternatively, I could forego my breakfast and leave now. I opted for the latter, pausing only for one last spoonful of porridge and to almost scald my mouth emptying the mug of tea.

Dragging my sack I joined the other two in reception, where one by one an S.O. spelt out the conditions of our early release, which boiled down to mean that if any of us received a custodial sentence before the full expiry of our present one, the remitted time would be automatically added to it. He also placed great emphasis on the fact we were forbidden to possess a firearm for the following five years, requiring us to sign a form stating we fully understood, then without even a goodbye, turned and vanished through a rear door. We stood there for a moment expecting someone to appear to and show us off the premises, but soon realised that was not to be, so decided to head out through the likeliest looking door. That took us into a yard where a row of sweat-boxes were parked, presumably in readiness to transport the court appearances. No screws were to be seen, so we dragged our sacks across the tarmac towards a big gate at the far end, looking round all the time for someone to let us out. We had got halfway when a yell to stay where we were made us turn to see four screws erupting from the doorway we had just left. It would appear we had taken the wrong route, and after checking our release papers, an impromptu debate took place as to what course of action to now take. There was a reluctance to take us back through the reception area, which would now be busy processing court appearances, so a decision was reached to get

319

rid of us through the big gate. While three walked the rest of the way with us, the fourth screw ran on ahead to arrange for another, seated in what looked like a big fish tank adjacent to the gate, to open it wide enough to let us through. Once on the other side we all took a deep breath to savour our conditional freedom, as the door slid shut behind us, then after shaking hands, my two companions headed for the nearest bus stop. It was barely 8.15am and I had told my youngest son I wouldn't need picking up before 9am. After three months of central heating, a chill wind blowing across the big car park fronting the prison felt it had come directly from the Arctic Circle. I decided to drag my sack over to the attendants' building, where I could shelter and have a smoke. The screw inside operating the barrier might even take pity and let me sit with him, but the look he gave me as I approached immediately killed off that idea. Huddled under his window, I spent the next hour alternatively gazing down the approach road for Joe's car, and watching early visitors arriving. Young mums pushing toddlers in buggies, all too often visiting arse-holes whose only concern was whether they had deposited enough of their benefits into their private accounts to enable them to buy a couple of spliffs. Elderly parents that had lost track of the different prisons they had travelled to over the years, for sons they had never given up hope on. Faithful wives, struggling to keep a home and family together, once again facing the men they loved, all with the unasked question hanging over them as to whether or not she was having a bit on the side. Occasionally a cab would deliver a smartly dressed passenger, indicating that someone was having a legal visit, or a banged-up businessman had summoned his accountant to assure him the company was coping in his absence. The first of the sweatboxes came roaring out, and remembering the promise I made to myself, stepped forward as they slowed at the barrier to give a thumbs up sign to faces peering out the windows. The screw in the hut didn't like that, probably thinking a mass rescue was in the offing.

Watching visitors going in made me realise that, if anything, Belmarsh looked grimmer from the outside than from within. Thinking back, I was glad my arrival had been after dark, otherwise the sight of the place would have made me more depressed than I already was. A car horn being overworked behind me prevented any further dwelling on that miserable night in December, and I turned to see the welcome sight of Joe and my wife waiting for me to get in his car. Having delivered me to start with, it seemed a nice touch for Joe to be taking me back home, albeit thirteen weeks later than we had hoped, but I didn't care, 'cos we were on our way now.

- *The End* -

Appendices

Appendix 1: Prison Hooch

Appendix 2: Terminology

Appendix 3: Categorisation and Acknowledgements

Appendix 1

PRISON HOOCH

<u>Ingredients:</u>

One clean bucket: two matchboxes of dried yeast (any type): three cartons of pure or sweetened juice: three tins of pineapple chunks in juice: two Kg. bag of sugar: two to three handfuls of raisins: one pint of cooked rice: five raw potatoes, peeled: two tea-bags: a further 2Kg. bag of sugar, to be added during fermentation.

<u>Method:</u>

Empty the yeast, juice, pineapple chunks and juice, sugar and raisins, into the bucket. Two thirds fill the bucket with cooled down boiled water, then add rice and sliced up potatoes.

Finally, drop in the tea-bags, to prevent the mixture turning into vinegar. The bucket must then be stood in a warm place, usually on the pipes running through the cell, for five days. During this time, the remaining bag of sugar is fed in on a daily basis.

On the sixth day, strain the liquid through a T-shirt, preferably a clean one, leaving it to stand a further day.

A longer period of fermentation would be very beneficial, but is ruled out on the grounds of security and the ever present threat of a cell spin, especially if a screw with a good sense of smell is prowling around. It has been known for additives, such as liquid floor polish or after shave, to be splashed in to enhance the "kick factor", but such practice is not recommended as the existing punch is more than sufficient for internal organs that have been alcohol starved for a considerable length of time.

Appendix 2

TERMINOLOGY

Brief:	Solicitor or Barrister
Screw:	Prison Officer
Bang-up:	Locked in cell
Sweatbox:	Prison lorry
Rub down:	Clothing search
Burn:	Cigarette
Puff:	Drug smoking
Two's:	Sharing cigarette

Belmarsh Bang-Up

Hot-plate:	Servery
Cell spin:	Search
Spur:	Small wing
Houseblock:	Contains three spurs
Bubble:	Houseblock admin. office
Bird:	Bird-lime = time (slang)
Nonce:	Child molester; rapist; etc.
Grass:	Informer
E-man:	Escapee
B.O.V.	Board of Visitors
O.C.A.: Allocations Unit.	Observation: Categorisation:
Canteen:	Shop
S.O.	Senior Officer
P.O.	Principal Officer

****

Appendix 3

CATEGORISATION and ACKNOWLEDGEMENTS

All inmates entering the prison system are placed in one of four security categories, the highest being A and the lowest D. During recent years there has been a steady growth in an unofficial Double A category of prisoners, who inevitably become the occupants of the Special Secure Units, the prisons within prisons. It is presumably easier for the Prison Service to do it that way rather than introduce a new E category, which would necessitate amending the records on 50-odd thousand inmates, plus creating a risk of confusion with the E-men.

The C. category is applied to those "who cannot be trusted in open conditions but who do not have the will or resource to make a determined escape attempt", whereas a D category is reserved for "those who can be reasonably trusted to serve their sentence in open conditions". In their infinite wisdom, the Prison Service deemed me to be a C. cat. Undoubtedly their decision was based on the fact that I had a previously unblemished record and a substantially shorter sentence than my co-defendants, whereas four of the five also had previous convictions. Furthermore, I had spent eighteen months on bail, during which I had received Court permission to visit relatives in the Irish Republic, which is outside British jurisdiction. Salt was added to the wound with the knowledge that millionaires possessing plenty of resources were swanning around Ford Open Prison, yet not only was I precluded from such facilities, I could not even move outside the houseblock without an escort. It was a very unsatisfactory situation which had to be challenged.

A week into my sentence and I had sent an application to the Office for Categories and Allocations (OCA), which is located within the prison, stating my reasons for requesting a D. category in line with my co-defendants. Their reply was that I had been made a C. pending the receipt of a letter from my Solicitor, detailing any previous convictions. I had waited a week for their response, but was able to telephone my Solicitor the same day. He informed me that the information would have arrived at Belmarsh on the same vehicle as myself, and even if it had not, the OCA could have asked for it to be faxed through. In view of their apparent inability, he agreed to have the information sent by special delivery to the OCA.

Xmas was now just days away when I contacted the OCA to find out what was happening, to be informed that they now had to obtain the details from the police. I was becoming very pissed off, having learnt during my years in local government what bullshit smelled like, in this case amounting to the residue of a sizeable herd.

327

At the outset, I was not to realise how many people would become involved in the issue, none of whom were to make any headway. Under the circumstances, it was just as well I had the time to pursue it. The finale was to come six weeks after my release, when the Prison's Ombudsman's report catalogued a saga of deceit, confusion and sheer incompetence, with a recommendation that I receive a written apology from the Prison Service. This they did, but so as not to spoil their previous track record, the two-sentence letter apologised for something completely different.

I realised by Xmas that not only was the information furnished by my Solicitor unacceptable, but additionally the OCA were not too sure what they were supposed to be doing to resolve the matter. A letter seeking assistance from my MP seemed a good idea and was promptly dispatched. Meanwhile, I continued my efforts locally, which included a meeting with a BOV representative, two interviews with the Deputy Governor and a chat with a Probation Officer. The BOV man fell at the first hurdle when, upon being told the matter was dealt with elsewhere, he proved unable to ascertain where "elsewhere" was. The DG didn't even get that far, as on both occasions he informed me of his failure to contact anyone at all, and fifteen months after my release, I'm still waiting to hear back from the Probation Officer.

With the end of January approaching and halfway through my incarceration period, I received a letter from my MP which included a copy of his reply from the Director-General of the Prison Service. Now we're getting somewhere, I thought. They won't muck the top man about. My optimism was soon knocked on the head though, when I read his reference to Belmarsh waiting for the necessary information from the police. He did not even think it slightly off that my five co-defendants were all able to be categorised within a day or two, yet after six weeks my case was still outstanding. Shortly afterwards he was sacked, but still received a substantial golden handshake for being a waste of space.

There was nothing for it now but to lodge an official complaint to the Governor. The regulation form was only available on request, and completed within minutes of receiving it, to be promptly lodged with the Principal Officer in charge of the houseblock. Nearly three weeks were to elapse with no reply, so I obtained another to complain of the lack of any response to the first. I also decided at that stage to submit my grievance to the Prison's Ombudsman.

The Ombudsman's office contacted Belmarsh on 23rd February to ascertain why I had not heard anything following my official complaint, dated 31st January, to be told a reply was outstanding. On 4th March, two days before my release, I received the reply, which was dated 15th February, eight days before the Ombudsman had been informed it was still outstanding. Needless to say, the signature on it could not be traced to anyone, but we knew it wasn't the Governor, as he was on a lengthy period of sick leave. The scribbled reply contained the enlightening news that necessary information was still awaited from the Inner London Crown Court. During subsequent weeks, the Ombudsman's investigation officer was to extract an admission that Prison Service regulations clearly state such information must only be obtained from the police.

On 17th May. the Ombudsman published his report, in which he upheld my two complaints regarding miscategorisation, and refusal to transfer. This was followed on 26th May by an apology from the Prison Service <u>for not giving me a security category at all.</u> Apparently my C. rating was a figment of everyone's imagination, including the staff at Belmarsh!!

I was messed about for a relatively short period of time and can only pity those who suffer much worse whilst in their clutches for years on end. My total appreciation goes to the Ombudsman's Office, whose powers to intervene and redress such situations must be maintained.

In closing, I would register my thanks to Mr Martin Meadows, of Hanne and Co., Solicitors, of Battersea, for his valuable assistance, not only in pursuing the Prison Service during the latter stages, but for his sterling efforts from the time of my arrest almost two years previously. A special thank you is also due to Mrs. Dee Whiston for her perseverance in transposing my hand-written account into legible type.

To both these fine people I gladly dedicate this book.

* *

Printed in Great Britain
by Amazon